THE TWO MICHAELS

THE TWO MICHAELS

Innocent Canadian Captives and High Stakes Espionage in the US-China Cyber War

MIKE BLANCHFIELD & FEN OSLER HAMPSON

SUTHERLAND HOUSE

TORONTO, 2021

Sutherland House
416 Moore Ave., Suite 205
Toronto, ON M4G 1C9

Sutherland House and logo are registered trademarks of The Sutherland House Inc.

First edition, November 2021

If you are interested in inviting one of our authors to a live event or media appearance, please contact publicity@sutherlandhousebooks.com and visit our website at sutherlandhousebooks.com for more information about our authors and their schedules.

Manufactured in Canada
Cover designed by Lena Yang
Book composed by Karl Hunt

Library and Archives Canada Cataloguing in Publication
Title: The two Michaels : innocent Canadian captives and high-stakes espionage in the US-China cyber war / Mike Blanchfield & Fen Osler Hampson.
Names: Blanchfield, Mike, 1964- author. | Hampson, Fen Osler, author.
Identifiers: Canadiana 2021032287X | ISBN 9781989555545 (softcover)
Subjects: LCSH: United States—Foreign relations—China. |
LCSH: China—Foreign relations—United
States. | LCSH: Cyberterrorism—United States. |
LCSH: Cyberterrorism—China. | LCSH: Espionage,
American—China. | LCSH: Espionage, Chinese—United States. |
LCSH: Geopolitics.
Classification: LCC E183.8.C5 B48 2021 |
DDC 327.73051—dc23

ISBN 978-1-989555-54-5

CONTENTS

CHAPTER ONE

An Ill-Fated Arrival

T HE SURREY DETACHMENT OF the Royal Canadian Mounted Police was short staffed on Friday, November 30, 2018, when Const. Winston Yep's cellphone rang. His supervisor told him to get down to the Department of Justice to swear out a provisional arrest warrant for a female traveller due to arrive in Vancouver from Hong Kong in less than twenty-four hours. It was mid-day and Yep, a member of the RCMP's foreign and domestic liaison unit, was in the middle of only his second extradition case, but he dropped everything and headed out to begin the process of swearing out and signing the necessary affidavit.[1]

Yep had never heard of Meng Wanzhou before that day. By the time he'd finished dotting the I's and crossing the T's on his affidavit, he'd learned that Wanzhou Meng ("Meng"), also known as "Cathy Meng," and "Sabrina Meng," was a citizen of the People's Republic of China. She worked as a top executive of Huawei Technologies Co. Ltd., which bills itself as "the world's largest telecommunications equipment company." She was also the daughter of Huawei's legendary founder, Ren Zhengfei.

In addition to her role as chief financial officer, Meng served as Huawei's deputy chairwoman of the board, among other roles at Huawei subsidiaries and affiliates. She also sat on the board of Hong Kong-based Skycom Tech Co. Ltd. ("Skycom") in or around 2008 and 2009. According to financial statements for Skycom for the years 2009 and 2010, the principal activities of Skycom were "investment holding" and "acting as a contractor" for undertakings in Iran.[2]

Yep's affidavit and an appended summary of facts described how US authorities came to believe that Huawei was using Skycom as a backchannel to trade with Iran in violation of American trade sanctions. The US and Iran have been enemies since 1979, when a group of radical students in Tehran stormed the American embassy and took hostages in a siege that lasted 444 days. The US immediately imposed trade sanctions which have evolved over the decades in response to a variety of crises, including the international effort in this century to prevent Iran from enriching the uranium it needs to create a nuclear weapon. On November 2, 2018, weeks before the Meng extradition request reached Yep, the Trump administration slapped Tehran with its toughest sanctions yet, targeting its oil exports—the cornerstone of Iran's economy—to punish it for support of militant groups.

According to Yep's documents, Huawei was running Skycom "as an unofficial subsidiary to conduct business in Iran while concealing Skycom's link to Huawei." There was no real distinction between Skycom and Huawei. Skycom employees working in Iran were employed by Huawei.[3] What's more, wrote Yep:

> *Documents show that multiple Skycom bank accounts were controlled by Huawei employees, and Huawei employees were signatories on these accounts between 2007 and 2013;*

> *Documents and email records show that persons listed as 'Managing Directors' for Skycom were Huawei employees;*

Skycom official documents, including several Memoranda of Understanding, bore the Huawei logo;

Email correspondence and other records show that all identified Skycom business was conducted using '@huawei.com' email addresses;

Documents show that a purportedly unrelated entity to which Skycom was supposedly 'sold' in 2009 was actually also controlled by Huawei until at least in or about 2014.

Records obtained through the investigation show that Skycom was used to transact telecommunications business in Iran for major Iranian-based telecommunications companies.[4]

Yep's affidavit was the culmination of months of work by American intelligence, which had long had Meng, as a senior official at Huawei, on its radar. The previous August 22, Magistrate Judge Roanne L. Mann of the Eastern District of New York had issued an arrest warrant for Meng to stand trial on criminal charges in the US. The full case against her was under seal while Yep was preparing his documents but it was later revealed that Meng was accused of bank fraud, wire fraud, and related conspiracy charges, while Huawei was formally accused of stealing telecommunications technology, trade secrets, and equipment from the American wireless company T-Mobile USA.[5] If convicted as charged, Meng would face substantial prison time. Before anything could be done toward a conviction, however, she had to be brought into custody, which was no simple matter.

"Huawei executives," Yep wrote, "appear to have altered their travel plans to avoid the United States jurisdiction since becoming aware of the United States' criminal investigation into Huawei in

April 2017. Meng, who previously visited the United States multiple times in 2014, 2015, and 2016, has not made a trip to the United States since March 2017, prior to Huawei becoming aware of the criminal investigation." That's where the Canadians came in.

American surveillance had learned that Cathay Pacific flight CX838, which Meng was scheduled to board that day in Hong Kong, was to land in Vancouver the following morning, December 1, at 11:30 a.m. After a brief stopover, Meng intended to carry on to Mexico City and Argentina. It was Yep's job to ensure that her journey ended in Vancouver. "Meng is not ordinarily resident in Canada and appears to have no ties to Canada," he wrote in his affidavit, and she was likely to have "access to large amounts of resources to escape the jurisdiction." She would also have a strong motivation to flee if not properly detained in Canada pending her extradition to the US to stand trial.[6]

Before the day was over, Yep was successful in persuading British Columbia Supreme Court Justice Margot Fleming to issue a warrant for him to "immediately arrest" Meng and bring her before a judge within twenty-four hours. The definition of "immediately" would become the source of extensive legal arguments in the months ahead. Yep and his partner also made a trip to the Vancouver International Airport to get the lay of the land.[7]

* * *

The next morning, Yep donned a suit and, warrant in hand, joined his uniformed partner at the Vancouver airport ready to execute the legal request of the US government to arrest its high-value target. About two hours before Meng's plane landed, the police and the border agents met to discuss how the morning should unfold. It was decided Canadian Border Services Agency officers should have the first crack at Meng so they could assess her legal admissibility to Canada. "This is your jurisdiction. We want to work with you guys," Yep said in his conversation with them. "What do you suggest we do here?"

The border agents, Yep remembered, told him they had immigration issues with the two multimillion-dollar homes Meng owned in Vancouver and wanted to talk to her about them.[8]

"I did not give CBSA any directions on what to ask Ms. Meng," Yep would later recall in court testimony. "We left it up to them to do their process and when they were done their process, I was going to execute the warrant. We let them do their job." He said the border agents agreed to confiscate Meng's electronics and store them in sealed bags supplied by US authorities.[9]

Yep's supervisor sent him a note suggesting that they board the plane immediately and arrest Meng in her seat. Yep didn't think that was a good idea. "We didn't know Ms. Meng," Yep later recalled. "We didn't know who she was travelling with and what she was capable of. Plus, you have other passengers there. It's a risky situation."

As Meng's flight was approaching Canadian airspace, the CBSA suddenly came to terms with the scope of what was about to unfold. "We had serious concerns," said border services officer Scott Kirkland, "and we knew that this was going to be a big deal and it was going to be a huge issue."

Kirkland, a former member of the Canadian army, was proud of his work at the CBSA. A photo of the bearded and trim border officer was once featured in a government public service announcement in which he says joining the border service was one of the best decisions he had made. He'd even been featured in the short-lived National Geographic Channel Canada reality television show, *Border Security*. On learning what was to happen when Meng's plane landed, he got on the internet and started doing his own research. He was shocked when he saw the fraud charges in the CBSA database and read news stories that filled in a few more gaps.[10] Kirkland wondered if it was wise for border services to delay Meng's arrest, rather than hand her over to the RCMP immediately; if the whole matter were to wind up in court, there might be objections raised under Canada's Charter of Rights and Freedoms. "But at the same time," he said, "we also have a job to do."[11]

As her long overnight flight from Hong Kong was in its final descent towards Vancouver on December 1, Meng Wanzhou enjoyed her final hour of freedom in a luxurious first-class cocoon. It was a self-contained pod in soothing beige; her seat folded out to a flat-bed. Suffering from what court documents would later describe as a bout of hypertension, the forty-six-year-old chief financial officer was comfortably dressed in a dark hooded tracksuit, white t-shirt, and white running shoes.

Meng had no reason to suspect anything was amiss when her Boeing 777 landed, seventeen minutes ahead of schedule, and began its taxi toward the terminal of Vancouver International Airport. She had already traveled to Canada six times in 2018, most recently on October 5, without incident. (That trip had apparently gone unnoticed by US law enforcement, even though a warrant for her arrest had already been obtained.) Meng was unaware of the contents of the sealed charges that had been filed against her and her company. She had no important business in Canada: the urgent part of her trip was her scheduled meeting in Mexico with its new populist president, Andrés Manuel López Obrador, who might be able to open his domestic market to Huawei equipment.

Meng unbuckled her seat belt, deplaned, walked out of Gate 65 into the terminal and presented her passport to Canada Border Services Agency officers, who directed her to a secondary inspection area where the unluckiest of travellers come face to face with the fine-tooth efficiency of the CBSA. There, her luggage, including two large cardboard boxes, was assembled and the border agents began a search of her belongings. Meng was carrying two mobile phones—a Huawei device and an Apple iPhone—as well as a rose and gold-coloured iPad, a pink MacBook laptop, and a USB stick. These digital devices were sealed in the Mylar bags provided by the Americans to block wireless signals and prevent anyone from cleansing data with a wireless signal from a far-off location. The Americans also asked the Canadians to retrieve Meng's passwords for her electronics.

The inspection took nearly three hours. Border agents have wide latitude to search and question inbound travelers, invasive powers that at least temporarily extend beyond what police are allowed to do. However, the distinction between routine detention and examination, and a pre-arrest search that amounts to an unlawful, arbitrary detention in violation of one's rights under the Charter of Rights and Freedoms, is an important one, as the CBSA's Kirkland had intuited.

A distraught Meng asked why she was being subjected to additional screening as the search unfolded. She said she was only making a twelve-hour stopover at her Vancouver house to drop off some possessions before continuing her journey to Mexico City and Buenos Aires. The methodical border agents did not engage with her. She was ordered to sit down and not walk around the secure secondary inspection area. When she needed to use the washroom, a CBSA agent escorted her. She wasn't allowed to contact a lawyer.

Near the end of the search, seven minutes before handing her over to the RCMP, Kirkland asked for and received from Meng the passwords to her electronic devices. He wrote the information down on a slip of paper and placed it with them. It would be established in subsequent court proceedings that those codes were passed on to the RCMP an hour later.[12] That raised the question, argued exhaustively in a Vancouver courtroom in the coming years, of whether or not Meng's rights had been trampled and information from her phones and computers had been passed to the FBI.[13]

Also, toward the end of the search, acting CBSA Superintendent Sanjit Dhillon, who had been overseeing the examination, joined

Meng and one of the border agents at 1:55 p.m. Dhillon and Meng had a fourteen-minute discussion, all of it captured on security camera video footage that would later be admitted as evidence at Meng's extradition hearing. Dhillon didn't make notes of the conversation, but Meng's lawyers later received his sworn declaration about the content of the conversation after filing a request under Canada's access-to-information law.[14]

Dhillon said Meng repeatedly asked his agents "why she had been selected for secondary inspection, and on this occasion, she had posed the same question to myself." Dhillon didn't answer Meng, nor did he tell her she was about to be arrested by the RCMP. But he did question her on sensitive topics.

Dhillon asked Meng what she did for work. She told him she was the chief financial officer for Huawei Technologies and that her father was the founder of the company. She said the company sold products in several countries around the world. Dhillon asked Meng if the company sold products in the United States.

"No, we do not," Meng replied.

Dhillon said Meng was "reluctant" to explain why her company sold products around the world, "but did not sell those same products in a lucrative market like the United States." Dhillon said Meng eventually replied: "the United States had security concerns regarding her company's products. The subject would not elaborate on those security concerns."

Dhillon asked Meng if her company sold products "in countries that they should not." Meng "appeared confused" by the line of questioning. "I rephrased the question and asked the subject if her company sold products or did business in Iran."

According to Dhillon, Meng replied: "I don't know."

Dhillon reminded Meng that she was the CFO of a multibillion-dollar company, "and that it would be hard for me to believe" that she wouldn't know that detail.

"The subject stated that her company does have an office in Iran. At this point my interaction with the subject ended and I had no further contact with her," Dhillon wrote.

Several minutes later, after close to three hours of interrogation, the border agents finished with Meng. At no time had they told her she was facing criminal charges in the US.

Yep was sitting patiently in an adjacent room with his partner when Meng was brought in. He addressed Meng through his partner, who translated his comments into Mandarin.

"Can you advise Ms. Meng, Ms. Meng here, there's an extradition warrant on behalf of the United States to arrest her for fraud in the United States? . . . We're arresting you and then you will be sent back to the United States," said Yep.

"Me?" Meng said.

"OK," said Yep. "I'm going to continue on with, OK, now this is a warrant for provisional arrest under Section 13 of the Extradition Act."

Yep's partner translated the comment, explaining to Meng in Mandarin about Section 13 of the Act.

"Sorry," Meng said, "I need to ask you. You're saying I committed fraud in the United States?"

Through his partner, Yep explained they had a signed warrant from Justice Fleming. "OK, do you have any questions now?"

Meng replied: "Right, I'm not clear what has happened. Why would I have an arrest warrant? And I have got involved in fraud?"

Yep's partner interjected: "So she said she's not sure why she has an arrest warrant. How she's involved in this fraud."

Yep told her she was going to be moved to the RCMP's Richmond detachment. "And then, uh, you will stay a few days and then go to the United States," the officer told her.

At 2:27 p.m., Meng made her first request to speak to a lawyer. She wanted to call her company lawyers to help her find a Canadian lawyer. "Yeah, if you find a lawyer sooner, you can go to the United States faster," said Yep. Meng's first contact with her company lawyer came at 3:20, barely an hour after she first asked.[15]

Yep cuffed Meng's hands in front of her body. He didn't think it necessary to cuff her hands behind the back. "It was always going to be me who was effecting the arrest because I had the warrant and this was an RCMP matter," Yep recalled later. "It went smooth." He believed it was the right decision not to arrest her on the plane: "You don't just rush in to arrest somebody without knowing your environment."[16]

This three-hour sequence of events prior to Meng's arrest by the RMCP would later form a pivotal part of her defence against extradition to the United States. An extradition hearing is not a trial. It is meant to be a court proceeding where a judge determines whether there is sufficient evidence against a person to justify sending them to another country where a formal trial can determine their guilt or innocence. Meng's lawyers would argue the pre-arrest search by Canadian border agents was a flagrant violation of her rights, conduct that fatally tainted the legal process brought to bear against her. Innumerable affidavits, motions, and pleadings in the months ahead would focus on those three hours.[17]

As Meng was settling in for her first night in a Canadian jail, the leaders of the world's richest economies were winding down the G20 summit in Buenos Aires, Argentina. Chinese President Xi Jinping, US President Donald Trump, and Canadian Prime Minister Justin Trudeau would enjoy one final dinner together before relations between their countries became infinitely more complicated.

CHAPTER TWO

Who is
Meng Wanzhou?

MENG WANZHOU'S FIRST court appearance was a low-key affair, although her lawyer, David Martin, correctly predicted "global interest" in her case. He told the hearing that arresting Meng was akin to apprehending Facebook chief operating officer Sheryl Sandberg.

The key question to be settled as the hearings unfolded over the early days of December 2018 was this: given that Meng was worth billions of dollars, could she be trusted not to flee if she were granted bail?[1]

On December 3, Meng pleaded for her freedom in a four-page affidavit, providing Canadians their first glimpse into her life, career, and connections to their country. The affidavit reported that she was born on February 13, 1972, in Chengdu, China. She was a citizen of China, and no other country, but also held a Hong Kong passport. She lived in Shenzhen, the southern Chinese city that is also the headquarters for Huawei. She joined the company in 1993 after earning a master's degree from the Huazhong University of Science and Technology.[2]

Meng started out in her father's company as a secretary but her rise through its senior ranks mirrored Huawei's own swift ascendancy to the highest levels of the global telecommunications market. For Meng, it led to a frenetic life of international travel, and like many well-heeled Asians, she was drawn to Vancouver and the oasis it provided her and her family:

> While I am a Chinese citizen and normally reside in China, my family has extensive ties to Canada, and Vancouver in particular. I first visited Vancouver approximately fifteen years ago. Since then, I have returned regularly, originally as a visitor but for some period of time I was also a permanent resident of Canada—status that I have since relinquished.[3]

In addition to the natural beauty of its Pacific Ocean setting, ringed by distant Rocky Mountains, Meng was lured by another of Vancouver's attributes: its skyrocketing real estate market. It was a great place to park money. In 2009, she and her husband, the venture capitalist Xiaozong Liu, bought a house on 28th Street in Vancouver. She had a $2.5 million mortgage on the house, which was assessed at $5.6 million in 2017. They bought a second home in 2016 at 1603 Matthews St. in Vancouver, and started to renovate it. She had a $5 million mortgage on the property. It was assessed at $16.3 million in 2017.[4]

The house on 28th Street served as a base to educate three of Meng's children in Canada. She has three sons from a previous marriage, about which little is known, and a daughter with Liu. The younger of the family's children lived with Liu in Vancouver while he worked towards a master's degree on a student visa. By 2012, the family had left the city but, says Meng, "my husband and my younger children spent many weeks, sometimes months, here during the summer."[5] Her mother and her older son also visited Vancouver.

While her work obligations and frequent travel kept her busy, Meng always tried to spend part of every summer in Vancouver.[6]

Despite her privileged rise in a family-owned company, Meng faced serious business challenges along the way. She and her younger brother, also named Ren, were at one point understood to be in line to succeed their father, Ren Sr. The elder Ren crushed that notion in 2013 in an internal email that was made public by a Chinese high-tech news website. In the missive, Ren said his successor must possess vision, character, and specific knowledge of their industry. "None of my family members possess these qualities," he wrote, and they "will never be included in the sequence of successors." He announced new measures to provide training to senior executives to prepare them for leadership roles in the company.[7]

It wasn't the first time Ren Sr. had publicly undermined his children. Two years earlier, in 2011, he disclosed to the company that his daughter had undergone cancer surgery twice in the previous eight years.

In a 2018 affidavit to a BC court, Meng also acknowledged "numerous health problems," including hypertension and cancer. "I survived thyroid cancer, for which I underwent surgery in 2011," she testified. "In May of 2018. I had surgery to remedy health issues related to sleep apnea. I currently have difficulty eating solid foods and have had to modify my diet to address those issues. My doctor has for years provided me with daily packages of medications that I have been prescribed to treat these ailments."[8]

Despite her challenges, Meng arrived on Canadian shores in December 2018 an accomplished, respected international business figure. She was named a top ten female business executive by *Forbes* magazine, and she is revered in her own country. The week of her arrest, the *Globe and Mail's* China correspondent, Nathan VanderKlippe, wrote that Meng "has become an important Chinese voice, both on the global stage—appearing on panels next to figures such as Ben Bernanke, the former chairman of the US Federal Reserve—and in giving a positive face to a company whose immense growth has been accompanied by suspicion about the security of its technology." VanderKlippe cited a speech Meng delivered two years earlier at Tsinghua University where she "drew on Einstein, Newton, and Nietzsche, calling Huawei a place of great opportunity for young people, with a work environment that has sought to do away with traditional hierarchies."[9]

* * *

On the morning of her second court appearance, international journalists, Meng supporters, and gawkers gathered on the downtown Vancouver courthouse steps, hoping for a glimpse of the celebrity prisoner. They also competed for seats in the large courtroom, which had been specially built for the Air India terrorism trial many years earlier. Amid the circus atmosphere, television cameras focused on three young men and two women brandishing a white placard emblazoned with red spray paint: "Free Ms. Meng."[10]

Meng arrived from the women's correctional centre in Maple Ridge, BC, wearing a drab green jailhouse uniform. She sat in the glassed-in prisoner's box with a translator. Her husband waited in the front row, surrounded by a group of Huawei employees.[11]

The US Justice Department made its position on bail crystal clear in a December 3 letter to the BC court: it wanted Meng behind bars. United States Attorney Richard Donoghue said Meng was a citizen of China with "no legal status in Canada," and given her family's wealth and connections she was a definite flight risk. Huawei was now on notice that it was the subject of criminal prosecution in the US, and this would only heighten Meng's desire to flee. She had seven passports and the advantages of being the daughter of the world's eighty-third richest man, Ren Zhengfei, who had a net worth of $3.2 billion. "As a result of Meng and her family's extensive net worth, there is no question that Meng has the resources to flee from prosecution and to remain a fugitive indefinitely."

Donoghue added that Meng had been avoiding travel to the US and that Huawei had pulled some of its people out of the country once it "became aware of a US criminal investigation when Huawei's US subsidiaries were served with a grand jury subpoena. As a result, Huawei executives began altering their travel patterns, to avoid any travel to or through the United States." Meng had often travelled to the US between 2014 and 2016. Her last trip was in late February and early March of 2017, one month before US officials believe Huawei learned of the investigation. "Meng has not travelled to, or through, the United States since, even though one of her children attends boarding school in the United States," said Donoghue.[12]

Meng professed her innocence, swearing in an affidavit that she would stay in Vancouver to contest her extradition, "and I will contest the allegations at trial in the US if I am ultimately surrendered." The accused said she had no criminal record and promised to live at the 28th Street house and "scrupulously abide" by all curfews and conditions. She offered to pledge the equity in her family's two Vancouver homes. "I understand that my husband and daughter, and my extended family members would come to Vancouver and reside with me as permitted by Canada's immigration laws."

Meng offered another reason for why she would not try to flee. "My father founded Huawei and I would never do anything that would cause the company reputational damage. I believe that breaching my bail conditions would cause such damage."

Others spoke in support of Meng in written submissions to the court. Sha Ye, a senior fellow at Fudan University in Shanghai, said Meng had devoted her life to Huawei and wouldn't damage her hard-earned reputation by absconding to China to avoid prosecution. "I am really saddened to hear the news that Ms. Meng has been detained in Vancouver over the past weekend. I have spoken to Ms. Meng's family. Ms. Meng firmly believes that the Canadian and US legal system will produce a just result that will prove her innocence. Ms. Meng has spent her entire career working for Huawei. She has gained an impeccable reputation over these years. This is her lifelong work!"[13]

A neighbour of Meng's in Vancouver also wrote to the court on her behalf, saying that she had a son in school in the United States and wouldn't do anything to jeopardize the child's future. "I first met Sabrina about eight years ago when she and her husband first purchased the house next door. The home has been largely used as a summer retreat for extended family including children and grandparents. Sabrina's visits were typically brief but understandably due to her involvement in business affairs internationally. Conversations with her gave one the impression of a quiet and modest individual who considered her family and children a priority."[14]

A week later, BC Supreme Court Justice William Ehrcke decided Meng could live in her Vancouver home on bail of $10 million. Ehrcke imposed strict conditions: her every move would be monitored by a private security detail, and a GPS tracker would be strapped to her ankle to record her every move. The bail hearing had heard evidence from Scot Filer, a retired RCMP officer and founder of the Lions Gate Risk Management Group, a private security firm specializing in risk management and surveillance services. Filer offered the court a pair of options on how Meng could be monitored. In his ruling, Ehrcke said he preferred "option two" which offered "continuous observation at any time when Ms. Meng would be outside of her residence." For every eight-hour shift, that would require one driver, one security officer, a security vehicle, and "technical devices."

"The advantages of this option," Ehrcke explained, "are that while still being minimally intrusive and less overt, it still provides continuous observation of Ms. Meng while at the residence and out in the community. The driver remains with the vehicle at the pick-up and drop off location, while the security officer accompanies Ms. Meng into whatever location she attends. The security officer remains in close proximity of Ms. Meng while still allowing her to conduct business and have private conversations. This option also utilizes secure software and hardware that tracks the movement of the operators while on duty. The device allows for constant two-way communications via secure text, and accurate GPS tracking. The device does not track Ms. Meng, which minimizes the intrusion of her Charter Rights. The device works in conjunction with a GPS tracking bracelet."

In making his decision, Ehrcke said no bail order could provide an "absolute guarantee" that an accused person won't flee. He also said that Meng had no criminal record, was a "well-educated busi-nesswoman," and that several people attested to her good character. He also took into account that at least five acquaintances of Meng had posted $3 million of her total bail of $10 million.[15]

Ehrcke also rejected the US Justice Department arguments that Meng was studiously avoiding travel to America. It was almost as if the judge was taking a swipe at President Donald Trump: "I put very little weight on the suggested inference that Ms. Meng's failure to travel to the United States since March 2017 is evidence of an intent to evade apprehension there. That inference is entirely speculative and without any reliable foundation. Residents of countries other than the United States, including Ms. Meng, may have myriad good reasons for choosing not to travel to the United States during the past two years."[16]

In the months and years that followed the grant of bail, Meng's lawyers spared no expense in arguing that her arrest was an abuse of power, and that a Canadian judge should throw out the charges against her and let her go free. That argument stretched what should have been a short extradition hearing into a lengthy legal proceeding that extended into the summer of 2021. An extradition hearing is not supposed to be a trial, but Meng's has all the appearance of one. It was clear from the earliest days of the affair that she was determined to stay in Vancouver for the foreseeable future. Prime Minister Justin Trudeau was alerted to this fact by his national security advisor in a December 18, 2018, memo: "Ms. Meng is preparing for a long stay and has reached out to the University of British Columbia (UBC) to indicate that she intends to pursue a PhD in business at UBC while resident in Vancouver," wrote Greta Bossenmaier.[17]

On December 11, Meng Wanzhou traded the formless green jailhouse tracksuit she had worn for ten days for a shiny red waffled coat over a plush purple tracksuit. She was also sporting the accessory that would define her international image for years to come: a GPS tracking bracelet locked to her ankle. Surrounded by British Columbia courthouse sheriffs and a small group of men in black, by all appearances a private security detail, Meng was ushered with her head down out onto the wet concrete and through a throng of journalists.

"Ms. Meng, what's your reaction to being granted bail today?"

No answer. The sheriffs and the men in black formed a wall around Meng as they reach the curb.

Someone asked of the men in black: "Who do you guys work for?" That question, too, was ignored.

Finding no vehicle at the curb, a member of the security detail was heard to say, "Let's move her back in." Suddenly a black SUV with darkened windows pulled up. The leader of the security detail, gray-haired and goateed behind black glasses, shielded Meng with his right arm while his left hand pressed his cellphone to his ear. He draped his arm around Meng like a protective father; she burrowed into his shoulder like a frightened child. "Wait a minute, the vehicle's here, the vehicle's here," he said.

The rear passenger side door suddenly swung open. Another journalist shouted out a question: "Ms. Meng, why should people believe you that you won't breach your bail? Do you have anything to say?" She silently disappeared into the SUV.[18] She was bound for a seven-bedroom mansion, where she would begin a new chapter in her life, not free, but in relative comfort compared to what was happening to two Canadians on the other side of the Pacific Ocean.

CHAPTER THREE

They Just Disappeared

EVEN BEFORE MENG'S plane touched down on Canadian soil, there were worries about the consequences of her arrest. The US Federal Bureau of Investigation had tipped off the Canadian Security Intelligence Service, Canada's spy agency, about the plan to pick her up when she reached Vancouver. But no FBI agents would be present "in an effort to avoid the perception of influence," CSIS said. The main conclusion of the Canadian spy agency was prophetic: "The arrest is likely to send shock waves around the world."[1]

Meng's December 1 arrest sparked immediate outrage from Chinese authorities, raising the possibility that China might retaliate with its own arrests of Canadians. When the story broke, the Chinese embassy in Ottawa branded her detention "a mistake" and called for her immediate release, claiming a serious human rights violation. In Beijing, Chinese foreign ministry spokesman Geng Shuang angrily complained at his daily media briefing that neither Canadian nor American officials had responded to China's concerns about the arrest. Chinese officials were clearly miffed when Prime

Minister Justin Trudeau said that his office wasn't talking to anybody about the file because "we are a country of an independent judiciary, and the appropriate authorities took the decisions in this case without any political involvement or interference." Trudeau said his office only received "a few days' notice that this was in the works."

Five days after Meng's arrest, David Mulroney, Canada's former ambassador to China (2009–2012) and an outspoken critic of the Chinese government, explained what was at stake in the unfolding drama. "I don't want to exaggerate the risk, but we should be alert to it," said Mulroney. "China will be furious and look for means of punishing us, in part as an example for others. That could include tit-for-tat moves against Canadians."[2]

On December 8 and 9, respectively, the Chinese foreign ministry in Beijing called in the Canadian and American ambassadors for a dressing down.[3] That was only the beginning.

* * *

Michael Kovrig was born Canada in 1972, after his family fled Hungary's communist regime in 1950. Kovrig was drawn back to Budapest in the mid-1990s where he taught English and worked as a journalist, joining the wave of younger westerners drawn to the bohemian allure of the newly thriving eastern European capitals that were exploding with newfound euphoria after the fall of the Berlin Wall. It almost seemed natural that Kovrig would end up the front man in a punk rock band. In 1996, he answered an advertisement for an English-speaking singer for an all-Hungarian group of musicians that wanted to broaden their appeal. He aced his audition, armed with a decent enough voice for a group that, in keeping with the punk ethos, could barely play its instruments.

The four-piece punk rock band, known as Bankrupt, introduced its lanky, leather-jacketed lead singer as Michael K. His onstage moniker was a play on Joseph K., the protagonist of Franz Kafka's novel, *The Trial*, the surreal allegory of totalitarianism. Balazs Sarkadi, the band's leader to this day, had auditioned singers from Britain, New Zealand, and the United States, but when he met Kovrig for the first time at a McDonald's restaurant, he knew he had found a musical brother. "You know, the leather jacket? He looked the part," Sarkadi recalled.[4]

The rehearsals started and Kovrig reliably showed up. "It was inspiring," said Sarkadi. But Kovrig offered more: he opened the band's eyes to music from the free world, including the Clash, the Pixies, and Leonard Cohen. He introduced Sarkadi to the legendary American rock music writer, Lester Bangs. He also wrote songs, including "Listen," the story a disaffected twenty-one-year-old that was recently released on a compilation of lost punk oddities.[5] "I'm sitting in my room and I think there's nothing I can do against this gloom," Kovrig sings in an aped British post-punk accent. "If you don't listen, I'll go crazy on my own."[6]

Three years later, Kovrig left Budapest and parted ways with Bankrupt, but he would maintain contact with its members in the decades to come. "I guess he kind of grew out of it as he got serious with his career in diplomacy," said Sarkadi. "The Michael I remember, I mean I always think of him as our singer, and a rock and roll kind of guy."

Kovrig traded his leather jacket for a suit and tie and spent more than a decade as a Canadian diplomat, serving in a variety of posts including Beijing, Hong Kong, and Canada's United Nations mission in New York City. He also spent four years in the Afghanistan capital of Kabul with the UN Development Program. In February 2017, he took a leave of absence from the Canadian foreign service and joined the International Crisis Group. The Brussels-based think tank is devoted to fostering world peace by understanding why countries and combatants fight, and what can be done to resolve their differences.

Based in Hong Kong, Kovrig, who speaks fluent Mandarin, visited China on a regular basis on behalf of Crisis Group. As senior adviser for Northeast Asia, he was able to meet government officials in an attempt to understand Chinese policy and how the Chinese view the world. He synthesized his learnings into public reports and analyses intended to deepen the pool of global knowledge on an ascendant and ambitious country.

Kovrig contributed to two major Crisis Group reports: one on conflict prevention in the Korean peninsula, which focused on "Chinese ideas" for easing the ongoing tensions between the United States and North Korea over its unchecked nuclear weapons program; the other was the group's analysis of China's role as a mediator in the long-running saga of war and humanitarian carnage in South Sudan.[7]

Five months before Meng's arrest, Kovrig had closely watched the historic meeting between US President Donald Trump and Kim Jong-un as it unfolded in Singapore. It was the first time that a sitting American president had met with a North Korean leader. The meeting was a coup for Kim, who had been denied facetime with Barack Obama, who didn't want to give the despot a soapbox or a platform. Previous American presidents had similarly snubbed Kim's father. Trump had no such compunctions. His ambassador to Canada at the time, Kelly Craft, said that her president was determined to "carry the water" for a Western world determined to make peace with North Korea; he was determined to succeed where others had failed.[8] So the president walked into a luxurious Singapore hotel to meet the waiting Kim. He mugged and deadpanned for the cameras, effusively shaking Kim's hand in a series of photo-ops, generally treating him as a legitimate politician. To this day, North Korea remains a dangerously armed nuclear state.

Kovrig offered a thoughtful take on what transpired during a split-screen panel discussion with two American pundits on the New

Delhi-based WION (World is One News) television program called *Gravitas*. Kovrig spoke carefully and lucidly. He pronounced the Trump-Kim summit a qualified success: "I think against a relatively low bar, given that we were mostly worried in many cases that it could have gone off the rails or been cancelled, or there could have been all kinds of unexpected outcomes. I think the three of us all agree that this is a broadly positive summit."[9]

The one thing Kovrig said he found striking was that as much as analysts such as himself had found Kim Jong-il reclusive, his son was "clearly relatively extroverted, jovial, likes to hug people, he's physical."

For all the bonhomie that had just taken place between Kim and Trump, Kovrig pointed out that Kim's key relationship was with China's Xi Jinping. The two had met four months earlier, and it was important to remember that any peace that might one day be achieved in the Korean Peninsula would most definitely bear the stamp of Xi.

Kovrig's final observation seems bitterly poignant in hindsight. He thought it was significant that Kim had placed his own personal safety, and potential liberty, in Xi's hands. The North Korean had accepted a flight on a Chinese airplane to the Singapore meeting with Trump. Kovrig was aware that no one, not even a dictator, ought to let one's guard down when it comes to personal safety: "Kim flew an Air China 747 down to the summit. I think that's a pretty strong signal that he feels comfortable now with his relationship with [the Chinese], enough to trust them with his life going through their airspace down here, building on those previous meetings."

Five months later, Kovrig boarded a commercial airplane from his base in Hong Kong for what he expected would be another informative research trip to Beijing. On December 10, he simply disappeared. He may have been arrested at his hotel, or outside of it, perhaps pulled away from a plate of steaming street food. No one knows. Meng's arrest generated an exhaustive trail of detailed court filings, sworn evidence, judicial orders, plans, documents, notes, and long sequences of videotape. Kovrig vanished into the opaque Chinese justice system. All that was known was that the Chinese alleged Kovrig had jeopardized their national security.

As soon as Kovrig was arrested, the Crisis Group moved to emphasize that his work had nothing to do with Chinese national security. "Michael's work included meeting several dozen times with Chinese officials, academics, and analysts from multiple Chinese state institutions. He had attended numerous conferences at the invitation of Chinese organizations. He frequently appeared on Chinese television and in other media to comment on regional issues," his employer said. "Nothing Michael did harmed China. On the contrary, Crisis Group's work aims to defuse any tensions between China and nearby states, and to give a fresh, independent appraisal of China's growing role in the world. Michael's detention is all the more perplexing to Crisis Group since it came after a decade of good and productive engagement with the Chinese authorities."[10]

At its core, Kovrig's work—travelling the world, interviewing people, gathering information, analyzing its significance—resembled journalism or academic research. He was not part of the intelligence apparatus of any country or organization. He was never a spy. He was a legitimate researcher for an organization determined to learn and explain the point of view of one of the most important countries in the world. But there was enough raw material on how Kovrig performed his work to give the Chinese government the fodder it needed to spin a fictional espionage narrative when it became necessary to retaliate for Meng Wanzhou's arrest in Canada.

* * *

Robert Malley had just arrived in Tokyo on December 11 after a long journey from the United States when his phone rang in the middle of the night. His chief of staff back in Washington had grim news.

"I was told one of our colleagues had been picked up on the streets of Beijing," Malley recalled. "We didn't have much information."[11]

Malley was the president of the International Crisis Group.* He was scheduled to travel from Tokyo to Australia, but he immediately changed his plans and caught a flight to Beijing to see what he could do to get Michael Kovrig out of detention.*

Kovrig couldn't have had a much heavier hitter in his court than Malley. The trim, bearded, soft-spoken New Yorker was a skilled and experienced American diplomat who had served as a special adviser to US president Bill Clinton (organizing the 2000 Israeli-Palestinian summit at Camp David) and on Barack Obama's National Security Council. The latter assignment had placed him at the heart of a major international security issue: the West's negotiations to prevent Iran from acquiring a nuclear bomb. Malley was the lead American negotiator for the 2015 Iran nuclear deal that included the five permanent members of the United Nations Security Council and the European Union—an agreement ripped up three years later by Donald Trump.*

"Maybe this is something that could be resolved quicker," Malley recalled thinking as he headed to Beijing. "But I had no contact with Chinese authorities when I was there. Nobody would respond to requests for a meeting." He spent a few days in Beijing meeting people who knew Kovrig, as well as foreign diplomats and Canadian embassy officials. Malley departed Beijing empty-handed. "It's one thing to know where he is. And it's terrible enough," said Malley. But the indeterminate nature of Kovrig's detention begged the question of whether this "was going to last a month, two months, three months, six months, a year, two years?"[12]

---

* By the spring of 2021, Robert Malley had joined the Joe Biden administration as the state department's special envoy to Iran as part of the new president's attempts to undo some of the political damage of his predecessor.

* * *

As a schoolboy, Michael Spavor absorbed the spectacle of the 1988 Winter Olympics in his hometown of Calgary, Alberta, followed by the summer games months later in Seoul, South Korea. That provided his introduction to the peninsula, and he became more captivated by Korea, north and south, as the decades passed.

In 1997, Spavor travelled to South Korea as a teenaged English teacher on a three-month contract. He stayed for two years and indulged in a variety of activities—co-hosting a radio show, doing voice work, and playing extras in movies. He worked as a marketing manager at the Korea Tourism Organization and the Seoul Tourism Organization. Returning to Canada to be with his mother as she battled cancer, he completed an international relations degree at the University of Calgary. His major? The Korean Peninsula and East Asian studies.[13]

In 2001, Spavor made his first trip to North Korea for a vacation. Four years later, he planted deeper roots in the country, taking a job with a non-governmental organization to teach English and graphic design. By 2011, he was working with a non-profit called the Pyongyang Project as its program director for Korea. As he told a Korean magazine in July 2011: "People might think I want to go to North Korea because it's adventurous and mysterious, but the truth is I fell in love with the North Korean people."[14]

Spavor eventually carved out a well-earned reputation as a leading China-based Western aficionado of all things Korean: he specialized in connecting people to the world's most isolated and despotic country. Known as the Hermit Kingdom, North Korea was an international pariah. It had sealed off its population from the rest of the world, leaving many to starve as it funneled its resources into building a nuclear weapons arsenal. Spavor based himself in the northern Chinese city of Dandong, which is separated from

North Korea by a short swim across a ribbon of river. In 2015, he helped found a non-profit organization called the Paektu Cultural Exchange, which organized events that allowed outsiders to meet the cloistered residents of North Korea and connected investors with opportunities in the country to position them for an eventual lifting of international sanctions. So far, that hasn't happened.

In 2013, Spavor became a pivotal figure in an audacious and memorable junket to North Korea by the flamboyant former NBA basketball player, Dennis Rodman. The trip marked ground-breaking contact between Americans and the cherubic, wildly reclusive Kim Jong-un. The generously tattooed and pierced Rodman, who had been a contestant on Donald Trump's television show, *The Apprentice*, and who supported his presidential bid, had no trouble getting along with the North Korean president. Rodman called the dictator a "friend for life" and said President Barack Obama ought to pick up the phone and give him a call. After all, Rodman figured, they both loved basketball. In the middle of Rodman's circus was an unassuming man with a wry grin and solid track record for plugging outsiders into North Korea: Michael Spavor. A fluent Korean speaker, Spavor served as interpreter between Rodman and Kim on that trip, and on Rodman's return visit the following year.[15]

Rodman's 2013 visit left Spavor with a claim very few in the Western world could make: he had forged a friendship with Kim. Four years later, he would post a photo on Instagram of himself sharing drinks at a small table with Kim, a small plume of smoke wafting from a glass ashtray, and a pack of cigarettes next to the leader. The caption: "LONG ISLAND ICED TEAS: Kim Jong Un shares cocktails with Michael Spavor of the Paektu Cultural Exchange on board the North Korean leader's private yacht in Wonsan in September 2013."[16]

"That was the most amazing experience I've had in my life," Spavor told *Reuters* in a 2017 interview. "We hung out for three days." Spavor and Kim had spent several hours jet skiing in the bay where the yacht was anchored. Mindful of the need for discretion, he did not talk politics with Kim. "For me, encouraging these sports engagement events, these non-political friendship interactions, promoting these kinds of events can show people that Americans and Koreans can get along very well," he told *Reuters*. "I guess if we can continue to increase these exchanges, then we hope that has an effect on politicians, too."[17]

Nevertheless, Spavor couldn't escape the political dimensions of the life he had built. Fourteen months before his arrest, he was eating brunch in the Chinese border city of Yanji. The restaurant started shaking and air raid sirens started blaring. Its patrons had just felt the effects of North Korea's sixth underground test of a nuclear bomb in twelve years. It was the country's most powerful test blast to date.[18]

On December 10, 2018, Spavor had next-day plans to fly to Seoul, South Korea. He had sent out an invitation to fifty people on Facebook letting them know he was going to be in town and looking to connect. He also posted a Twitter message rallying his friends to meet for drinks. He never made it to Seoul. He was also a no-show at a planned appearance at the Royal Asiatic Society on December 11 where he was scheduled to give a lecture on his North Korean experiences.

Three days later, Chinese authorities confirmed Spavor had been arrested. As was the case with Kovrig, nothing was disclosed about the circumstances of the arrest, or the reasons for it. Experts such as Andrei Lankov, who had known Spavor for a decade, tried to fill in the blanks. He said China and Canada were now clearly playing a "hostage game." Lankov was surprised that China had picked a target with such "humble origins." He described Spavor as a likeable extrovert who didn't much care for politics. "He sees North Korea as a misrepresented underdog, and as such he wanted to basically improve its image, while making some money in the process."[19]

Jon Dunbar, a reporter with the *Korea Times* newspaper, met Spavor at a house party in Seoul a decade before his arrest. Spavor shared his contagious enthusiasm for North Korea and the two became friends, with Dunbar accompanying Spavor to the Hermit Kingdom on two occasions. Ten days after Spavor's no-show in Seoul, Dunbar called in his newspaper for China to release his friend: "He is no agent for any government or ideology, and is only pursuing his love for Korea."[20]

Dunbar had made his second trip to North Korea with Spavor only three months earlier, in September 2018. He had been nervous because he was a newspaper reporter but Spavor assured him that if he wasn't travelling in any "official" capacity, everything would be fine. On their return, Dunbar was reluctant to write about North Korea in case he somehow undermined the connections Spavor had cultivated through the Paektu Cultural Exchange. Spavor encouraged him to write anyway. Dunbar extended the unusual courtesy of letting Spavor see what he had written ahead of publication to avoid causing problems for his friend. "But it turns out it wasn't North Korea we needed to worry about. It's a bitter irony that it would be China detaining him, while he was en route to South, not North, Korea."[21]

CHAPTER FOUR

The Toilet is a Hole in the Floor

MICHAEL KOVRIG AND MICHAEL SPAVOR had established significant ties to China years before their arrests. Those connections, the work they did, and the lives they lived while in the People's Republic would provide useful facts for Chinese authorities to repurpose into their own narrative that the Two Michaels were spies. The Chinese government initially offered few details on how the Two Michaels were supposedly engaged in espionage, or what they could have done to compromise China's national security, beyond a vague suggestion that Kovrig had passed on to Spavor illicit information of some kind. It was only later that Dominic Barton, Canada's ambassador to China, offered some scant details of why the Chinese believed Spavor committed a breach of their state security. Barton says Chinese authorities accused Spavor of taking photos "around airports or those places where one should not take photos" and that some of them were of military aircraft.[1]

Western intelligence sources rebuffed Chinese allegations that Kovrig and Spavor were spies, or that they even knew each other, despite the unsubstantiated claim of a Chinese state-controlled newspaper that Spavor was an "important intelligence contact" of Korvig's.[2] Spavor's supporters also wrote a passionate defence of their friend on a website dedicated to freeing him:

> Each and every one of us who write accounts of our friendship with Michael Spavor are one hundred percent certain that he is not, and never has been, any sort of spy or intelligence asset or national security threat to China, or to any other country for that matter. Suspicions to this effect are specious and completely without merit or foundation, and anyone actually acquainted with Michael knows these allegations about him cannot possibly be true. Michael is a gregarious and big-hearted man of bounding entrepreneurial verve, endearing mild eccentricities, and above all an intense and abiding love for all things Korean. Between China and Korea, he is an interlocutor not an informer, an operator not an operative. His passion for Korea is played out openly in the ballroom, not indulged sub rosa in the cloakroom. He has neither the temperament nor the inclination to be secretive or manipulative in his love affair with Korea.[3]

Kovrig's wife, Vina Nadjibulla, also debunked the spying allegations. "They're baseless. Their detention was arbitrary since day one. That is what our government and that's what many other governments around the world have clearly stated. There is no doubt why this happens. Even Chinese officials in various elaborate ways have made it clear that there is a link between what took place on December 1, 2018, with the arrest of Meng Wanzhou and subsequent detention of the Two Michaels."[4]

Kovrig and Spavor did cross paths years before they were arrested. Kovrig served in the Canadian embassies in Beijing and Hong Kong between 2012 and 2016. Spavor was living in northern China and would intersect with the Western expatriate crowd when he visited Beijing. "Both Michael and I met Michael Spavor socially in Beijing as part of the expat community when he traveled, when Spavor traveled to Beijing," Nadjibulla said in a September 2021 interview. Did that crossing of paths provide fodder for the Chinese spy narrative about the two men? "That's just speculation. And the fundamental facts of the case don't change," said Nadjibulla, who advocated publicly for the release of the two men. "It doesn't change anything that I'm doing, or for that matter anything for Canadian government is doing."[5]

One of the only other known connections between Kovrig and Spavor was their deep and abiding interest in North Korea. Spavor was drawn to its people and way of life, disconnected from the outside world yet linked by a shared humanity. Kovrig was all about the geopolitics: understanding global conflict and the existential threat North Korea posed to the world because it possessed nuclear weapons to counter its sworn enemy, the United States; also, how China might figure in turning back the doomsday clock and de-escalating the conflict, maybe even ridding North Korea of its nuclear weapons, or at least downgrading its capabilities. The nuclear threat hung over the heads of the Two Michaels as it did for everyone else in the world.

With the imprisoning of the Two Michaels in China, their families and loved ones struggled privately and incessantly with the pain of their ordeal, clinging to scant contact with the captives through diplomatic channels, building bridges wherever possible, and trying desperately to understand what was happening behind prison walls, starved as they were of reliable information.

With China offering only silence, the best clues as to what had befallen the Michaels came from others who endured similar ordeals. Canadians Julia and Kevin Garratt, for instance, demonstrated that retaliatory hostage-taking is nothing new for the Chinese. The Garratts had lived peaceful, uneventful lives in China for the better part of three decades, running a coffee shop and performing missionary work in the border city of Dandong, near North Korea. They were picked up in 2014 and accused of espionage and stealing military secrets, one month after Canada extradited to the US a Chinese national named Su Bin, who held permanent residency in Canada.[6] In 2016, Su pleaded guilty in a US court to taking part in a lengthy criminal conspiracy to steal US military secrets and was given a forty-six-month prison sentence. The Garratt's ordeal ended the same year when Kevin was released from prison (Julia was granted bail a few months after their initial arrest).

The experience of Peter Humphrey, meanwhile, is testimony to what awaits prisoners thrown into the Chinese prison system. Humphrey was a former foreign correspondent with *Reuters* who pivoted from journalism to a fifteen-year career as an anti-fraud consultant for Western companies operating in China. For ten of those years, he owned his own company. Humphrey and his wife were locked up in Chinese prison cells for twenty-three months between 2013 and 2015. On the first-year anniversary of the imprisonment of the Two Michaels, Humphrey recollected his own experiences in an attempt to shed light on how Kovrig and Spavor were suffering:

> To ensure full shock and horror, detainees are almost always thrown into a crowded cell in the middle of the night, after at least one full day or more of interrogation in a police cell without any legal counsel. Alternatively, they may be placed into solitary confinement. Usually, prisoners are held in small and crowded unfurnished cells with no beds or chairs. Detainees are forced to spend the whole day sitting or squatting on the floor, which causes joint and muscle deterioration. At night, they sleep on a hard, rough wooden floor without enough bedcovers to keep warm. The toilet is a hole in the floor in the corner of the cell. No hot water is provided, and prisoners must wash in cold

water from a crude tap. The cells are hot in summer and freezing in winter. Beyond the cell bars, the corridor windows are left open. In winter it is often colder in the cell than it is outdoors. In hot weather there is no heating or air conditioning."[7]

What several sources have said privately about the life of the Two Michaels behind Chinese bars is confirmed by Humphrey's descriptions:

No privacy is ever allowed, for the use of the toilet, for washing, or for contemplation. If a prisoner is held in solitary, he is permanently watched over by menacing guards and cameras every single minute. Strong lights are kept on 24/7, causing sleep deprivation and eyesight deterioration.[8]

Humphrey's account of Chinese prison also includes forced "propaganda lessons," coercion into fake confessions, and endless years locked up without being formally charged. "The key drivers of all foreign detention cases in China are either revenge or political/diplomatic leverage. China has made clear that the Two Michaels are tit-for-tat hostages."[9]

Humphrey lays the blame for the Chinese practice of hostage diplomacy firmly at the feet of President Xi Jinping, who revived, with verve, the former practice of Chinese emperors of throwing people in jail to further political ends. He bemoans the West's lack of "sufficient leverage and reverse reciprocity, combined with a sense of vulnerability or a sheer lack of courage."[10] Polite diplomacy, Humphrey maintains, will not work against this new form of coercive diplomacy. He evokes British Prime Minister Winston Churchill, who offered a memorable justification for not negotiating with Adolf Hitler on the eve of the Second World War: "You cannot reason with a tiger when your head is in its mouth."[11]

* * *

There is no escaping the harsh, punishing conditions designed to break Michael Kovrig's and Michael Spavor's spirits as human beings. Degrading misery is a fact of life for inmates in China's penal system,[12] as is confusion and uncertainty. There are no public court hearings, no public records of their trials—no affidavits, no testimony, no transcripts—and no visits from lawyers or family members throughout their incarceration.

It did not go unnoticed in the Western world that those conditions were starkly different from Meng Wanzhou who had been allowed to live in her Vancouver mansion, sleep in her own bed, surrounded by loved ones, with space to indulge her literary, artistic, and culinary pursuits as she awaited her fate in a lengthy, but utterly transparent Canadian court proceeding. She has even been allowed out for the occasional massage.

On being granted bail, Meng was driven to tears. Her outburst came while waiting in the downtown Vancouver courthouse and going through the "formalities," she said in a later public statement on her company's website. One of her lawyers was telling her about the various people who had contributed to her $10 million bail. One of her sureties was a yoga teacher who pledged $50,000:

> My lawyer told me that many strangers had called his law firm and offered to put up their properties as a guarantee against my bail. Even though they had never heard of me, they knew Huawei and they trusted Huawei, and were therefore willing to believe in me. My lawyer said that he had been practicing law for over forty years and had never seen anything like this, with so many strangers willing to issue guarantees for a person that they don't know personally.
>
> Listening to the lawyer's words, I couldn't help but burst into

tears. I wasn't crying for myself; instead, I was moved by the thought that so many people had trust in me.[13]

In late January 2019, a BBC reporter visited Meng's "gilded cage," the less expensive of her two Vancouver homes, to try to get a better idea of how she was living and coping on bail. He was turned away by the two private security guards assigned by the court to make sure Meng didn't skip bail. They had another function, as far as the BBC journalist could tell: keeping outsiders away from Meng.[14]

Undaunted, the journalist Michael Bristow turned to a local businessman who built luxury homes for wealthy Chinese clients in Vancouver to get the flavour of Meng's life. The builder took Bristow on a tour of one of his architectural creations. Bristow said it looked like something out of a celebrity magazine. "Light bounced off shiny marble and polished wood. In the basement alone there is a bar, a temperature-controlled wine cellar and a grand piano," he wrote. The house had two kitchens: one for show, perhaps to boil water for tea, the other, sealed off in another part of the home to isolate odours, for serious cooking.[15]

Several months into her detention, Meng grew tired of the conditions of her house arrest, even though she could travel around Vancouver under the watch of her private, court-appointed security detail, except during a modest 11 p.m. to 6 a.m. curfew when she was confined to her home. In May 2019, the BC court modified Meng's bail conditions to allow her to move to the larger, more expensive of her properties. The renovations had apparently been completed. Her lawyers successfully persuaded the court that the mansion provided better security than the six-bedroom, five-bathroom house she had previously been living in.[16]

On the first anniversary of her arrest, Meng penned another letter reflecting on how slow her life had become compared to the hurly-burly of her previous life as a busy executive. "It is so slow that I have enough time to read a book from cover to cover," she wrote in December 2019. "I can take the time to discuss minutiae with my colleagues or to carefully complete an oil painting."[17]

In January 2021, the *Washington Post* revealed that Meng had enjoyed Christmas dining at an upscale Vancouver restaurant with an entourage of fourteen people, including her husband and two of her children, in apparent violation of British Columbia provincial guidelines limiting indoor gatherings to control the spread of COVID-19. Her family meal with friends came during a Christmas season that had separated most Canadian families, preventing children from seeing elderly grandparents, among other sacrifices.

Meng's festive holiday was consistent with the gilded quality of her "confinement." She had also been to outdoor concerts and an art teacher had been permitted visits to her mansion. She had been allowed to shop at expensive Vancouver shops that were opened just for her. All this while most Canadians were subjected to lockdowns mandated during the COVID-19 pandemic. Schools, offices, stores, and gyms were closed, and strict limits were placed on direct, in-person interaction.

* * *

Whatever the differences in their circumstances, Michael Kovrig, Michael Spavor, and Meng Wanzhou were now bound by one shared reality. All three were pawns in a full-blown technology war for control over global communications and the future of the internet. This cyber war is the defining global conflict of the early twenty-first century—less life-threatening, but every bit as definitive in its time, as were two world wars and the Cold War between the Soviet Union and the United States in the last century.

China and the United States are the leading combatants. China is determined to see Huawei Technologies consolidate its position as the leading provider of the next generation 5G communications equipment on which so much of the world's communications and business will operate. It believes the US is simply trying to block the rise of one of the few successful multinational tech firms that isn't American owned.

The US views Huawei as an arm of Chinese military intelligence and has warned its main intelligence allies (Canada, Britain, Australia, and New Zealand) not to allow its equipment into their communications infrastructure. America's concerns are long-standing. More than a decade ago, the Obama administration raised alarms about Chinese cyber espionage, threats to US critical infrastructure, and the growing role of companies like Huawei in China's bid to control the 5G future. Under the Trump administration, the US pursued a vigorous investigation of Huawei. Opposition to Huawei and China's attempts at technological dominance are one of the few points on which Democrats and Republicans have agreed in recent years.

When the RCMP picked up Meng at Vancouver's airport on December 1, 2018, it opened Canada as a new front in the cyber war—indeed, one of the main battlegrounds between the two global giants. And when they were subsequently arrested, a new Cold War over internet technologies and geopolitical ambitions ensnared two innocent Canadians, giving the conflict a human scale.

CHAPTER FIVE

A Brief History of Underestimating China

O N DECEMBER 14, 2015, black-clad Chinese police officers wearing white N95 respirators were gathered in front
of a Beijing courthouse under an overcast, soot-soaked
sky. Inside, the trial of Chinese human rights lawyer Pu Zhiqiang
was underway. Supporters and demonstrators had rallied to support
Pu, while journalists, camera crews, and diplomats from Western
embassies joined them in the street to document their dissent. The
Chinese police were having none of it. The officers broke into the
crowd, shoving and pulling people out of their way. One thick fire-
plug of an officer pushed several people, punched one, and ripped
a large television camera out of the hands of its operator. In the
middle of the scuffles and hollering, BBC Beijing correspondent
John Sudworth, whose camera operator was recording it all, narrated
the scene: "This is a trial that's all about free speech. And China was
keeping journalists well away. But this was forceful even by China's
usual standards for press access."[1]

"Even diplomats, who had hoped to observe the court proceedings were pushed and hassled away," says Sudworth.[2] The Canadian embassy in Beijing was among those to dispatch two diplomats to witness the scene. A third diplomat was assigned to write a report on what they witnessed: his name was Michael Kovrig. Eight days later, relatively good news emerged from Pu's trial. He was banned from his profession but handed a three-year suspended sentence. Kovrig wrote a two-page memorandum that was circulated widely within the Canadian foreign ministry, and to colleagues across China, Hong Kong, and Geneva, the seat of the United Nations Human Rights Council.

"Renowned human rights lawyer Pu Zhiqiang given suspended sentence, barred from practicing law," Kovrig wrote in the subject line. The file was entitled: "BEIJING-262 Diplomats and foreign journalists manhandled outside trial of human rights lawyer Pu Zhiqiang." The documents were stamped "SECRET" but were subsequently released under Canada's access-to-information law.[3]

Kovrig's dispatch analyzed the implications of Pu's trial. The three-year suspended sentence, he wrote, was "lighter than what many observers had feared." Pu's lawyer told the Canadian embassy that a ten-day appeal period had now been triggered, but there were no plans to proceed. When the ten days expired, Pu was expected to be released from prison and allowed to return home under "certain rules," such as reporting to police if he wished to travel. The Beijing Intermediate Court had found Pu guilty of charges of "inciting ethnic hatred" and "picking quarrels and provoking trouble." His "alleged crimes," as Kovrig detailed them, consisted of seven posts on the Chinese microblogging website Sina Weibo, China's version of Twitter, between July 2011 and May 2014. The posts totaled just 600 characters.[4]

"Pu," wrote Kovrig, "was particularly critical of China's ethnic policies against Uyghurs, writing in one post, 'If you say Xinjiang belongs to China, then don't treat it as a colony, don't act as conquerors and plunderers. This is an absurd national policy.'" He had also "mocked Chairman Mao's grandson Mao Xinyu and a senior National People's Congress deputy and accused now-purged CPC security czar Zhou Yongkang of abusing human rights."

Pu admitted to his posts but insisted none warranted the charges that had been brought against him. His lawyer "also noted that he appreciated the support and attention that Canada and likeminded governments had given to the case."[5]

Kovrig's memo was symptomatic of the Canadian government's disjointed approach to Beijing. As front-line diplomats such as himself were documenting serious human rights cases in China, the government pursued its economic aspirations to increase trade, investment, and the mobility of people between the countries. Kovrig's memo was filed little more than a month after Prime Minister Justin Trudeau's first encounter with Chinese President Xi Jinping at the G20 summit in Turkey. That meeting was amiable and full of promise. Xi was pleased to know the son of the man who had helped pave the way for the West's relations with the People's Republic some forty-five years earlier.

* * *

Pierre Trudeau's establishment of Canadian diplomatic relations with China in October 1970 and his memorable visit in 1973, in which he was granted an unexpected audience with Chairman Mao Zedong, opened the floodgates for other Western nations to engage China. Notably, US President Richard Nixon paid his own historic visit to China in 1972, paving the way for the establishment of formal diplomatic relations seven years later. The elder Trudeau's motives were partly a personal fascination with China, which he had travelled extensively in his youth, partly an ambition to bring the

Chinese into the international family of nations, and partly a desire to expand Canada's international trade opportunities and strike a foreign policy course independent of the US. Human rights were not high on his agenda. As Trudeau's biographer John English explains, "Trudeau had ridiculed China's exclusion from international organizations and its non-recognition by many Western democracies, including Canada. It would be a mark of the 'independent foreign policy' many Canadian intellectuals and journalists were demanding if the Canadian government broke with the Americans and others and recognized China."[6]

In the 1980s, human rights concerns barely registered in Brian Mulroney's pre-Tiananmen Square engagement with Beijing. The Progressive Conservatives under Mulroney enthusiastically pursued trade and people-to-people ties with the Chinese, disregarding at least publicly China's totalitarian ways.

Declassified cabinet documents show how the Progressive Conservative government had been eager and full of purpose as it set out to build economic bridges with China. On March 16, 1987, Mulroney and his cabinet met to consider a secret memo titled *A Canadian Strategy for China*. It laid out a clear economic goal: "How to capitalize on Canada's fascination with China to seize opportunities created by its modernization drive and to position ourselves for the year 2000 when China will be a major world power with a GNP approaching $1 trillion."[7]

The document called for a "coordinated drive" to promote Canadian trade with China, laying out marching orders for ministers holding the portfolios of external affairs, trade, national defence, employment and immigration, and international development. They were to consult with the provinces, business, academics, and other China experts to get Canadian companies into China, and to get people moving between the countries in a series of exchanges spanning the arts, academia, sports, and the media. The document also called for Canada to help expand defence relations with China, consult on security issues, and shepherd its new friend into the General Agreement on Tariffs and Trade (GATT).[8]

The Progressive Conservatives wanted to keep their grand China plan under the radar. While the strategy sought to "enhance Chinese awareness of Canada's potential" as a trading and investment partner, it displayed little appetite for stimulating broad public discussion in Canada. "The impact of the China strategy will be localized to the segments of the Canadian society and media who have an inherent interest in developing and expanding the Canada/China relationship. Media in general will not be inclined to give more than passing reference to the issue," it said. "There is a slight chance that Canada might be censured for promoting the commercial/economic/cultural aspects of the relationship while ignoring the question of human rights."[9]

Mulroney was no doubt mindful of that "slight chance." A *Globe and Mail* news story of his trip to China in the spring of 1986 had been headlined, "Mulroney, Chinese Premier discusses human rights, clergy." It reported that Mulroney had discussed an imprisoned Chinese clergyman in a meeting with Premier Zhao Ziyang. The prime minister was forced to acknowledge at a press conference that the topic had arisen, but he offered no details of what was said. "Quiet diplomacy" was the mantra when it came to China's sensitive issues. As far as Mulroney was concerned, the highlight of his trip had been a seventy-minute meeting with Chinese leader Deng Xiaoping, which had echoes of Pierre Trudeau's historic audience thirteen years earlier with Chairman Mao. Mulroney said meeting Deng "was like meeting Churchill."[10]

Months later, the China strategy presented to the federal cabinet put forth a government plan to bypass the mainstream media as Canada pursued its trade ambitions with China: "There is little requirement to raise the awareness of Canadians to the importance of our relationship with China." Communications were to be "tightly targeted to groups already involved in the China relationship," particularly businesses, which would be urged to "take a fresh and realistic look at China." It said the "communications tools of choice" were speeches by ministers and top officials "to prestige audiences," with detailed briefings only to "specialized national media." National television and other "mass audience tools" were to be mainly avoided. "The messages are sophisticated ones targeted by and large at sophisticated audiences."[11]

The internationally televised slaughter of innocent students by Chinese tanks and soldiers in Tiananmen Square on June 4, 1989, put an end to the under-the-radar approach. The students had occupied the square calling for more democratic freedom, political reform, and an end to state corruption. Canada's external affairs minister, Joe Clark, was one of the first Western foreign ministers to speak out against China's abhorrent behavior. Clark briefed Mulroney and his cabinet colleagues forty-eight hours after the massacre, which at the time was believed to have cost thousands of lives.

Mulroney called for swift action on several fronts. His top instruction was to have Canada's mission at the United Nations call for the matter to be referred to the UN Security Council. A series of cabinet meetings in the following weeks firmed up Canada's actions, which included joining Britain and Australia to broadcast radio signals directly into China. Canada's contribution was through Radio Canada International and the intent was to "transmit factual reports into the country," according to cabinet meeting minutes.[12]

It wasn't long before the Conservative government began coming to terms with the implications of the massacre. At a June 19 meeting of the cabinet committee on foreign and defence policy, the government discussed the need for Canada to balance a strong response to China's vicious behaviour with the imperative of playing the long game with a country of strategic economic importance. "Essentially the question we need to ask is what sort of relationship does Canada want with the China that appears to be emerging from these tumultuous events," Clark said in talking points for his presentation to the committee. "For example, how permanent is this reversal in the democratization process? Will another shoe drop?"

One thing was clear in Clark's view: "The Canada-China relationship is on a fundamentally new footing." What that meant was, "we are not accepting China's international call for 'business as usual'."[13] Still, he hoped Canada could find a way to renew some sort of constructive relationship with the Chinese, having invested the better part of two decades building a relationship. "I would hope that our approach will be conscious of the importance of the bilateral relationship, and indeed of the importance of preventing China from sliding back into international isolationism," he said. "We do not have to accept the Chinese position on any part of the crisis but there will be advantages if it is clear that what we are doing is clearly Canadian and conscious of the special relationship that we have had with China . . ."[14]

The following year, at a G7 summit in Houston, Mulroney and his counterparts agreed in their final communiqué that the "prospects for closer cooperation [with China] will be enhanced by renewed political and economic reform, particularly in the field of human rights."[15] In many respects, that marked the beginning of the end of the West's diplomatic deep freeze with China over Tiananmen Square. Mulroney welcomed Premier Zhu to Canada three years later in hopes that engaging with someone who was seen as a reformer might spur reform in China. Such reform has yet to happen. Relatively normal economic relations were restored between China and Canada before Mulroney's nine years in office ended in 1993.

* * *

By the time Jean Chrétien's Liberals came to power in 1993, Canada was very much back on its familiar path of economic engagement with China. Memories of Tiananmen Square had faded from public and official consciousness, and human rights barely warranted lip service. Canada became the first G7 country to host a visit from Chinese Premier Zhu Rongji, part of an effort to build relationships with the "newer breed of Chinese leaders."[16] Canadian journalists badgered Chrétien on China's human rights record every time he visited the country—six trips over the course of his ten years in power—but to little apparent effect.

Chrétien's first trip to China in November 1994 was a major trade mission. He brought nine premiers and an entourage of senior business executives. They did not leave empty-handed. The marquee deal was a letter of intent signed between Atomic Energy of Canada Ltd. and its Chinese counterpart to sell two Candu reactors, worth between $1 billion and 1.5 billion. Other deals totaling in the hundreds of millions of dollars were also signed in the medical technology, forestry, petroleum, telecommunications, and transport sectors. Among the benefitting Canadian companies were the Quebec-based powerhouses, Power Corp. and Bombardier Inc., which inked a deal to build passenger rail cars. Two lesser-known firms signed $135-million contracts to help build a telecommunications tower in Chengdu, Sichuan province where a then twenty-two-year-old Meng Wanzhou was residing.

In a speech to students at Beijing University, Chrétien lauded the progress that had been made between the countries since Pierre Trudeau's 1970 breakthrough, in which, he reminded his audience, he had served as a cabinet minister. Reporters pushed Chrétien about whether he raised human rights in his meeting with Premier Li Peng. Chrétien said he did, but the Chinese side said he did not. "The resulting furore saw one Canadian premier use Chinese security guards to avoid the press and another at first denied human rights had been raised and then recanted," wrote Southam News correspondent Jonathan Manthorpe, who covered the visit.[17]

On his February 2001 trip to China, Chrétien made his most overt attempt at addressing human rights during a speech at the National Judges College in Beijing. Chrétien said China had new legal obligations because of its entry into the World Trade Organization and its planned ratification of the UN Covenants on Human Rights. "Chinese citizens, as well as visitors and businessmen, will look to the courts in cases of disputes or violations of their rights. For no matter how well the laws are written, there can be no justice without a fair trial overseen by a competent, independent, impartial and effective judiciary," Chrétien said. "Because we believe that China lives by its word, these ratifications will contribute to greater respect for basic freedoms and individual rights. This, Canadians would applaud. For they have been disturbed by reports of the lack of such respect in the past."

But a day earlier, Chrétien's rhetoric on human rights had been noticeably lighter. He said there had been a "big improvement in China" since Tiananmen. *Ottawa Citizen* journalist Jack Aubry noted that Chrétien "also joked at a reception for businesspeople on the trade mission about (how) the Canadian media is pushing him to tell densely populated China what to do while warning him that he can't tell Canadian provinces what to do."[18]

When Chrétien bade farewell to China in October 2003, less than two months before leaving politics, there were no premiers in tow, but the trip had the feel of a trade mission anyway. There was the usual butting of heads with the travelling corps of journalists over human rights and democratic reform. The government did its best not to engage. Chrétien was given a hero's welcome with a full military parade outside the Great Hall of the People facing Tiananmen Square. Inside, Chinese Premier Wen Jiabao told Chrétien: "You will stay forever a good friend, an old friend of China and the Chinese people." Chrétien joked that he would soon be an unemployed politician, and that, "I will keep coming and visiting."[19] Before the trip ended, he officially opened the two new Candu reactor sites.

On December 10, 2003, on his final day as Canada's prime minister, Chrétien hosted Wen in Ottawa on a return visit. Chrétien gave Wen his own military parade, albeit a much more modest one, at the downtown Ottawa Cartier Drill Hall and fêted him with a gala dinner at the Canadian Museum of Civilization in Gatineau. The next morning, the prime minister visited Gov. Gen. Adrienne Clarkson and formally tendered his resignation.[20]

During Chrétien's tenure, there was an appearance of behind-the-scenes engagement on human rights engagement between Canada and China. Little, if anything, was accomplished. A review of 1997 federal Liberal government documents, including cabinet affairs, released under the federal access-to-information law, demonstrates one inescapable fact: the Chrétien government got played by Chinese officials who appeared to take advantage of the Liberal government's renewed enthusiasm to engage. Canada wanted to formalize a series of high-level dialogues on human rights and democracy and entrench a joint effort to help China build a more open, Western-style judicial system. There would be seminars on legal processes, including "criminal law procedure," "the adversarial trial system," and "development of evidence law," to name a few, and exchanges involving Canadian lawyers and judges.[21]

To this end, on May 21, 1997, Gordon Houlden, head of the China division at the Department of Foreign Affairs and International Trade (DFAIT), wrote an internal department memo announcing the first meeting of the Canada-China Joint Committee on Human Rights (JCHR). It was to be held in June 1997 during the visit of China's vice-minister of foreign affairs, Li Zhaoxing. "The timing is not ideal due to competing priorities at that time for both DFAIT and other participants, but we believe it could be

managed and allow us to maintain important forward momentum
on the human rights package," Houlden wrote in an email. Li's visit
would be brief, but the Chinese delegation was expected to include
representatives from its foreign ministry and "other agencies." If all
went well, Houlden wrote, "we would intend to take up the Chinese
invitation to send a delegation to China in the fall, 1997, for a second round of JCHR."[22] (Houlden's involvement in the formation
of Canada's China policy would come full circle decades later when
he would find himself part of a delegation to China that would try
to bring the Two Michaels home.)

The documents detailed a broad and ambitious agenda, at least
from the Canadian side: "political and civil rights, including fundamental freedoms; religious freedoms; economic, social and cultural
rights; women's and children's rights." The major focus remained on
reforming China's justice system, including "practical training" for
defence lawyers and "technical assistance to reform trial processes
generally." There was also a plan to provide "technical assistance to
draft an evidence law" and an exploratory talk with China's Ministry
of Justice and Public Security Bureau to establish "an educational
program for police and other legal personnel."[23]

The documents noted that Canada was already running a project through the International Centre for Criminal Law Reform and
Criminal Justice Policy that was aimed at changing China's criminal procedure law to help strengthen the rights of accused people,
focusing on the "presumption of innocence," the right to contact
a defence lawyer early in the legal process, and abolishing a system
"which allows police to detain a person for up to three months without trial or right to contact a lawyer."[24]

Canada also proposed to help strengthen Chinese police conduct
by publishing a how-to booklet and holding an educational program
for police on how legal changes "should affect their daily conduct."
Another suggestion was greater cooperation between the RCMP and

China's Public Safety Bureau "on ethics issues and conduct as well as other police activities."[25]

While all these plans were being drawn up, rank and file Canadian diplomats were dutifully highlighting emerging concerns about China's human rights failings. On April 24, 1997, the Canadian embassy in Washington, DC alerted its missions in Beijing and Hong Kong to a joint report by Human Rights Watch/Asia and Hong Kong-based Human Rights in China that was due to be made public. This was in the pre-internet era, so a summary of the report was shared by fax. It said that changes to the Chinese criminal code "represent the culmination of a ten-year effort to strengthen authoritarian controls and have ominous implications for Hong Kong," which was due to be handed over from British to Chinese control in little more than two months. It gave three examples. The first was the "punishment of contact with individuals and organizations outside China," which gave broad powers to prosecute people for harming Chinese state security by giving information to so-called outsiders. The second was "highlighting crimes of separatism" by sabotaging national unity in Beijing's efforts to control Tibet, Xinjiang, and Inner Mongolia. The third was to increase the limits on freedom of expression, broadening what would be considered "subversive, seditious or secessionist expression" in a clawback of what was already established in China's 1979 criminal code. The report's authors warned that the broad new national security provisions "will be cold comfort to those fighting to protect Hong Kong's freedoms after the July 1 transfer of sovereignty."[26]

The report did nothing to dim the wide-eyed optimism and unabashed self-importance of the Chrétien government as it attempted to single-handedly reform China's human rights record. In a bold move, it broke a six-year commitment by abandoning a joint international effort to co-sponsor a resolution at the United Nations Commission on Human Rights that would have been critical of China's rights record.

On April 24, 1997, the same day the new human rights warnings were being circulated between Canada's diplomatic missions in Washington, Beijing, and Hong Kong, Canadian foreign minister Lloyd Axworthy wrote to a leading US congressman to explain why Canada had changed course on the international effort to condemn China's human rights record. Benjamin A. Gilman, the chair of the House of Representatives committee on international relations, had written to Axworthy ten days earlier asking about the decision. Axworthy's letter refers to his visit to China a year earlier when he was able to get "unprecedented agreement on a whole package of initiatives" on human rights, including the creation of the Joint Committee on Human Rights. "This committee will provide a formalized forum in which we can regularly address human rights concerns," wrote Axworthy. "Furthermore, we have obtained agreement with the application of evidence and criminal law, the development of an adversarial trial system and a legal aid system, and the implementation of corrections reform. The package also includes cooperation in the area of religious freedom."

In a press release on April 14, Axworthy said Canada was still "very concerned" about the human rights situation in China but "concluded that Canada could have a greater influence on the state of human rights in China by pursuing and intensifying our promising bilateral measures."[27]

Behind the scenes, a confidential cable from the Canadian embassy in Beijing provided a clue to the real reason Beijing was being so co-operative. The Chinese had agreed to take part in the Canadian human rights process in return for Canada withdrawing its support of the UN human rights statement with its allies in Geneva as it had done for the previous six years. The April 25 cable refers to a meeting the previous day between a Canadian diplomat and a senior Chinese official in the Ministry of Foreign Affairs, Shen Yongxiang. They were discussing the "busy path ahead" in the wake of the UN human rights commission decision. In the block letter format of the day, the cable reads: "AFTER THANKING CDA FOR ITS DECISION NOT TO COSPONSOR A RESOLUTION AT GENEVA, SHEN TOOK THE OPPORTUNITY TO STRONGLY UNDERLINE THAT CHINA IS TAKING THE BILATERAL DIALOGUE AND ALL OTHER ACTIVITIES OUTLINED IN DFAIT BACKGROUNDER VERY SERIOUSLY." Shen then confirmed that Vice Minister Li would come to Canada in early June for the first joint committee meeting—but he wouldn't be staying long. "THEN TALKS WOULD CONTINUE AFTER HIS DEPARTURE GIVEN THE BREVITY OF HIS STAY AND LONG LIST OF AGENDA ITEMS TO BE COVERED."

The great fear of Canadian diplomats at the time was that their bold program to advance justice reform and human rights in China would be seen as "window dressing." Once China had wheedled the vote it wanted out of Canada, persuading Chrétien and Axworthy to stand down from the multilateral effort to condemn its human rights record, these fears were realized. The Chinese had deftly manipulated the Canadians. International solidarity on human rights had been diminished as China skillfully redressed the window to suit its interest.

CHAPTER SIX

Xi has a Dream

STEPHEN HARPER AND HIS Conservatives came to power in 2006 and immediately set a new tone to Canada's international relations. Harper expressed disdain for China and spent his first three years in office snubbing the Chinese. Communism, in his view, was a historic evil. He derided those who considered the unseemly pursuit of the "almighty dollar" more important than principled opposition to China's denial of political freedoms and human rights.

Harper's hard line eventually crumbled. It was one thing to rail against an economically insignificant totalitarian country such as Cuba, and quite another to give the world's second-largest economy the cold shoulder. Canadian business leaders were apoplectic. And when Harper got around to visiting China in 2009, he received a stern public rebuke from China's premier, Wen Jiabao, who noted this was the first meeting between a Chinese premier and Canadian prime minister in five years: "Five years is too long a time for China-Canada relations and that's why there are comments in the media that your visit is one that should have taken place earlier."[1]

Harper changed his mind and joined the pursuit of the almighty dollar. He began speaking about the importance of building economic relations with China, and he eventually forged a new foreign investment protection agreement with Beijing in 2012, arguably the most substantive economic agreement between Canada and China in the twenty-first century. More importantly, as far as the public was concerned, he "capped" a visit to China in 2012, as the CBC noted, with "the long-sought loan of two giant pandas." Harper next reached for the fences, openly musing about one day achieving a free trade agreement with China.[2]

With Harper's conversion, the long-standing Canadian policy of doing business with the world's fastest growing economy while giving short shrift to democratic reform and human rights became unanimous. Successive Liberal, Progressive Conservative, and Conservative governments salved their consciences by telling them-selves and Canadians that greater trade, along with exchanges of students and tourists with China, would somehow nudge the People's Republic toward greater democratic tendencies and freedom. This belief that free markets and democracy were natural complements of each other, and that over time China's political and economic system would converge with the West, would prove to be mistaken.

The second-generation Trudeau government, beginning in 2015, followed the China template of its predecessors, adding a marked nostalgia for the senior Trudeau government's daring (for the time) embrace of China, and the grand, if futile, reformist ambitions of the Mulroney and Chrétien years. But Trudeau failed to factor in the significance of the rise of Xi Jinping as China's new leader, a hardened authoritarian presiding over an iron-fisted totalitarian transformation of twenty-first century China.

China's rise under President Xi has been characterized by an underlying desire to unseat the United States as the world's dominant economic and political power through a bold and forthright rejection of Western democratic values. Xi laid down his marker when he was sworn in as party president in 2012 and evoked, for the first time, the concept of the "China Dream." Xi was clearly positioning China as a direct rival to the "American Dream." In a follow-up speech, he declared, "we must make persistent efforts, press ahead with indomitable will, continue to push forward the great cause of socialism with Chinese characteristics, and strive to achieve the Chinese dream of great rejuvenation of the Chinese nation. To realize the Chinese road, we must spread the Chinese spirit, which combines the spirit of the nation with patriotism as the core and the spirit of the time with reform and innovation as the core."[3]

Spreading the Chinese spirit clearly meant extending China's global influence, politically and economically. In 2013, Xi announced an ambitious new foreign policy centered around the Belt and Road initiative, a massive Eurasian infrastructure project estimated to cost between $50 billion and $100 billion per year, linking four billion people across several countries.[4] This was a twenty-first-century updating of the classic Silk Road which facilitated westward expansion of China's Han Dynasty starting in 206 BC. The old Silk Road wound its way through Central Asia to Europe through what is now Afghanistan and Uzbekistan as well as through India and Pakistan, almost 6,500 kilometers long. The new version proposed a land route combined with a vast Indian Ocean maritime route connecting East Africa and Europe. It would involve investment in some seventy countries and encompass a huge network of ports, energy pipelines, railways, superhighways, and other border crossings backed by new financing tools such as the Asian Infrastructure Investment Bank, and the New Development Bank.[5] The Belt and Road would massively expand China's political and economic influence in what was widely viewed as "an unsettling extension of China's rising power," and "nothing less than the rewriting of the current geopolitical landscape."[6]

"Xi's ambitious initiative has three drivers: (1) energy, (2) security, (3) markets. Like the silken strands on a loom, these drivers will weave together to create a fabric of interconnected transport corridors and port facilities that will boost trade, improve security, and aid strategic penetration," writes Theresa Fallon, a China foreign-policy expert, in *The Journal of the National Committee on American Foreign Policy*. "The overarching 'Belt and Road' concept attempts to sew together these interests in one mega–foreign policy project. The 'Belt and Road initiative is a flexible formula and can even be expanded to include past projects as there are no deadlines or clear parameters. China's leading academics have been recruited to celebrate Xi Jinping as the 'designer of China's road to being a great power.'"[7]

Like the Belt and Road strategy, Huawei and its telecommunications technology are part and parcel of Xi's strategic vision, crucial to the future of China's prestige, national identity, wealth, and security. As a result, the war with the US over 5G technology is not just another trade dispute. China is on what it considers a sacred mission to play *the* leading role in the future of the internet, a campaign that not only companies like Huawei, but the entire Chinese government and military, are engaged in.

Simultaneously, China's massive naval build-up in the South China Sea has left no doubt that the "China Dream" includes a formidable projection of Beijing's military might outside its borders. More than $3 trillion of the world's ship-laden trade passes through the South China Sea every year, or about one-third of the world's maritime trade. Vietnam, the Philippines, Taiwan, Malaysia, and Brunei also lay claim to parts of the vast disputed waters. Xi pushed forward with the creation of what are essentially fake islands, built upon reefs and dredged sediment, to house large landing strips and bases for the Chinese military. China's navy stepped-up patrols of the sea, chasing away ships from other countries that it unilaterally deemed were trespassing its waters. The United States became embroiled in the high-seas showdown sending its own ships to the region. In July

2016, the international tribunal in The Hague rejected China's claims of sovereignty in the South China Sea and denounced its build-up of fake military islands. The ruling said China was in violation of international law by endangering Philippine ships and interfering with its oil exploration and fishing, as well as causing "irreparable harm" to the ocean's marine life.[8] It marked one of the sternest condemnations of Chinese conduct by any international body.

Beijing and Xi had to decide whether or not to abide by that ruling. Five years later, nothing has changed. Beijing continues to patrol the waters of the South China Sea, putting it in bitter conflict with the Philippines. The war of words reached new heights in May 2021 when Teodoro Locsin Jr., the exasperated foreign minister of the Philippines, took to Twitter to blast China for what he viewed as the trespassing of hundreds of Chinese boats inside his country's two-hundred-mile territorial waters. "China, my friend, how politely can I put it? Let me see . . . O . . . GET THE F**K OUT," Locsin tweeted. "What are you doing to our friendship? You. Not us. We're trying. You. You're like an ugly oaf forcing your attention on a handsome guy who wants to be a friend; not to father a Chinese province . . ."[9]

Under Xi, China snubbed and manipulated the international rulebook to suit its grand ambition. He has jailed his political opponents in record numbers, shattering any façade of adhering to any Western notion of the rule of law, and perpetuated what many would come to label as genocide against the ethnic Muslim Uyghurs of China's Xinjiang province. He has also mounted a systematic campaign to crush democratic freedoms in Hong Kong. In 1997, Britain and the world negotiated the handover of Hong Kong to mainland China, signing an international treaty that was supposed to safeguard Hong Kong's political and economic future. Xi unapologetically trashed the "one country-two systems" agreement in 2019 with a draconian national security law that has essentially outlawed democracy.

In his book, *Chinese Politics in the Era of Xi Jinping*, the Hong Kong political scientist Willy Wo-Lap Lam highlights two memorable European appearances by Xi that provide insight into his thinking and ambitions. "The lion has woken up," Xi said in a speech in Paris in March 2014. This referenced an assessment attributed to Napoleon Bonaparte that "China is a sleeping lion, and when she awakes, she will shake the world." This, says Lam, was Xi's signal of "his intention to shake up the trajectory of twenty-first century history." While he went on to reassure his audience that China would be a "peaceful, pleasant, civilized lion," the undisputed leader of 1.3 billion people had served notice that change was coming.[10]

Also in March 2014, in a speech at the College of Europe in Belgium, Xi announced that "socialism with Chinese characteristics" was the optimal form of government for his country. "Constitutional monarchy, imperial restoration, parliamentarianism, a multiparty system, and a presidential system, we considered them and tried them, but none worked," Lam quotes Xi as saying. Xi also made clear that he would not adopt the political system of another country "because it would not suit us, and it might even lead to catastrophic consequences."[11]

* * *

In certain respects, Canada's foreign ministry appreciated the implications of Xi's rise and what its envoys were now dealing with in China. Among the warnings it had received was a dispatch from front-line diplomat Michael Kovrig. His December 2015 note on the scene outside Pu Zhiqiang's sham of a trial noted that the fifty-year-old defendant, in addition to being a defender of the Uyghur minority, was a veteran of the 1989 Tiananmen Square protests. He had been in detention since attending a May 2014 gathering commemorating the twenty-fifth anniversary of that incident. Chinese authorities were determined "to silence Pu and restrict him from practicing law, and the actual allegations were merely a convenient excuse."[12]

Kovrig reflected on the sad state of Chinese legal reforms, the cause that had been so enthusiastically embraced by the Chrétien government a generation earlier. "Ironically, on Dec. 20 the CPC central committee and the state council general offices issued a joint opinion pledging to reform the system of qualifications for entering the legal profession," Kovrig wrote, referencing a report by China's state-run Xinhua news agency. The new system created a new single unified exam for judges, prosecutors, lawyers, and notaries that extended to other professions. "It also unifies legal training, defines the suspension and revoking of law licenses and is intended to ensure that people working in the legal system are 'faithful to the Party, the country, the people and the law.'"[13]

Global Affairs Canada, as the Department of Foreign Affairs is known, further commented in a January 2017 human rights report that while there had been some "positive developments" in China over the previous two years, "the overall trend for human rights continues in a decidedly negative direction."[14]

If those weren't clues enough for the Trudeau government, China's ambassador to Canada, Lu Shaye, spelled out his nation's position in an interview with Canadian reporters. The Chinese embassy compound in Ottawa sits behind a foreboding gray wall on the banks of the Rideau River. It is a short walk from some of the city's best addresses—historic mansions, diplomatic residences, and upscale homes of Ottawa's elite Rockcliffe Park neighbourhood—yet just as close to a large men's emergency shelter and a wooded area on the banks of the Rideau River that serves as a seasonal encampment for the homeless. A pair of reporters and a photographer from *The Canadian Press* passed through the embassy's gates on June 29, 2017, for an interview with the Chinese ambassador.

The journalists were escorted through a winding corridor to a roomy high-ceilinged sitting room and motioned to one of two sofas, opposite an entourage of Chinese diplomats. Lu Shaye sat in a large white leather armchair framed by a giant painting, ready to hold court. Lu was trim and short in a light blue suit with wire rim glasses. He spoke in Mandarin as the photographer Justin Tang circled the room, clicking away. Lu spoke deliberately, with occasional inflection, pausing briefly to allow a young man seated opposite him to provide English translation. Over the course of ninety minutes, the translator would grow increasingly nervous as Lu sternly interjected in English to correct his work. Translation issues aside, Lu's meaning and message were crystal clear. The only coaxing needed was a polite, open-ended question and he would respond in great detail.

After four months at his new diplomatic post, Lu had concluded that his country wasn't especially popular with Canadians. China and Canada had begun exploratory talks towards launching full-scale free trade negotiations. Both sides saw the talks evolving differently: the Trudeau government still wanted to link human rights and good governance issues to any free-trade pact with China, priorities China firmly rejected in favour of a business-only deal. That the talks were going nowhere was already evident when Lu spoke to the visiting reporters.

"I feel that in Canada, and especially its media, there seems to be some misunderstanding about China, which is detrimental to bilateral cooperation," he said. Canadians "look down" on China and "don't see any merit" in it. They don't consider it a worthwhile trading partner, he continued, and view it as a country with no democracy, human rights, or freedom.[15] In Lu's view, these impressions, standing in the way of friendly relations, were the fault of the media.

"I think the Canadian government is pressured by the media on this issue," Lu said. Journalists have an anti-China agenda, and they are forcing the government to abide it. Asked how he would like to see Canadian media behave, Lu recommended the journalism model favoured by the Chinese communist party: reporters should essentially behave as an organ of the government to help promote and disseminate its agenda. "The Chinese Communist Party is good at listening to public opinion and also they do their part to lead and mobilize people for a common cause." Canadian journalists, he said, are representatives of the Canadian people. "And I think your questions also represent the confusion of the Canadian people."

Lu used the interview to drive a stake through the heart of that core assumption of Canadian policy engagement with China dating back to Prime Minister Pierre Trudeau. The axiom, followed by subsequent Liberal and Conservative leaders, was that if you traded and engaged economically and socially with China, exposure to Western democracy would over time expose its people to values of freedom and democracy and nudge an ancient Chinese society away from its totalitarian, authoritarian, one-party form of government. Canada wasn't the only Western country that bought into this idea, and it wouldn't be the only one disillusioned in the coming years.

Lu said his country saw no connection between the values of human rights and democracy and the hard interests of strong economic and trade ties. There would be no linking values to trade deals, he insisted, and any politician that believed otherwise was going to miss out on the chance for an all-encompassing trading relationship with China and its mighty economy. "Politicians should have the courage and responsibility to explain to people where the overall and fundamental interest of the country lies."

Lu was not denying that many human rights and free-press watchdogs had criticized Xi and his party's clampdown on media and political dissent. As Reporters Without Borders had said around that time: "The planet's leading censor and press freedom predator, Chinese President Xi Jinping, is the instigator of policies aimed at complete hegemony over news coverage and the creation of an international media order heavily influenced by China." Rather than argue these points, Lu airily brushed them aside. Presiding over the interview from his armchair, he was the personification of China's bold, assertive, and confrontational diplomatic posture. He wasn't trying to hide anything, or play nice. He articulated a clear understanding of China's values and its place in the world, and made it clear that anyone who wanted to engage with China had to accept its terms.

That warning was not enough to dissuade Prime Minister Trudeau and his inner circle from pursuing Canada's problematic but time-honored, values-laden approach to China. Rather, the Trudeau Liberals tried to up the ante later in 2017 by pressing for a "progressive" free trade deal with Xi's China.

A model for the agreement was the renegotiation of the North American Free Trade Agreement between Canada, Mexico, and the United States. The Canadian side had successfully pushed for the inclusion of a section to protect labour rights in Mexico. Both Canada and the US desired to level the playing field in the auto industry, which had seen manufacturing plants close in their countries and move to Mexico where it was far cheaper to build cars because of paltry wages and few labour protections. A similarly values-laden approach was used in Canada's comprehensive pact in goods and services with the European Union, which included provisions to protect labour rights and the environment. The Trudeau government was optimistic that it could succeed where Chrétien had failed in marrying trade and human rights in a deal with the Chinese.

A month before Trudeau touched down in China in December 2017—his second visit as prime minister—Xi had had himself written into the Chinese constitution alongside Chairman Mao and Deng Xiaoping at the gala meeting of the 19th National Congress of the Communist Party of China. It marked the solidification of the "personality cult" of Xi in Chinese society, an attempt to elevate him to a status not seen since Mao. A village where he had once worked as a teen was transformed into a shrine. A Chinese newspaper dubbed him the "The Great Leader Xi Jinping." A provincial government where Xi once served launched a public campaign called "What's My Favourite Xi Jinping Quote," a play on Mao's legendary "Little Red Book." Another village established a permanent exhibition of Xi's writings and speeches and created a visual exhibit to illustrate the China Dream.[16]

In several rounds of preliminary discussion prior to his visit, Trudeau had made it clear he was keen to forge a comprehensive deal with China, rekindling many of the formal, joint mechanisms that had been in place during the Chrétien years (they had been largely dismantled by the Stephen Harper Conservatives). He also broached the notion of a free-trade deal with "progressive" elements, not seeming to realize, despite the warnings of its own diplomats, that workers' rights, collective bargaining, and labour unions weren't part of the Xi Jinping vision of socialism with Chinese characteristics. Nor had he heeded the public pronouncements of China's ambassador to Canada, who made it clear four months before Trudeau's trip that "non-trade" issues had no place in an economic agreement. "I have stated many times that we're not afraid of discussing the issues, such as democracy and human rights," said Lu Shaye, in his summer 2017 interview with *The Canadian Press*. "FTA is FTA itself—we just don't want to add too many non-economic or non-trade factors into it."[17]

In a move that stands as the culmination of five decades of Canadian leaders grossly overestimating their ability to bring change to China, failing to recognize that China is uninterested in embracing so-called Western values, and getting mercilessly played by Chinese leaders, Trudeau made his pitch regardless. It was met with deafening indifference. Premier Li Keqiang registered his government's formal rejection of the Canadian proposal over dinner in Beijing early in Trudeau's visit.

On the final morning of his final day in China, Trudeau attended the Chen Clan Academy, an ancient temple in the southern city of Guangzhou. He was treated to a traditional performance of the "lion dance," a percussive and athletic display by six skilled dancers in heavy and colourful masked costumes. Trudeau took part in an "eye dotting" ceremony prior to the performance, dabbing the eyes of one of the costumed lions with red paint. It was supposed to symbolize the awakening of the lion. The symbolism of this act and its relation to the Napoleonic prediction that an awakened China lion would shake the world was apparently lost on Team Trudeau. They returned home without any commitment to commence free trade talks between Canada and China.

Four months later, Chinese ambassador Lu Shaye told a group of Canadian journalists that the two countries had reached "extensive" consensus on a number of trade issues (he didn't offer specifics) but added there "still remain some differences on the so-called progressive trade factors." He left no doubt about his country's position: "For the Chinese side, we have stressed many times . . . we really want so-called, non-trade-related factors or issues to not be included in the negotiation of an FTA."[18]

After a half century of failing to push China to adopt Western values, especially regarding human rights and legal reforms, the arbitrary detention of two Canadian nationals in retaliation for what the Chinese saw as an extradition hearing dangerous to its own commercial and political objectives should not have been a surprise in Ottawa.

CHAPTER SEVEN

Lambs and Wolf Warriors

WITH 2020 DRAWING TO a close, Germany's ambassador to the United Nations bid farewell to the security council. Germany's temporary two-year term on the council was also coming to an end, along with Ambassador Christoph Heusgen's four-decade career as a diplomat. In his final speech on December 22, Heusgen pointed out that Meng Wanzhou was being held in far more favourable conditions than the Two Michaels, and suggested that maybe the time had come for the Chinese government to show mercy on the Canadians:

> While the Chinese executive spends her time in a seven-bedroom mansion in Vancouver, Michael Kovrig has been confined to an isolated small cell in Beijing. This council will lose its legitimacy if it ceases to be concerned about the fate of individuals, about their protection and security, their human rights and their freedoms, their well-being and their aspirations. Therefore, let me end my tenure in the security council by appealing to

my Chinese colleagues to ask Beijing for the release of Michael Kovrig and Michael Spavor."[1]

The Chinese response to Heusgen's words bore little resemblance to the polite diplomatic exchanges he had been accustomed to over his long career. It came from Geng Shuang, China's deputy UN ambassador, who in his former role as one of Chinese foreign ministry's deputy communications chiefs and a fixture at their daily press briefings in Beijing, had established himself as one of his nation's marquee "Wolf Warrior" diplomats. These high-profile purveyors of China's aggressive new diplomacy were skilled at shoving Beijing's unapologetic worldview back in the faces of anyone who dared question it. In the words of the *Global Times*, the Chinese state-owned newspaper that is an organ of the Communist Party, Geng was one of three foreign ministry spokesmen who had been "applauded by the Chinese public for refuting Western charges with harsh tones."[2]

Six months before Heusgen's speech, Geng had ended his four-year assignment in Beijing and was moved to China's UN mission in New York as its deputy. He told the German diplomat that his remarks represented "malicious attacks against" other council members. "[Heusgen] abused the platform of the security council in an attempt to poison the working atmosphere of the council."

Geng wasn't finished:

> Now, I wish to say out of the bottom of my heart: good riddance, Ambassador Heusgen. I hope that the council, in your absence in 2021, will be in a better position to fulfill the responsibilities and mandate for maintaining international peace and security.[3]

The moment was typical of how Canada and its Western allies often found themselves outgunned by China after December 2018.

Beijing's aggressive next-generation envoys practice a unique brand of shock-and-awe diplomacy, sparing no insults or threats in service of their foreign policy objectives, which are every bit as aggressive as their rhetoric.

Canada had a taste of the new diplomacy shortly after the Two Michaels were imprisoned. Ambassador Lu Shaye, the same man who had warned Trudeau about linking values to trade, responded aggressively to requests by Canada and its Western allies, including the US, Britain, Australia, and the European Union, for Beijing to release the captives. In an article placed in the *Globe and Mail* newspaper, Lu called Meng's arrest a "miscarriage of justice" and insisted that Canada was taking part in a US "witch hunt" by executing what was a lawful arrest warrant under an extradition treaty between two allies.[4]

That was mild compared to the column he wrote a month later in the *Hill Times*, a bi-weekly newspaper widely read on Parliament Hill. Lu questioned whether countries like the US and Britain were truly representative of the international community. He accused the West of employing a "double standard" in judging his country. "The reason why some people are used to arrogantly adopting double standards is due to Western egotism and white supremacy," he wrote. "What they have been doing is not showing respect for the rule of law but mocking and trampling the rule of law."[5]

Lu's tenure in Canada came to an abrupt end in June 2019 (two and a half years is shorter than the three or four years ambassadors usually serve). Before leaving Ottawa, he granted the same two CP reporters another interview, and this time seemed more relaxed, offering warm smiles to his guests, but his message was unchanged. He continued to blame Canada for the decline in relations with his country over the Meng affair.

* * *

Ottawa's diplomatic response to the arrest of the Two Michaels in China was problematic from the start. Four days after Kovrig was picked up, Canada's ambassador to China, John McCallum, visited him for the first time in prison. Two days later, Canadian diplomats were granted access to Spavor. A cone of silence enveloped these meetings and subsequent ones that would take place, roughly once a month, until their abrupt halt in January 2020 because of Chinese concerns about COVID-19, but some of what has transpired diplomatically has leaked, and none of it is especially surprising to those who have followed Canada-Chinese relations in recent years.

The first casualty in the diplomatic warfare that erupted in December 2018 would be John McCallum, an economist and university professor who had entered politics in 2000 as a member of parliament for a Toronto-area riding. He had served as the chief economist at the Royal Bank of Canada and was dean of arts at McGill University when his future boss, Justin Trudeau, was a student there. Two years into his political career, McCallum was Liberal Prime Minister Jean Chrétien's minister of national defence. He found himself standing beside his leader during his historic, and last minute, decision in March 2003 to keep the Canadian Forces out of the US-led war on Iraq. McCallum went on to serve Chrétien's Liberal successor, Paul Martin, as minister of Veterans Affairs and, subsequently, National Revenue. He returned to cabinet as Immigration, Refugees, and Citizenship minister in 2015 when the younger Trudeau won power.[6]

Throughout 2016, Immigration Department employees coming to and from work in their downtown Ottawa headquarters would grow accustomed to seeing their minister in the drab courtyard between their Slater Street and Laurier Avenue West twin office towers. He took his smoke breaks in the concrete courtyard and waved at his colleagues as they arrived and, later, went home in the later afternoon. McCallum's hours were notably longer, responsible as he was for implementing the Trudeau government's decision to bring 45,000 Syrian refugees into Canada. The first planeload arrived in Toronto on December 10, 2015, and McCallum joined Trudeau for a photo-op with a young Syrian family, and numerous selfies with other new arrivals.

Grueling as the assignment was, McCallum succeeded in helping the prime minister fulfill his promise on Syrian refugees. Not long after, in January 2017, he was rewarded with another key assignment. McCallum became Canada's ambassador to China. The appointment of one of the government's senior politicians as ambassador was intended as a signal to Beijing that its relationship with Canada was a top priority for Trudeau.

McCallum seemed especially well-suited to the job, given strong personal ties to China, and decades of high-level business and political experience. His wife, Nancy Lim, is of Malaysian- Chinese origin, and their three sons, Andrew, Jamie and Duncan, all have Chinese wives. McCallum's federal riding, Markham, also has a large Chinese population. Proud of these connections, McCallum was known to speak openly and enthusiastically about the opportunities for Canada in China. One such occasion was when Trudeau visited the country late in 2017. Notwithstanding the implosion of Canadian hopes for free-trade talks with China, McCallum held court for reporters on the top floor of an office tower in Guangzhou at the tip of the Pearl River Delta, China's southern industrial heartland. He spoke of the large groups of street dancers that had been out in Guangzhou the evening before, and how his wife liked to join in with them, and insisted that it was still conceivable that Trudeau would manage to convince the Chinese to engage in formal trade talks before returning home.[7]

On January 21, 2019, a month after his initial visits with the Two Michaels, McCallum spoke to a group of Chinese-language journalists in Canada about the Meng case. He offered his opinion on how Meng's legal team might defend her against the extradition order and concluded that there were some "quite good arguments" for her lawyers to pursue. "One, political involvement by comments from [US President] Donald Trump in her case. Two, there's an extraterritorial aspect to her case. And three, there's the issue of Iran sanctions which are involved in her case, and Canada does not sign on to these Iran sanctions," said McCallum.[8]

He kept going: "I know this has angered China, but we have a system of extradition treaty, a system of rules of law, which are above the government. The government cannot change these things, and as I said, I think Ms. Meng has quite a strong case."[9]

McCallum was giving voice to what many were thinking at the time, but what the government was not saying: that if a way could be found to allow Meng to go free, it could pave the way for China to release the Two Michaels. Days later, McCallum issued a statement saying that he misspoke during that media briefing. Foreign Affairs Minister Chrystia Freeland attempted to address the confusion, stating that "Canada is conducting a fair, unbiased, and transparent legal proceeding. There has been no political involvement in this process. Canada respects its international legal commitments . . ." There had been calls for McCallum to resign but his job was safe, momentarily.[10]

Four days later, McCallum was at a charity luncheon in Vancouver when a reporter asked him about the Meng case. McCallum did the one thing politicians and diplomats almost never do: he told the reporter from *StarMetro Vancouver* exactly what he thought. He said it would be "great for Canada" if the US dropped its extradition request for Meng. Furthermore, any deal between the US and China on Meng would have to take into account the fate of the Two Michaels. "We have to make sure that if the US does such a deal," says McCallum, "it also includes the release of our two people. And the US is highly aware of that."[11]

Having once again raised the specter of political interference in a case that his government was insisting was subject entirely to the rule of law, McCallum found himself later that night, on the phone with Trudeau. The prime minister told him he'd made one comment too many and asked for McCallum's resignation. As the *Toronto Star's* Susan Delacourt opined at the time: "The firing throws a bucket of cold water over speculation all last week that McCallum was saying what the Trudeau government could not say publicly" since Meng's arrest.[12]

McCallum's diplomatic freelancing continued months after his career as a diplomat and politician came to a crashing end. In a July 2019 interview with the *South China Morning Post*, he offered some speculation on the upcoming Canadian federal election. He told China not to do anything to hurt the Liberals' chances ahead of the election. "Anything that is more negative against Canada will help the Conservatives, [who] are much less friendly to China than the Liberals." Freeland, who had previously expressed mixed feelings about her former cabinet colleague's necessary firing in January, appeared angry and said there was no way McCallum was speaking for the government. "I think it is inappropriate for any Canadian to be advising any foreign government in ways it ought or ought not to behave to secure any particular election outcome in Canada," she said.[13]

McCallum would later reflect on his time as Canada's man in China. He had some regrets, but not many. "I think I've done some useful things in my career, such as in the case of Syrian refugees, as defence minister under Chrétien when we said no to Iraq," he said. "But I've never claimed to have led an error-free career."

In the summer of 2019, after departing his position, he was invited to a meeting of Chinese government officials and accepted. He offered few details about what occurred but suggested his closed-door discussion mirrored his comments to the *South China Morning Post*: "My purpose was to try to get them to release the Two Michaels or at least improve their living conditions. I painted a dark picture of plummeting support for China among Canadians, and I also mentioned as part of this darkness an impending election. In hindsight, I regret having spoken of the election. I don't think it was appropriate. I don't think it made any difference, because at the end of the day the Chinese refused to release or even improve the living conditions of our two detainees. But that was an error I made."

McCallum also later took back his apology for offering his armchair legal analysis of Meng's case to the group of Chinese Canadian journalists in Markham. "I made some comments about how the burden of proof is lower for extradition cases, so that went against her, but I also commented on some of the legal arguments she might have, which I just picked up from the media. The case was not at that point before the courts, so I'm not sure that what I said was inappropriate. I know some people thought it was, but I was really just trying to give to this group the overall lay of the land of the situation with regard to China at that time," McCallum told a special House of Commons committee on Canada-China relations in November 2020. "The comment about the election was, I think, inappropriate. The overall comments about the situation with regard to detainees and Meng Wanzhou in Markham I thought were OK."

McCallum also told the committee that "as one of relatively few Canadians who have actually visited the Two Michaels in detention, I was determined to do whatever I could to secure their release. On more than one occasion, I tried to convince the Chinese that if they were unable to release Kovrig and Spavor, they should at least improve their living conditions. Sadly, as you all know, Canadian efforts in this area have so far been unsuccessful."

Asked whether there was anything the current government could do, McCallum was sanguine. "You have to put it in perspective. Yes, we want to have a relationship with the Chinese government, and Canada cannot control who the government is. While it isn't easy, it is what it is. So, we have to accept it."

CHAPTER EIGHT

Canada Pushes Back

THE CANADIAN GOVERNMENT replaced John McCallum as its ambassador to China, although it took most of 2019 to do so. Once more, it reached outside the ranks of its foreign service, this time to recruit an accomplished, well-travelled business executive with no direct experience in government. Dominic Barton, at least, was no stranger to the Trudeau team. He had been appointed by Trudeau's first finance minister, Bill Morneau, to head the government's economic advisory council on growth, and had briefed the Liberal cabinet at one of its retreats.[1] His pitch to cabinet had been about the importance of China to the future of the world economy and Canada's economic advancement.

Born in Uganda, Barton is the son of an Anglican missionary who fled to Canada with his family. Their escape from the horror of Idi Amin's slaughter of his political opponents in the late 1960s is said to have exercised a powerful effect on Barton's worldview. He grew up in the town of Sardis, British Columbia and attended the University of British Columbia where he studied economics. He won a Rhodes Scholarship and continued with his studies in economics at Oxford. He worked briefly for the firm N.M. Rothschild & Sons before joining McKinsey & Company, the international consulting giant.

The trim, silver-haired Barton began his McKinsey career in Toronto but by the late 1990s was prominent in its Asian business, initially leading its operations in South Korea before moving to China. He served a five-year stint as McKinsey's China chairman based in Shanghai and was simultaneously an adjunct professor at Tsinghua University in Beijing and an advisory board member of the China Development Bank. Barton capped his career at McKinsey when he became the managing director of the firm, serving three consecutive terms from 2009 to 2018.

Questions about Barton's leadership at the firm would later be raised when it was revealed in 2019 that McKinsey's American operations had advised Purdue Pharma how to promote sales of its drug OxyCotin, a highly addictive painkiller that has been responsible for thousands of deaths. McKinsey denied any wrongdoing, although it did agree to a $600-million payment to US state authorities. Barton firmly denied having any "knowledge of the work undertaken for Purdue by my former colleagues."

Barton was also forced to defend himself during testimony at the Canadian House of Commons special committee on Canada-China relations in February 2020, where he sparred with opposition politicians who criticized his appointment as Canada's ambassador to China.[2] Their attack was largely based on a report in the *New York Times* that described how McKinsey held a lavish retreat in 2018 in China's western region, not far from where Uyghurs were being rounded up, and alleged the firm was carrying out "contentious" work with authoritarian clients in China, Russia, Saudi Arabia, and elsewhere.[3]

In September 2019, Barton began his mission in China as Canada's ambassador with one overriding priority: get Kovrig and Spavor out of prison.

Barton entered his first diplomatic meeting with his Chinese counterparts guns blazing. The exchange was heated and draining.

"We're angry. We're very angry because our people have been taken. China is very angry as well. Furious. We're both furious," Barton said during in-person testimony before the House of Commons Canada-China committee on February 5, 2020. "I'll just say that the first conversation I had there was probably one of the most unpleasant conversations I've ever had. I mean, the shaking and anger . . . it wasn't a conversation—it was a two-way reading of things."

Things were only slightly smoother when Barton presented his diplomatic credentials to Xi Jinping. "When I was presenting my letters of credence to President Xi, I told him what my priorities were. He said that in restoring a relationship like this, it takes two sides. That there are things we need to do and there are things they need to do. There is clearly a lot of work there."

Barton and the Chinese were eventually able to move beyond the shouting and speechifying and take steps toward bridging their core difference: Canada sees the imprisonment of the Two Michaels as arbitrary and wrong; China sees Meng's detention much the same way.

Barton says all he heard from China was: "You are lapdogs of the US. You've done this and that and the other."

His reply: "We're following the rule of law in what we did. We have an extradition treaty, and this is how it works."

Barton tried to push his conversations into more positive areas, leaning into a history of good cooperation between the Chinese and Canadian people, and even the legacy of Canadian doctor Norman Bethune, who is revered in China. He told the Canada-China committee of parliament that he'd said to the Chinese, "Do you know what? We actually have this long-standing relationship. Our people like each other. . . . Let's go back to what we like about each other. Let's not forget that. Let's talk a bit about why that is the case. What are some of the things we did for each other in the past?"

The ambassador's intent was to "build trust and open the ears on both sides. . . . There are going to be differences. We're never going to be singing from the same hymnbook on this, but we can start to find some common areas that we can work on. We have a lot of things to work on and a common agenda out there. When we think about this challenge we have, let's not lose the forest for the trees."

The next day, the new Chinese ambassador to Canada, Cong Peiwu, sat for an interview in a high-windowed room overlooking the frozen Rideau River. Cong was warm and welcoming; he smiled and spoke English. By now, the novel coronavirus had ravaged the Chinese city of Wuhan and was spreading towards the rest of the world. More than 28,000 people worldwide had been infected with COVID-19 and 560 had died from it. Naturally, it came up as a topic of discussion, and Cong was the one who linked it to Meng and the Two Michaels: "Anything that your side has done and will be doing in the next few weeks in our fight against the disease, of course, that's much appreciated, and that's good."

Cong thanked Canada for its help in battling the outbreak so far. "We like to coordinate with the Canadian side because we want to make sure it's an international campaign against the disease. From the very beginning we have adopted an attitude of being open and transparent to the outside. So we isolated the virus, we sequenced the genome of the virus and we shared the information with the outside, promptly. Canada has adopted a fairly objective reading of the situation, and it has taken the advice of the WHO not to impose unnecessary trade and travel restrictions. So that's good."

The ambassador hoped that both sides would "take measures to address the problems in the bilateral relationship so that we can remove the obstacle and move the relationship back on track." He also extended an olive branch to the media, saying he was happy to have an opportunity to do the interview because the media had an important role to play in fostering understanding between the two countries. "That role is very much appreciated."

The remark was a stunning contrast to the tone Lu had tried to set three years earlier, even if the core message regarding the Meng affair remained unchanged.[4]

The softer tone was clearly noticed in Beijing. Five weeks later, just as the World Health Organization had declared a global pandemic and Canada and the vast majority of the rest of the world had closed down, shutting borders, schools, and businesses, the Chinese embassy sent a long statement to *The Canadian Press*, attributed to Cong. It was emphatic that the Chinese position on the Meng file was unchanged:

> For some time, a few people in Canada have been hyping up the cases of Michael Kovrig and Michael Spavor and comparing them to the case of the innocent Chinese citizen who was arbitrarily detained by Canada. I would like to reiterate that Michael Kovrig and Michael Spavor are suspected of engaging in activities endangering China's national security and their cases are being handled in accordance with law, while the Canadian government cannot explain which law of Canada Ms. Meng Wanzhou violated.
>
> China's judicial authorities have ensured that Michael Kovrig and Michael Spavor have received adequate humanitarian treatment as other suspects of the same kind. In line with the *Consular Agreement between the Government of the People's Republic of China and the Government of Canada*, the relevant authorities have arranged multiple consular visits by the Canadian Embassy in China. Both of them are physically sound and mentally stable. Their lawful rights are fully protected.
>
> I also want to inform that, so far as I know, after the outbreak of the COVID-19, the relevant Chinese authorities have overcome the inconveniences and difficulties caused by the epidemic, and taken the following measures promptly to ensure the

safety and good health of the said Canadians and tried its best to address their reasonable concerns: First, the authorities have provided better food for all the detainees, including Michael Kovrig and Michael Spavor, so as to help strengthen their immunity. Second, given the relevant detention centers have been totally enclosed due to the epidemic, to ensure their contacts with the Canadian Consular agencies in China, the frequency of transference of letters and parcels to Michael Kovrig and Michael Spavor has been increased as interim arrangements. Third, the Chinese authorities, proceeding from humanitarian consideration, have allowed Michael Kovrig to have a phone conversation with his father as a special arrangement within the law, when they learned that Michael Kovrig's father is very ill. The aforementioned measures have fully demonstrated China's goodwill, and Michael Kovrig and Michael Spavor have expressed their gratitude."[5]

Kovrig and Spavor were now cut off from human contact, due to COVID-19. They hadn't had a consular visit since Barton saw them in January.

During his parliamentary committee appearance, Barton had reflected on that visit, during which he also saw Robert Schellenberg, a Canadian convicted of drug smuggling whose sentence was converted to capital punishment weeks after Meng's arrest. "The comment I would just want to make—and I'm not used to doing this type of thing—is that I am unbelievably inspired by their resilience. Each of these three people is incredible, as a human and as an individual. I want to say that. That's how I mark my time in China, by my visits that I do to see them. It's not usual for ambassadors. They typically will do one. Every single time I am allowed to visit, I'm going to go."

After the pandemic struck, Barton was forced to mark his time in China differently. He wouldn't be allowed to see the Canadian prisoners for another ten months. China insisted it was too dangerous to allow foreign diplomats into its prisons with COVID-19 circulating. The push for access continued. Canada claimed China wasn't living up to its international legal obligations to allow consular access to detained nationals. Could it be done virtually, perhaps over a video, Canada asked? "As far as we know from the science, the virus doesn't go through televisions. How does that work? We pushed them on that," Barton later told Canadian MPs. "I think our understanding of why it was the case is that the Chinese are completely paranoid about the virus." He mentioned that during a video visit with a different Canadian inmate on an unrelated case, he had asked the prison warden how things were going with COVID-19. "He said, 'Zero, zero.' That's zero cases and zero risk of a case. I asked, 'What happens if that doesn't happen?' He said, 'I'll be fired.'"

China dragged its heels for months, pondering the request, as the country slowly opened up and life returned to a semblance of normal, including in Wuhan, where the outbreak had begun. In October 2020, Barton was finally allowed to see the Two Michaels again, but only by remote. Kovrig was being held in a prison outside of Beijing, while Spavor was being held in the northern Chinese city of Dandong, near the North Korean border. Barton saw them on large video screens and found it disconcerting. He described the scene during a second round of parliamentary testimony, this time by video link. "It's a strange thing," he said. "We fly to these places, or drive to them in the case of Beijing, and I know that the Michaels are literally on the other side of the wall, but you've got, you know, two big TVs."[6]

* * *

As Barton was dealing directly with the Chinese throughout 2020, another Canadian diplomatic colleague was fighting the battle in another forum. Bob Rae, also a Rhodes scholar, the former interim leader of the federal Liberal party, and an ex-premier of Canada's largest province, Ontario, had been appointed ambassador to the United Nations in the summer of 2020. The following October 5, the seventy-two-year-old Rae was in the general assembly when ambassadors from China and Syria criticized Canada for speaking out on human rights violations in their countries. The Chinese representative accused Canada of trying to bully China. When he was appointed to his new position, Rae informed a press conference that anyone who wanted to better understand China today ought to read George Orwell's *1984*.[7] When his Chinese and Syrian counterparts had finished their speeches, Rae fixed his gaze squarely ahead and spoke without reference to the notes and memos on his desk:

> In response to the comment by the representative of China, I would say this to this assembly, he is the one who's raised the particular case of Mme. Meng, who was under house arrest, and limited in her movements because of an extradition treaty that Canada has with the United States, pursuant to the rule of law in Canada.[8]
>
> In response to this, the Chinese government arbitrarily arrested and detained two Canadian citizens, Michael Spavor and Michael Kovrig. And they have been living in terrible conditions, without consular access, without any humane treatment whatsoever, in a Chinese prison.
>
> And I can say to my friend from China . . . when you say to a country of 35 million people, that we are somehow bullying a nation of over a billion, one the great superpowers of the world, and they have chosen to treat these two Canadian citizens in this way . . . this is something which we shall never forget.
>
> And we shall continue to raise their case. And we shall continue to raise other cases of people who have been harshly

treated and arbitrarily detained. And if you think that insulting us or insulting my country or insulting anyone is going to help in resolving the situation, you are sadly mistaken.

Rae's words were not going to get the Two Michaels out of prison anytime soon, but they did represent a valiant attempt to claim the moral high ground.

It was nevertheless clear that the Canadians were unlikely to match the Chinese in vehemence or invective, and that even if they could, it was unlikely to sway Beijing. It was also apparent that an ambassador with the skills of Houdini would be unable to spring the Two Michaels from their Chinese prison cells. Another approach was required.

To that end, Canada began building an international coalition of support for the Two Michaels not long after they were arrested. The United States, Britain, and the European Union were quickly brought on board, and several dozen nations soon followed. Canada at least now had numbers on its side, allies presenting a united front against Beijing's unlawful arrests. It was probably the best strategy available to Canada given its own limited leverage over China.

CHAPTER NINE

Huawei to the Top

A S MENG WANZHOU ENTERED her second full year under Canadian house arrest, firmly grounded from her high-flying executive lifestyle, her father was taking centre stage at one of the last, major in-person international meetings held before the full force of the COVID-19 pandemic locked down the planet. The Davos World Economic Global Forum in the luxurious Swiss Alps resort was a meeting of what Canada's deputy prime minister Chrystia Freeland once described as "the plutocrats," the world's "A-listers," the elite of industry and finance, government, banking, along with a few notable thinkers and celebrities.[1] One of the hottest tickets at the 2020 meeting was a panel chaired by the *Economist's* Zanny Minton Beddoes, a sharp British journalist, the first woman to become managing editor of the venerable weekly, and one of *Forbes'* "Most Powerful Women in the World." She presided over a half-hour discussion with Huawei's CEO and founder Ren Zhengfei and the brilliant young Israeli academic Yuval Noah Harari. They debated whether a new arms race was emerging between China and the United States in artificial intelligence, information-based technologies, and 5G. Beddoes introduced Ren as the head of a company "blacklisted by the US and Exhibit A in the technology arms race."[2]

Harari argued that the race for technological dominance and the control of information and people's minds and bodies has real parallels to the nuclear Cold War rivalry between the United States and the former Soviet Union. The only two combatants in this twenty-first century fight were the United States and China, and Harari saw it shaping up like this: a competition between the state surveillance to which China subjected its citizens and the "surveillance capitalism" the US imposed on its masses.[3]

"To hack human beings, you need a lot of biological knowledge, a lot of computing power, and especially a lot of data. If you have enough data about me, and enough computing power and biological knowledge, you can hack my body, my brain, my life. You can reach a point when you know me better than I know myself. And once you reach that point—and we are very close to that point, then democracy, the free market and, actually, all political systems . . . we have no idea what happens, once you pass that point," Harari calmly stated. "And the outcome of the arms race is really going to shape how everybody on the planet is going to live in twenty to fifty years, humans, other animals, new kinds of entities."[4]

In stark contrast, Ren, whose company stands at the commanding heights of network communications and R&D, tried to assuage the suspicions of the room that his company was part of China's nefarious plan to control the internet and the world. Speaking through a translator, and frequently smiling through a deeply etched face, Ren was doing his best to project a benign, avuncular presence. If there was a race, Ren argued, it was to better the planet and improve the lives of its citizens by harnessing the wealth-generating potential of new information technologies based on AI.[5]

"Humanity will be able to use new technologies to benefit society instead of destroying society because the majority of people in society aspire for a good life, instead of a miserable life. When I was born, that was the time when the atom bomb exploded in Japan.

When I was six, or seven, the biggest fear people had was around atom bombs," Ren explained. But if we take a step back, "we see enormous benefits from atomic energy," including the use of radiation in medical treatments. "Today, we're seeing fears about artificial intelligence, but we should not exaggerate. The explosion of atom bombs would hurt people. But people can manage that. And AI is not as damaging as atom bombs, right?"[6]

During the conversation, Ren reminisced about his humble beginnings growing up in a small village in southwest China and how, when he was setting up his company, he lived in a modest one-room apartment and put all of his savings into his fledgling enterprise.[7] He acknowledged the importance of American management practices and know-how to the rise of his own firm. It was an impressive performance, part of an ongoing charm offensive by a company that had run afoul of the US justice system and the administration of President Donald Trump.

Ren's upbeat remarks came as no surprise to the cognoscenti. As a major Brookings Institution study has documented, external Chinese government and commercial messaging on information technology is quite different from its domestic messaging: "The former stresses free markets, openness, collaboration, and interdependence," whereas the "internal discourse emphasizes the *limits* of free markets and the dangers of reliance on foreign technologies." [8]

If the world is embarked on a new arms race driven by an ineluctable quest for technological superiority in artificial intelligence, IT, and the adoption of 5G networks, it is a race in which many countries have stumbled badly attempting to balance the competing pressures of commercialization and economic growth with the demands of national security and the importance of keeping their citizens safe from those who seek to do them harm.

* * *

To understand the race and its stakes, and how it applies to Meng and the Two Michaels, we need to start with the basics. What is 5G? How did Huawei become the world's biggest and most important player in 5G networks? Why did Huawei become the bête noire of the American government? And how have Canada's own 5G policies and those of its key allies, most of whom are struggling to cut ties with Huawei, contributed to the conflict?

In simple terms, 5G stands for "fifth generation" mobile network technology. It is supposed to revolutionize the way people and devices hook up to the internet. It is a technology that will not only speed up the transfer of data but also ease access and enhance connectivity for the billions of devices (cellphones, cars, drones, home appliances, robots, heart monitors, wearable devices), critical services and infrastructure (electricity grids, pipelines, water and waste management systems), and transportation networks that are now or will in the future be connected to the internet. 5G also involves the creation of a new telecommunications architecture that will more closely align cellular software operating systems with the hardware (the computers, cables, switches, cellphone towers, and satellites) that carry the gazillions of bits and bytes of data across the internet and around the world.

5G networks are expected by many to transform our lives and the way we work and communicate with each other, and perhaps even the global balance of power. As *Wired* magazine somewhat breathlessly opined, "The future depends on connectivity. From artificial intelligence and self-driving cars to telemedicine and mixed reality to as yet undreamt technologies, all the things we hope will make our lives easier, safer, and healthier will require high-speed, always-on internet connections."

The fifth generation of wireless networking technology promises download speeds of 10 gigabytes per second which is 600 times faster than currently available 4G technologies. That means someone could potentially download an ultra-high-resolution 4K movie on a smartphone in less than half-a-minute while streaming another movie at the same time, although, as *Wired* cautions, the first generation of 5G networks operate at considerably lower speeds because they lack the infrastructure for the millimeter wave signal transmission that allows carriers to operate at much higher speeds. [9]

Another important feature of 5G is greatly reduced latency: the time it takes for any device on the network to respond to another device. Reduced latency times are vital for systems where milliseconds can mean the difference between life and death, as in the case of a remotely operated heart pacemaker or self-driving cars.[10]

5G also stands to have a major impact on productivity and innovation, which are critical to growth, prosperity, and competitiveness in today's hyperconnected world. McKinsey & Company's Global Institute has identified seventeen different commercial domains that will greatly benefit from 5G. Foremost among them are transportation, healthcare, manufacturing and retail, which together could increase global GDP by USD $1.2 trillion-$2 trillion by the beginning of the next decade with the widespread application of 5G connectivity. As the institute explains, "In mobility, vehicles will communicate with infrastructure, other vehicles, and networks, improving safety and traffic flow. In healthcare, connectivity-enabled innovations can make it possible to monitor patients remotely, using AI-powered tools for more accurate diagnoses, and automate many tasks so that caregivers can spend more time with patients. Manufacturers and other industrial companies can run highly precise, high-output, and largely automated operations using low-latency commercial and private 5G networks. Retail can offer a more seamless and personalized in-store experience while making inventory management and warehouse operations more efficient."[11]

Countries that are already deploying high-band 5G networks, including China, the United States, Japan, and South Korea, can expect to reap the biggest economic gains and social dividends. They will be followed closely by countries such as Canada, France, Britain, and India, which have modern mobile networks in their cities but not in the countryside. In the middle of the pack are countries like Brazil and Poland, which are still in the process of building fibre optic networks and where 5G will be mid-band and thus slower than those countries which are building faster millimeter-band wireless systems. Poorer developing countries, like Pakistan or Bolivia, will take much longer to develop these capabilities and run the risk of losing out on the growth opportunities that come with 5G.[12]

The world leader in 5G is the Chinese firm Huawei, which has made huge investments in R&D to push itself to the frontier of cellular network development. Huawei is now the largest telecommunications company in the world.[13] It makes and sells more smartphones than Apple. It is the major purveyor of telecommunications equipment in Europe, Asia, and Africa, and its products and services are found in more than 170 countries around the world. As *Forbes* magazine writes: "Underlying the story of 5G is the rise of Asia and particularly China in the broad transformation of the post-American world." Asia will have the majority of the world's 5G users and by 2025 many of those users will be in China, which is estimated to have 1.2 billion users of 5G networks.[14]

Huawei has risen to market dominance on the back of China's own extraordinary economic growth and development. When Huawei was founded in 1987 in Shenzhen, China as a satellite marketing firm for a Hong Kong-based phone and cable network company, China was almost entirely dependent on foreign suppliers for its telecommunications equipment. But the company was quick to expand its operations throughout China to meet the burgeoning needs of its cities and urban consumers. Eager to boost China's domestic capacities in telecommunications, its government promoted research and development ventures with foreign firms. Huawei was an exception, however, preferring to build its own in-house R&D capacity, especially in the development of large-scale switching equipment which foreign companies refused to sell to China.

In the early 1990s, Huawei developed its first high-capacity switch and found an eager customer in the Chinese Liberation Army. As that relationship blossomed, Huawei was soon supplying telecom equipment in rural areas with the support of local governments, and ▉▉g major contracts with state-owned entities, such as China's ▉▉l railway. Those contracts opened the door to major loans from China's state banks and helped pave the way to Huawei's entry into global markets. In the three decades since its founding (1987–2018), Huawei received US$30.6 billion in credit lines, US$15.7 billion in state loans, export credits, and other sources of financing and direct financial support, amounting to an estimated US$75 billion.[15] Huawei was also helped by the Chinese government in overseas markets which provided market intelligence, directly lobbied foreign governments to buy Chinese-made IT products and services, and greased the wheels for various kinds of joint ventures.[16] Huawei also leveraged its position as a provider of relatively low-cost fourth-generation networks in some seventy-five countries to promote the sale of its new 5G network technologies.

Although Huawei publicly denies that it has been the recipient of financial assistance from the Chinese government, it recognizes the importance of China's industrial policies to its phenomenal growth and development, which have given it a privileged position in China's own market by locking out foreign competitors.[17] Huawei's corporate governance structure underscores its close ties to the Chinese Communist Party. As Thomas Lairson explains, "The ownership of Huawei is often said to be with Huawei employees. However, the best evidence indicates this is not correct; instead, Huawei is arguably a near-99% indirectly state-owned enterprise, with the founder Ren Zhengfei holding slightly more than 1% of the shares . . . ownership shares for employees were converted into virtual shares that gave employees a right to profits, but not voting control or rights to the liquidated assets of the firm. The actual near-99% ownership shares were vested in a trade Union Committee that is itself controlled by the local Chinese Communist Party. The 1% shareholder, founder Ren Zhengfei, does retain a veto power over the actions of the Trade Union Commi   [18]

Huawei's business model is another   securin global success. By being vertically integ   nation sales and services throughout its four core operations, it has been able to offer a full range of products and services to its customers. Its carrier network business group offers combined "wireless networks, fixed networks, global services, carrier software, core networks and network energy solutions that are deployed by almost all major communications carriers worldwide," while its enterprise business group, "a perfect complement," carries data which is "analysed, translated, stored and saved, by Huawei's data center and storage products." Its consumer business group sells personal handset and smartphone products, and it now has a separate cloud computing business which it offers in partnership with local operators such as Germany's Deutsche Telekom.[19] Huawei also became the leading equipment provider for the world's other telecommunications carriers. Even some companies that don't use Huawei products are reliant on Huawei patented technology. Huawei's early research into 5G telecommunications at the beginning of this century means that its proprietary-based technology is used everywhere. As one study notes: "At the end of 2018, Huawei was granted 87,805 patents, 44,434 of them granted outside China. Additionally, one-third of these patents were critical for 5G development."[20]

As a market leader, Huawei has also come to occupy the commanding heights of network and cloud storage standardization by holding key positions in many international standard-setting technical bodies and organizations. This has allowed Huawei to set the prevailing technical standards in 5G wireless networking, giving it a distinct competitive edge over other firms—much as the Remington typewriter did with its QUERTY keyboard when the typewriter was first invented. All of this has given Huawei what the Oxford Digital Group calls a "first-mover advantage" in 5G technology, buoyed by the fact that Chinese companies have the resources—including a favourable regulatory structure and financial capital—to run large 5G testbeds, tightly control supply chains, develop vertical markets, and access a wide variety of global markets. As the group further explains, "In technology markets, first-mover advantage generally leads to a winner-takes-all scenario, due to economies of scale, network effects, and switching costs—these factors help to explain why the race to 5G has become a zero-sum game."[21]

But Huawei's gatecrashing success in networking technology is also due to the fact that its major Western competitors over the years have grown complacent. As Keith John and Elias Groll explain, "When 3G and 4G networks were being built, Huawei was playing catch-up to its established rivals, licensing much of their technology. To some extent, that lured Ericsson and Nokia, which today are Huawei's main rivals in the race to develop 5G, into a state of complacency, said Thillien of Fitch Solutions. They had invested a lot of money into what were then cutting-edge technologies and sought to squeeze the most they could out of them rather than racing ahead to the next stage, making their own developments obsolete. At the same time, they felt they had little to fear from what was then regarded as a nonthreatening Chinese firm. Now the situation is reversed. Huawei has more 5G-related patents than any other firm, according to IPlytics, a German-based company that tracks intellectual property development. That means other companies will have to pay Huawei to use key bits of 5G technology"[22]

All those patents are backed by a corporate culture of militaristic zeal. On the walls of Huawei's buildings, and the "cardboard sleeves on the campus's Illy coffee cups," writes *Wired* magazine's Garrett Graff, are images of "a battered World War II fighter, its wings and fuselage shot to pieces, still flying triumphantly. As the poster says, 'Heroes are forged, not born.'"[23]

CHAPTER TEN

Spies and Backdoors

THE ADVENT OF 5G involves a major shift in the architecture of the internet from a hardware-based system to a software system that relies heavily on cloud-based computing. This has prompted major concerns about computers, servers, and data processing systems which support 5G and their vulnerability to cyberattacks. In recent years, cybercriminals and some states such as Russia, China, North Korea, and Iran have developed increasingly sophisticated ways to steal data and target core systems, such as industrial control systems, with the aim of disrupting or even destroying them. Among the best-known forms of cyberattacks are distributed denial-of-service (DDoS) attacks, where an army of bots overwhelms computer servers with access requests that cause the system to crash, and phishing attacks where a user inadvertently downloads malware through an email or a website that disables the operating system of a computer or an entire network (or is used to steal, corrupt, or alter the data in the system). Damage from a well-planned cyberattack can cause major disruptions, as in the case of Russia's attack on Ukraine's eastern power grid in 2015, which left many without heat or light in the middle of winter.

The physical architecture of 5G creates additional vulnerabilities. As the Oxford University's Information Lab explains, "Due to the nature of 5G, the attack surface is significantly greater than previous networked technologies. It is projected that there will be twenty times more radio antennae to relay information, each representing a potential vulnerability. This will increase the threat from devices connected to and data on the network, putting the services and systems the network enables at risk." Both the operation and maintenance of 5G systems is a highly complex and technical undertaking, giving those firms responsible for securing 5G networks access to both the hardware and software that operates the system and the data that flows across the network. Even more serious, "Network equipment can be a backdoor in itself, potentially providing vendors access to data, information, services, and systems. Additionally, 5G could allow for more targeted manipulation of that network."[1]

Huawei began its American operations on Valentine's Day 2001 in Plano, Texas. It had formed a joint venture with the US firm 3COM (founded by Internet pioneer Robert Metcalfe, best known for pioneering "Metcalfe's Law" about the value of a communications network). Expansion was quick, and Huawei would soon have eleven branch offices across the United States and seven major R&D centers. Its commercial operations extended to Alabama, Alaska, Arizona, California, Georgia, Hawaii, Illinois, Iowa, Kansas, Maryland, Massachusetts, Minnesota, Missouri, Nebraska, New Hampshire, New Jersey, New York, North Carolina, Ohio, Oklahoma, Oregon, Pennsylvania, Texas, and Wyoming, and before long it had signed sizeable contracts with major US firms, such as Texas Instruments, Motorola, IBM, Intel, Agere, ALTERA, Sun, Microsoft, and NEC.

Huawei's rapid rise was probably enough to put it on a collision course with the US government and its US competitors, but the company's own actions and allegations of theft of intellectual property were also a major cause of its troubles. The first formal allegations against Huawei were levelled by US telecom giant Cisco, headquartered in San Jose, California. In 2003, Cisco filed a lawsuit against Huawei for stealing its proprietary routing source code. The theft was so brazen that even some of the bugs in Cisco's system showed up in Chinese operating systems. Several months after filing its suit, Cisco successfully obtained a worldwide injunction against the sale of Huawei products that used its code. The litigation was eventually concluded in a confidentiality agreement after Huawei agreed to remove the source code from its products. Years later, Huawei would continue to deny publicly that it had stolen Cisco's intellectual property. Charles Ding, Huawei corporate senior vice president and chief representative in the United States, said publicly, "If I remember well, that happened in 2003, when Cisco sued Huawei for intellectual property rights infringement . . . at that time, Huawei provided our source code of our products to Cisco for review and the results were that there was not any infringement found and, in the end, Cisco withdrew the case . . . this is the basic situation of that case." When pressed about the matter, he added, "As specifically to the source code, the source code of the issues was actually from a third-party partner that was already available and open on the internet."[2]

A year later, at the major IT trade show Supercomm in Chicago, a late-hours security camera caught a China-based employee of Huawei photographing the circuit boards of an optical networking device after removing its casing. The device was manufactured by the Texas-based firm Fujitsu Networking Communications. Convention security guards were summoned and memory sticks were confiscated from the individual; it was discovered that he also had notes in his possession that contained proprietary diagrams of AT&T's head offices and a list of other vendors at the exhibition, including Ciena Corporation, Lucent Technologies, Tellabs Inc., Nortel, White Rock Networks, and Turin Networks. In addition to Fujitsu's optical network networking devices, which was highlighted on his list, Nortel's Optical Multiservice Edge 6500 system was another prime target.[3]

Huawei's connections with the Chinese government and military were of mounting concern to the US military establishment. It is often noted that Huawei's founder Ren Zhengfei, who studied civil engineering at the Chongqing Institute of Civil Engineering and Architecture, is a former member of China's military's engineering corps. His links with the Chinese Communist Party reportedly began with the 1982 National Congress of the CCP, a year before he left the army.

A major study of Chinese technology companies undertaken by the independent, non-profit RAND research organization for the US Air Force, revealed the intricate connections between China's "private" companies, including Huawei, and the Chinese state. It pointed out that firms like Huawei and their research institutes are designated as "national champions" in China, and not only receive direct R&D funding as well as lines of credit from government entities in order to build their "global market share," but are also staffed by Chinese officials. The report added that "Huawei maintains deep ties with the Chinese military, which serves a multi-faceted role as an important customer, as well as Huawei's political patron and research and development partner."[4]

Active measures to block Huawei's expansion soon followed. In 2008, Huawei made a bid to acquire 3COM jointly with Bain Capital, a Boston-based private equity firm, but the deal collapsed because the officials in the Pentagon and the Department of Homeland Security worried that Huawei would get control over 3COM anti-hacking computer software, which was sold to the US military, giving the Chinese a backdoor into sensitive electronic equipment and software.[5]

Pressure on Huawei grew under the Obama administration. The company was forced to divest itself in 2011 of its acquisition of an insolvent US server technology company, 3Leaf Systems, by the Committee on Foreign Investment in the United States (CFIUS) following a review of the deal that considered its national security implications.[6] When Sprint, the third biggest US wireless carrier, was considering bids to upgrade its cellular network, Huawei and another Chinese firm, ZTE Corp., offered highly competitive bids on the contract, offers that were much lower than such competitors as Alcatel-Lucent SA, Telefon L.M., Samsung, and Ericsson, but following a telephone call by US commerce secretary Gary Locke to Sprint's CEO Dan Hesse expressing the government's security concerns about Chinese suppliers, Sprint dropped both firms from consideration. (Sprint's decision was dressed up to reflect the company's concerns about the quality of Huawei's technology). Locke's call came on the heels of a letter that had earlier been sent to administration officials from eight senators expressing their own apprehensions about the deal on the grounds it would give Huawei or ZTE access to critical US telecommunications infrastructure and internet traffic. (Revisions to the National Defence Authorization Act made in 2010 at the request of the US Department of Defense give military agencies the authority to force technology vendors to exclude suppliers and subcontractors that the US government deems to be a security risk).[7]

Facing growing heat from the US government and increasingly negative publicity, Ken Hu, Huawei's chair of US operations and deputy chair of its parent company, published an open letter calling for "a formal investigation" by the US government to address "any concerns it may have about Huawei." The letter was published several days after Huawei was forced to cancel its purchase of 3Leaf Systems.[8] The offer was quickly taken up by the House permanent select committee on intelligence, which initiated its investigation into Huawei and China's other major Telcom ZTE in November 2011. The bipartisan committee was co-chaired by Michigan Republican

Mike Rogers, a no-nonsense expert on national security affairs who had served in the US army and as an FBI special agent, and his Maryland Democrat counterpart, C.A. "Dutch" Ruppersberger, who would go on to cosponsor a House bill to establish a national cyber director in the executive office of the president to coordinate cyber policy across the federal government.

* * *

A year later, the bipartisan committee delivered a scathing report. Huawei's public relations stunt had backfired. The committee accused Huawei of not "fully cooperating" with its investigation and being consistently evasive about its relationship with the Chinese government and Chinese Communist Party. It also found "credible evidence" that Huawei had failed to comply with US laws. It noted that "Huawei admits that the Chinese Communist Party maintains a Party Committee within the company, but it failed to explain what the Party Committee does on behalf of the Party or which individuals compose the Committee." It criticized the company for failing to explain its ties to the Chinese military, its relationship with Western consulting firms, and for not providing documentation on "its claims to be financially independent of the Chinese government."

The committee also found that "Huawei exhibits a pattern of disregard for the intellectual property rights of other entities and companies in the United States," and that "former and current Huawei employees provided evidence of a pattern and practice of potentially illegal behaviour by Huawei officials." The report recommended that the United States government not do any further business with Huawei or ZTE and block any further mergers and acquisitions. It also called upon American companies to shun equipment and services from either Chinese company.[9] Landing in the middle of the presidential campaign, the report was something of a bombshell. It stiffened the resolve of both candidates, Democratic presidential incumbent Barack Obama and his Republican opponent Mitt Romney, to take a tough stand against China.[10]

Following the election, Obama's re-elected administration introduced new measures requiring major departments and agencies of the US government, including NASA, the Department of Justice, and the Department of Commerce, to seek prior approval for IT purchases or contracts for services from federal law enforcement officials. Although China voiced its "strong dissatisfaction" with US actions, it is worth remembering that China had adopted similar tactics when it threatened to ban Chinese government agencies from using Microsoft products over similar concerns about using "backdoors" in their equipment or software that would allow the United States government to spy on China.[11]

Donald Trump was elected in 2016 with China in his sights as part of his "America First" foreign policy, and Huawei's fortunes took a sharp turn for the worse. The US launched a trade war and resorted to punitive measures against Chinese tech companies operating in the US. One of the key architects of that strategy was now retired brigadier general Robert Spalding, director of strategic planning in the National Security Council. A former bomber pilot who had studied in China and was fluent in Mandarin, "Spalding's wariness of Beijing had grown over time," reports *Wired*. "He'd spent a year on a fellowship with the Council on Foreign Relations in New York, where he met with countless business leaders concerned about China's intellectual property theft and economic espionage. He was also troubled by how entangled US military supply chains were with China."[12]

Spalding was one of the key figures to lead the charge against Huawei in the battle over 5G. In a secret White House briefing memo that was leaked to the press, Spalding argued that "China ha[d] achieved a dominant position in the manufacture and operation of network infrastructure" and become "the dominant malicious actor in the Information Domain." Among the various options outlined in Spalding's memo was for the US government to support the construction of the 5G network (much as President Eisenhower's administration funded the building of the US interstate highway system in the 1950s through the Federal Aid Highway Act of 1956) and then rent it to the telecommunications sector. At the very least, however, if this option was not tenable, the report argued that the United States Government had to "provide clear direction and strong leadership" and if US carriers were to build the network, the government had to "standardize siting requirements . . . [and] strongly signal to equipment manufacturers our intent to build a secure supply chain."[13] The leak of Spalding's memo, which was characterized in the media as an attempt to nationalize the development of the 5G network, subsequently led to his dismissal from the NSC on the grounds that he had exceeded his authority.

Later, in an August 2021 interview with the authors of this book, Spalding would restate his Cassandra-like warnings about the dangers of leaving 5G in the hands of the Chinese: "We know how important these systems are to preserving our civil society. We've become so dependent on the electrical grid and particularly telecommunications that it's really very important for our way of life. And so, if the lights go out, people don't really know how to act . . . we had a cash-based society now most of it is done via electronic transactions, which aren't going to be possible [if there is a network disruption or attack] . . . Police, fire [stations], you know, all the first responders require the same networks . . . We need that infrastructure to be to be there, when we have . . . any kind of natural disaster and [it can't] be taken down by an adversary."

Spalding, of course, was not alone in expressing his concerns about Huawei and the use of Chinese equipment in US networks. The US firm Finite State conducted a major study of the cybersecurity-related risks of using Huawei network devices. After analyzing over a million files embedded in almost 10,000 firmware images, it found that over half of them had backdoors that could be used to gain access to the network and of the 102 "known vulnerabilities," most were deemed to be "high or critical in their severity."[14]

Major US carriers meanwhile began to distance themselves from Huawei, refusing to purchase or sell its products. In 2018, at one of the largest technology trade fairs, the Consumer Electronics Show, Huawei's CEO of consumer business, Richard Yu, had hoped to announce a new partnership with AT&T to see its new Mate 10 Pro Smartphone. But AT&T pulled the plug on the impending deal at the last minute, leaving Yu to sputter on stage about the virtues of Huawei's new smartphone and what the loss of US carrier support would mean for American consumers. Rumours that Verizon would follow suit soon proved to be true.[15]

In February 2018, appearing before the Senate Intelligence Committee, the heads of six intelligence and law enforcement agencies, including the FBI, the CIA, and the NSA, warned American citizens about the dangers of buying products and services from Huawei and other Chinese firms. As FBI director Christopher Wray testified, "We're deeply concerned about the risks of allowing any company or entity that is beholden to foreign governments that don't share our values to gain positions of power inside our telecommunications networks. That provides the capacity to exert pressure or control over our telecommunications infrastructure . . . provides the capacity to maliciously modify or steal information. . . . And it provides the capacity to conduct undetected espionage."[16]

That warning was followed in May by Trump's executive national security order giving the federal government the authority to block purchases of foreign telecommunications equipment on national security grounds and placing Huawei on a blacklist prohibiting American firms from selling technology and parts to it. One of the immediate consequences was that Google suspended Huawei's Android license, cutting it off from Google apps and services for consumers outside China.[17] These restrictions took a big billion-dollar bite out of Huawei's US revenues. Huawei laid off hundreds of workers because of its blacklisting.

The company would face more problems when the US Federal Communication Commission voted in November 2019 to ban Huawei and ZTE from its $8.5 billion a year universal service fund, effectively preventing US carriers from using Huawei equipment to upgrade their networks, while classifying both companies as a national security risk.[18] The FCC's action was followed by passage of a bill in Congress that barred the US government from buying any telecommunications equipment from companies deemed national security threats.[19]

Early the following year, the FCC announced that it was collecting data on US carriers that were already using Huawei and ZTE network equipment with the aim of helping those carriers remove their equipment following a vote in the US Senate to do so. (Those removal costs were subsequently estimated at $1.8 billion). In May, Donald Trump extended his earlier executive order banning US companies from buying Chinese telecommunications equipment or services until the following year. The order invoked the International Emergency Economic Powers Act, which gives the president the authority to regulate commerce in a national emergency. Even though the executive order did not specifically mention Huawei or ZTE, it was clearly targeted at them.[20] In June 2020, the FCC formally designated the two companies as national security threats even though the commerce department at the same time granted permission to US companies to work with Huawei in developing 5G networking standards. Defending the move, US commerce secretary Wilbur Ross said that his department was "committed to protecting US national security foreign policy interests by encouraging US industry to fully engage and advocate for US technology to become international standards."[21]

By 2021, US actions were hampering Huawei's growth, even though the company continued to post healthy sales and profit margins. As the *Associated Press* reported, the company was "struggling to keep its global markets after then-President Donald Trump in 2019 cut off access to US processor chips and to other technology." The Chinese government's response has been to claim that the US is trying to sabotage Huawei's dominance of the world's telecommunications market to make up for the shortcomings of its own companies. It has upped its technological and economic assistance to Huawei, taking specific measures such as exempting chipmakers from import duties while elevating China's self-reliance as a "technology power" to the country's "top economic priority."[22]

CHAPTER ELEVEN

Trump Makes His Move

WHILE THE TRUMP ADMINISTRATION was taking steps to shut Huawei and Chinese IT firms out of the US market, it was also putting its boot to key allies to do the same. There was nothing subtle about its tactics. US ambassador Richard A. Grenell, a former well-placed media adviser, political consultant in Republican circles, and Trump appointee, warned Germany that it might lose access to American intelligence unless it banned Huawei from its networks. As the *Wall Street Journal* reported, the letter was the first time the United States had told an ally that "refusing to ostracize Huawei could lessen security cooperation with Washington."[1]

Grenell's bombastic, undiplomatic manner had irked the Germans more than once. He controversially tweeted that German companies should stop doing business in Iran and told the Trump-friendly *Breitbart* news website that he saw his mission as empowering other conservatives in Europe. Grenell would later go on to serve as Trump's acting director of national intelligence.

After two years of deliberation, Germany announced that it would still allow foreign companies such as Huawei to participate in its 5G rollout. At the same time, it introduced a two-stage technical assessment and review mechanism requiring vendors to clearly demonstrate their products could not be used for "sabotage or espionage." After companies had registered and issued their declaration, the German government would then conduct reviews and decide about their participation.[2]

America's most trusted spycraft allies, the Five Eyes intelligence coalition of countries, includes Britain, Canada, Australia, and New Zealand. They, too, met mounting pressure to stop dealing with Huawei. For several years, the British government had managed its security concerns with Huawei through the UK-based Huawei Cyber Security Evaluation Centre (HCSEC), which analyzed "Huawei equipment to identify potential vulnerabilities." It was largely staffed by Huawei personnel. The government had resisted calls to place government security and intelligence personnel into HCSEC, preferring an oversight board of senior government officials.[3] Cybersecurity officials in the British government had also made it clear that "the issue was not one country or company, but that national networks had to be able to withstand any attack, malicious action or simple error," and that the best way to achieve this was "by diversifying suppliers" among the big three: Huawei, Nokia, and Ericsson. Inclusion of Huawei gear in the US network mix, according to the UK, would "counter-intuitively, result in higher overall security."[4]

Despite mounting pressure from the White House and a London visit by senior Trump officials who warned that there could be repercussions to UK trade and intelligence sharing, the British government announced in late January 2020 that Huawei's components would remain in their earlier generation networks (2G, 3G, and 4G) and could be used for non-core elements of its new 5G networks.

The government defended its policy on the grounds that a review conducted by Britain's National Security Council had come to the conclusion that the security risks associated with the use of Huawei products and services could be managed while denying claims that its equipment could be used to spy on sensitive communications or debilitate key infrastructure in a cyberattack.[5]

British government officials, speaking with *The Canadian Press* on condition of anonymity in order to speak candidly about a sensitive topic, said Britain was dealing with a "market failure"—there are not enough reliable companies to meet the country's 5G economic ambitions. They were hoping to create enough space for new European, American, or Canadian companies to emerge, diminishing their reliance on Huawei. Ultimately, they decided to limit Huawei's overall participation to less than 35 per cent. As one official put it: "That's the way you get security."[6]

But London's middle-of-the-road approach did little to assuage Washington. The US was especially worried that if its closest intelligence partner accepted Huawei 5G equipment, it would send the wrong message to other countries.[7] The British were all too aware of this. On January 28, 2020, the day of its decision, British Prime Minister Boris Johnson spoke with Trump by phone, and Britain's foreign secretary updated his Canadian counterpart, François-Philippe Champagne, in a call the same day. As one British official explained, the calls were intended to "keep our important Five Eyes partners informed of the decision and the logic behind it."[8]

The British were anxious to keep both China and the United States, the world's two biggest economies, in their wheelhouse as Brexit's D-Day approached, but the balancing act proved increasingly difficult. Within six months of saying Britain would continue to do business with Huawei, Johnson's government did "a major U-turn," announcing that Britain would ban Huawei from 5G and remove all critical Huawei gear from its existing networks by 2027.[9]

Defending the government's new policy in the House of Commons, Oliver Dowden, secretary for digital, culture, media and sport, stated that "keeping the country secure is the primary duty of a government to its people. This consideration precedes all others. There is of course no such thing as a perfectly secure network. But the responsibility of the government is to ensure that it is as secure as it can possibly be."

Dowden went on to explain that the decision had been affected by the introduction of new US sanctions which could "potentially have severe impacts on Huawei's ability to supply new equipment in the UK." He also noted that the National Cyber Security Centre had reviewed the consequences of the US's actions and "now reported to ministers that they have significantly changed their security assessment of Huawei's presence in the UK 5G network."[10]

It was likely that the UK's rapidly deteriorating relationship with China over its repressive actions in Hong Kong played into the decision, as did mounting pressure from Johnson's own Conservative party backbenchers. Trump was quick to brag that he was personally responsible for the decision: "I did this myself, for the most part," he crowed, although UK officials were quick to rebuff such claims. "We all know Donald Trump, don't we?" then-UK health secretary Matt Hancock said to Sky News.[11]

But it was not just Huawei that was now in Prime Minister Boris Johnson's crosshairs. In 2021 reports surfaced that Britain was looking at ways "to remove China's state-owned nuclear energy company China General Nuclear Power Group (CGN) from all future power projects in the UK."[12]

If there was one country in the Five Eyes that might have expected to buck American demands and stay firmly in Huawei's orbit, it would have been Australia. In 2015, the Australians had signed a free trade agreement with China. Trade had tripled within a decade, making China Australia's most important trading partner, accounting for 40 per cent of its exports by 2020. Australia is also the second most important destination for Chinese investment after the United States. In 2017, there were 131,000 Chinese students enrolled in Australian universities, proportionately five times the number enrolled in American universities. However, as its commercial and human ties with China have grown, Australians have become increasingly concerned about China's growing influence on their soil. Unlike Britain, Australia had few qualms about slamming the door in Huawei's face.

In August 2018, the Australian government took the unprecedented step of blocking foreign vendors from the rollout of its 5G networks. In a joint statement by Australian communications minister Mitch Fifield and acting home affairs minister Scott Morrison, the government announced that it considered "vendors who are likely to be subject to extrajudicial directions from a foreign government that conflict with Australian law" to have failed an important risk test. The directive expressly covered telecom carriers who could not "adequately protect a 5G network from unauthorized access or interference."

The government further justified its actions by referring to Australian telecommunication sector security reforms legislation requiring it to "take necessary steps to safeguard the security of Australians' information and communications at all times."[13]

Then-prime minister Malcolm Turnbull would later say that he tried to find ways to include Huawei and ZTE in the country's future high-speed mobile internet plans but that the risks were too high because a company providing and maintaining a 5G network would have "constant access" and an "enormous capability, if it chose to act adversely to your interest."[14] Huawei retaliated by lodging a complaint with the World Trade Organization on the grounds that the ban was "obviously discriminatory," and because "Australia had failed to notify the WTO of its decision to ban the Chinese operators."[15]

Australia's decision was a prescient one. It was subsequently revealed that Australia's signals directorate had advised the government that it would have to make at least 300 special hardware and software fixes on Huawei equipment to render Australia's 5G network secure from Chinese eavesdroppers and, even then, the network could still be shut down on orders from Beijing.[16]

New Zealand quickly followed Australia's lead. In November 2018, its communications security bureau ordered New Zealand's local carrier, Spark, not to use Huawei equipment for its 5G upgrade on the grounds that it posed "a significant network risk." This came after Huawei with great fanfare had constructed a 5G test site across the street from New Zealand's parliament. The Chinese government was quick to express its "severe concerns" about the decision, reminding New Zealand, the first western country to sign a free trade agreement with China in 2008, of the "mutually beneficial" nature of the two countries' relationship. In a bid to rally public support to reverse the decision, Huawei took out full-page advertisements in New Zealand's major newspapers, which treat the sport of rugby like a religion, suggesting the ban on Huawei was like a rugby tournament without New Zealand's All Blacks team.[17] Some New Zealand opposition critics chastised the government for scaremongering and falling into line with Washington.[18]

A year later, the government was spinning its earlier decision as a temporary one. Said Andrew Little, the minister responsible for the government security communications bureau: "New Zealand does not ban any telecommunications vendor. . . . [but] we do have a well-established and independent regulatory process to ensure the security of our networks under the Telecommunications (Interception Capability and Security) Act 2013 (TICSA)."[19] This verbal dance was undoubtedly motivated by the government's desire to protect New Zealand's trade with China, which had quadrupled since the signing of the free trade agreement.[20]

* * *

If the struggle by other Five Eyes members to deal with Huawei resembled something of an egg-and-spoon race with governments struggling to keep economic and security concerns in balance, Canada couldn't get its egg on the spoon to start. At the beginning of 2021, when all of its Five Eyes partners had more or less closed the door to Huawei's participation in their 5G networks, Canada had yet to announce whether it would let Huawei supply its equipment despite years of internal study and mounting pressure from its allies to toe a tougher line.

One reason, in the early days of the Trudeau government, was its desire to establish free-trade negotiations with the Chinese. Later, the delay was sheer opportunism. As the drawbridge for Huawei went up in the United States, Canada saw commercial gain by lowering its own. A third and perhaps overriding factor is the Meng affair. Canada worried that a negative decision on Huawei would jeopardize the fate of the Two Michaels. At the same time, it didn't want to antagonize the volatile Donald Trump so, in classic Canadian fashion, it punted the decision.

Canada was a late bloomer in its dalliance with Huawei. It was almost a decade after the company's US debut before it formally launched operations in Canada, which initially involved selling low-cost routers and switches to small carrier networks. Within two years, however, Huawei had opened an R&D centre in the suburban high-tech enclave of Kanata, a suburb of Ottawa, taking advantage of the region's access to major academic and research institutions. Then-mayor Larry O'Brien was "thrilled that Ottawa has been recognized by Huawei as the ideal place to focus its Canadian R&D efforts." His enthusiasm was no doubt reinforced by a visit he and other city dignitaries had paid to "Huawei's very impressive worldwide headquarters in Shenzhen." Hopes were high that Huawei would "leverage Ottawa's R&D talent globally" and help develop the "Ottawa's knowledge-based economy."[21]

Less than a year later, Huawei opened its Canadian headquarters in Markham, Ontario, just north of Toronto. As the Chinese-communist party organ *China Daily* reported, the facility is 47,000 square feet and includes "sales and marketing capabilities as well as a test lab." Charles Ding, president of Huawei's North American operations, stressed that the new headquarters in Markham "underscore[d] [Huawei's] long-term investment in the Canadian market and, on a broader scale. . . . Huawei's continued growth in North America." The venture received a $16 million commitment through the Ontario government's Job and Prosperity Fund to complement Huawei's $212 million investment.[22]

Another facility would open four years later in Waterloo, Ontario, best known for its world-class engineering, mathematics, and computer studies programs at the University of Waterloo, and for being the home of BlackBerry (originally known as Research in Motion, or RIM), the pioneer of the smartphone. By the second decade of the twenty-first century, BlackBerry was no longer a world leader, having lost most of its market share to far nimbler companies such as Apple, and Android device makers such as Samsung, Xiami, and Huawei itself. As BlackBerry turned to a new business model, focused on providing secure mobile services and AI-based solutions for self-driving vehicles, it shed many highly-skilled employees. Waterloo and its sister city, Kitchener, became a magnet for top ICT companies, including Google, OpenText, D2L, Vidyard, and then Huawei, eager to scoop up the best and the brightest who had left BlackBerry or had graduated recently from the University of Waterloo. As the *Globe and Mail* reported, "Huawei is looking to hire numerous engineers in the area to focus on security software for mobile devices and 'enterprise security' for businesses. Those skills were at the center of BlackBerry's global rise selling mobile devices and secure services to businesses . . ."[23]

Huawei's entry to Canada came in the Stephen Harper years, after the former Conservative prime minister had reconsidered his initial hard-line against China and was seeking to promote closer economic ties. On his 2012 visit, Harper said that he was "honoured" to have observed the signing of major contracts by Telus and Bell with Huawei for high-speed wireless network equipment.[24]

Even in those early days, there were dire warnings from Washington about Huawei's Canadian operations. In an interview with CBC News, the former head of US counterespionage in the Bush administration, Michelle K. Van Cleave, said "the involvement of Huawei Technologies in Canadian telecom networks risks turning the information highway into a freeway for Chinese espionage against both the US and Canada."[25]

After he left office, Harper's enthusiasm for Huawei cooled. In a December 2018 interview with Fox News, Harper said he supported American efforts to ban the company: "I obviously note that the United States is encouraging western allies to essentially push Huawei out of emerging 5G networks and my personal view is that this is something western countries should be doing in terms of our own long-term security issues."[26]

Many more warnings and expressions of concern would follow from other parties. In May 2019, with the obvious backing of Washington, former homeland secretary Michael Chertoff, a guru of cybersecurity who had served as Homeland Security secretary in the George W. Bush administration, warned Canadians that adoption of Huawei technology for their 5G networks would have major consequences for Canada-US relations because American officials would not want to share intelligence information with their Canadian counterparts if their networks could be compromised.

Chertoff also cautioned that the Chinese could "find or embed pathways in to compromise networks and allow the theft of intellectual property. They could introduce disruption or latency into the network because it's not just the hardware and software that you first install. It's all of the updates, the patches, everything you do to them to tend to and monitor the system going forward." 5G networks, Chertoff added, will be part of "your industrial control systems and your operating systems. So, the person who dominates that, in a way, has the ability to affect everything from your power grid to your air traffic control system to even your sensitive national security infrastructure."[27]

As Huawei's footprint in Canada grew, its business shifted from devices to providing Canada's major telecommunications companies with technology and equipment for their fast-growing cellular networks. All of Canada's major telecoms were soon using Huawei equipment in their networks. Two of them, Bell Canada and the Telus Corporation, entered into major contracts with Huawei for their 4G wireless networks, and subsequently looked to it for their 5G upgrades. Huawei's move upmarket was accompanied by a slick marketing campaign to boost its image and profile, which included promoting its phones at concerts through a contract it signed with Live Nation Canada to sponsor American singer Katy Perry's cross-country tour. The company became the major corporate sponsor of *Hockey Night in Canada*, which prominently featured the Huawei logo on pre-game and second-intermission broadcasts along with frequent shout-outs by the program's hosts. Huawei's first major sports sponsorship was with the Ottawa Senators in their 2015-16 season, giving it an out-sized presence in the nation's capital.[28]

Huawei's reach into Canada's university research community also accelerated. A special investigation by the *Globe and Mail* found that "Huawei has established a vast network of relationships with leading research-heavy universities in Canada to create a steady pipeline of intellectual property that the company is using to underpin its market position in 5G." The *Globe* noted that Huawei had spent $150 million on research and development in Canada as compared to "almost nothing" in the United States. Furthermore, "filings with the US Patent and Trademark Office . . . show that in forty cases, the academics—whose work is largely underwritten by taxpayers—have assigned all intellectual property rights to the company. In addition, Huawei licenses intellectual property from Canadian university researchers, often giving the company exclusive rights to their publicly-funded research. Huawei appeared as a co-author with a Canadian university on 350 peer-reviewed papers between 2010 and 2018."[29]

Ottawa itself was also contributing to Huawei's sponsored research in Canadian universities. Through the Natural Science and Engineering Research Council (NSERC), Canadian researchers working with Huawei received nearly $7 million in grants, funding that continued even after Meng's arrest. The grants were defended by NSERC on the grounds that they contributed to creating jobs and advancing scientific knowledge, even though some critics argue that Huawei is the main beneficiary and not Canada.[30] In February 2020, the *Globe and Mail* revealed that NSERC was putting up an additional $4.3 million in research partnership funding that included Huawei. The company's matching funding exceeded that amount. Critics such as former Research in Motion co-chief executive Jim Balsillie were stunned. "It boggles the mind," he said, "that in 2021 we continue to use taxpayer funds to advance China's priorities at the expense of our economy, security, and Five Eyes partnership."[31]

By 2018, Huawei employed close to 600 research employees in Canada compared to seventy when it began its Canadian operations in 2010. That number continued to grow with the introduction of US sanctions in 2019. Huawei announced that it was moving its US research operations to Canada. Although the company provided few details about the move, the announcement came as the company cut jobs at its Silicon Valley research centre in Santa Clara, California.[32]

Huawei's rapidly growing presence in Canada occurred without ringing any major alarm bells in Canada. The first real inkling that the Trudeau government was finally taking notice of the security risks in its wireless networks came in September 2018, when public safety and emergency preparedness minister Ralph Goodale announced that Ottawa was conducting its own national security review of potential threats to its telecommunications infrastructure from foreign-sourced equipment and suppliers, including Huawei. Goodale had visited Australia a few months earlier where he discussed with Australian authorities their ban of Huawei. Though few details about the review were publicly available, Goodale hinted that it had been underway for some time: "We are examining the issue of security in relation to supply chains right across government very carefully. It is a topic that many countries—our allies in particular—are taking a very close look at and have been for a considerable length of time . . . We have not arrived at those decisions yet, but obviously we are very sensitive to this issue."[33]

Part of the reason for Ottawa's indecision may have laid within the bureaucracy itself. Scott Jones, head of the Canadian Centre for Cybersecurity, publicly boasted that the government has sophisticated technology and the know-how to detect and prevent security breaches on Canada's networks, including new 5G systems. "We have a very advanced relationship with our telecommunications providers, something that is very different from most other countries to be honest from what I have seen," he told the House of Commons committee on public safety and national security. "We have a program that is very deep in terms of working on increasing that broader resilience piece especially as we are looking at the next-generation telecommunication networks."[34]

Jones would walk back some of his statements a week later, just before the annual SecTor conference in Toronto. In an interview with *IT World Canada,* he raised the possibility that Canada might follow the US and Australia on Huawei because there was a difference, as he was at pains to point out, between "Ottawa's strategy for current 4G/LTE networks, where carriers use some Huawei equipment . . . and faster 5G networks."[35] Some suggested that there was a major rift in the Canadian intelligence community about the security risks posed by Huawei. Whereas officials with the Canadian Security Intelligence Service (CSIS) were wary and said so openly, officials in the government's Communications Security Establishment (the national cryptologic agency) took the position that the cybersecurity risks were manageable.[36]

Whether the divisions were deep or not, they were not the only reason why the government was stalling for time. Ottawa was also under intense pressure from Bell and Telus to leave the door open to Huawei's participation in Canada's 5G networks because the two companies, which share a network, had invested heavily in Huawei gear in their existing 4G systems. The companies said that if Ottawa introduced restrictions on Huawei, they would have to tear out existing Huawei equipment because it would not be compatible with 5G suppliers, such as Ericsson or Nokia. Because the cost to both companies was estimated to run to a billion dollars or more, they also indicated that they would be looking for direct compensation from the federal government (although some legal experts doubt they would have legal grounds to do so).[37]

With an October 2019 election looming, the Trudeau government made it clear that it would postpone again a decision on Huawei and 5G. Public safety minister Ralph Goodale revealed the delay after meeting with the Five Eyes in London. Goodale played down suggestions that jeopardizing the fate of the Two Michaels played into the decision.[38] The fact remains that the Canadian government has left its 5G future hanging with the Two Michaels locked up.

In the meantime, Telus, after previously announcing that it would use Huawei technology to launch its 5G network, later reversed itself

in June 2020 and declared that it would use the Western manufacturers Nokia and Ericsson instead. Bell, too, announced that it
would be ditching Huawei. The decision was probably motivated
more by uncertainty around Huawei's status in Canada than any
official pressure.[39]

In November 2020, the House of Commons passed a Conservative
motion sponsored by the party's foreign affairs critic Michael Chong
calling on Trudeau to decide within thirty days whether to allow
Huawei to supply equipment to Canada's 5G wireless networks.
Citing the example of Australia, the motion also urged the government to "develop a robust plan, as Australia has done, to combat
China's growing foreign operations here in Canada and its increasing
intimidation of Canadians living in Canada, and table it within 30
days of the adoption of this motion."[40]

The motion was symbolic and non-binding. It, too, was eventually brushed aside. Canada remained in limbo, anxious to avoid
offending the Chinese and jeopardizing the fate of the Two Michaels,
yet failing to build the political capital with Beijing that would
help secure their release, and disappointing its Five Eye partners
who remain anxious for Canada to show some mettle and join the
Huawei ban.

Ironically, Huawei may already have received most of the value
available in Canada's telecom sector. At the turn of the millennium,
Canada was the global leader in developing the technology and
source code for fibre-optic data transmission systems and wireless
devices. Much of that sensitive and highly advanced networking
equipment had been developed by Ottawa-based Nortel Network
Corporation, a global giant that employed 90,000 people and had
a market value of $250 billion before it imploded. In 2004, it
was discovered that the company had been hacked at the highest
level and that much of its intellectual property was stolen by the
Chinese. Suspicions remain to this day that much of this wound up

at Huawei.[41] The company has strongly denied these allegations. We are unlikely to ever know exactly what transpired.

As for the future, the January 2020 conversation at Davos between Ren and Harari attempted a bit of crystal balling on how the new AI war might play out. It all came down to one ominous exchange that appeared to fly over the heads of Davos attendees near the end of the session, when they were eyeing the exits and weighing their evening party options. Harari returned to his core thesis: the world was approaching the point where "Facebook, the government, or whoever" will be able to know people "better than they know themselves."

Beddoes, the *Economist* editor, put the question squarely to Ren. "Is Huawei at that stage yet? Do you know people better than they know themselves?"

Ren's reply: "What Mr. Harari perceives about the future of science and technology, we are not sure whether that can become a reality. And we do not rule out that possibility at this point of time."[42]

CHAPTER TWELVE

As Meng Sits Quietly

FORTY-FIVE DAYS AFTER Meng Wanzhou was placed under house arrest in Vancouver, the law-and-order establishment of the United States laid its cards on the table. Acting attorney general Matthew Whitaker, FBI director Christopher Wray, homeland security secretary Kirstjen Nielsen, United States attorney for the eastern district of New York Richard Donoghue, assistant attorney general of the justice department's criminal division Brian Benczkowski, and assistant attorney general of the justice department's national security division John Demers all gathered in Brooklyn, New York on January 28, 2019 for a press conference to reveal the results of their intensive surveillance and investigation of the Huawei executive and the details of the thirteen-count indictment against her and her company.

The world learned from this press conference that a formidable team of cyber intelligence officers had been targeting Meng for several years. The first public hints that Huawei was somehow doing business in Iran came from a *Reuters* news agency in December 2012. It claimed that an Iranian-based company called Skycom had sold or attempted to sell US products in Iran in violation of US sanctions. The article linked Skycom to Huawei, which owned and operated

Skycom. A second *Reuters* article in January 2013 contained Huawei's denial that it had violated any sanctions against Iran.

Hong Kong-based banking executives with HSBC had read these reports with alarm. Meng requested a meeting with them to clear the air. It was held in August 2013 in Hong Kong. Several months later, Meng was on US soil, passing through John F. Kennedy International Airport where customs agents stopped her briefly and her electronic devices were temporarily seized. US cyber sleuths managed to scan those devices and swipe from the drive of one a file in "unallocated space," suggesting it may have been deleted, about the Hong Kong meeting.[1]

The file was a PowerPoint presentation written in Chinese and, according to the indictment, it stated that Huawei "operates in Iran in strict compliance with applicable laws, regulations and sanctions" of the United Nations, the US, and the European Union, and that the company's engagement with Skycom was "normal business co-operation." It added that "through regulated trade organizations and procedures, Huawei requires that Skycom promises to abide by relevant laws and regulations and export controls." The document further suggests as "key information" that "in the past" Huawei had "ceased to hold Skycom shares," and also that "Skycom was established in 1998 and is one of the agents for Huawei products and services. Skycom is mainly an agent for Huawei."[2] It was signed by Meng Wanzhou.[3] Those and other assertions in the document "were all false," according to the US indictment.[4] Meng was accused of lying to her customers.

"Today, we are announcing that we are bringing criminal charges against telecommunications giant Huawei and its associates for nearly two dozen alleged crimes," said acting AG Whitaker.

"Companies like Huawei pose a dual threat to both our economic and national security, and the magnitude of these charges make clear just how seriously the FBI takes this threat," said the FBI's Wray.

"As charged in the indictment, Huawei and its chief financial officer broke US law and have engaged in a fraudulent financial scheme that is detrimental to the security of the United States," said homeland security's Nielsen.

"As charged in the indictment, Huawei and its subsidiaries, with the direct and personal involvement of their executives, engaged in serious fraudulent conduct, including conspiracy, bank fraud, wire fraud, sanctions violations, money laundering and the orchestrated obstruction of justice," added US attorney Donoghue.[5] In addition to trying to conceal her company's ownership of Skycom in order to end US sanctions against Iran, Meng and Huawei were accused of plotting to steal technology and equipment from the Washington State offices of US cellphone provider T-Mobile USA. These charges relied on more internal company documents and emails.[6]

Another member of President Donald Trump's cabinet joined the who's-who of US law enforcement for the conference: the taciturn octogenarian and commerce secretary Wilbur Ross, who had this to say: "For years, Chinese firms have broken our export laws and undermined sanctions, often using the US financial systems to facilitate their illegal activities. This will end. The Trump Administration continues to be tougher on those who violate our export control laws than any administration in history. I commend the department's office of export enforcement, and our partners in the FBI, Justice Department, Department of Defense, and Department of Homeland Security for their excellent work on this case."[7]

That Ross joined the press conference was significant, so far as Meng's lawyers were concerned. They took it a clear sign that the US prosecution of her was more than a law-and-order exercise. It was part of a broader foreign policy campaign by then-President Trump to cripple China, an economic and political rival. "His presence at that event is telling," Richard Peck stated later. "It's an indication, clearly, of the economic concerns influencing this matter, influencing the president's words."

"What becomes very clear," Peck would argue in court, "is that Huawei is seen as a threat by the US, a threat to its historical place as the world's economic power, its dominance in the field of technology."

Since that press conference, the US had been elaborating its charges against Meng and Huawei while the defence was building its case that the Americans were wrongfully prosecuting a trade war through the criminal courts. Most of the back-and-forth, distilled in pleadings, transcripts, and affidavits filed in the Supreme Court of British Columbia, occurred in Courtroom 55 of the Vancouver courthouse before Associate Chief Justice Heather Holmes. She was appointed to her position seven months before Meng's arrest, after seventeen years as a BC jurist on its Supreme Court. "She brings to her new role as associate chief justice a strong sense of public service and a natural ability to bring people together," Prime Minister Justin Trudeau said on elevating her.[8] Holmes had dealt largely with criminal cases on the court, including high-profile murder and money laundering cases. She is esteemed as one of the "good judges who know the law and are happy to apply it well," says Martin Peters, an attorney who has argued cases before her.[9]

Courtroom 55 was not sealed from the outside world as the painstaking legal proceedings unfolded. The sounds of traffic from downtown Vancouver sometimes bled into the courtroom. Police sirens and horns periodically punctuated the lawyer's arguments with uncanny timing. The noise made it especially difficult for those attorneys, reporters, and observers participating in or watching the proceedings remotely because of COVID-19 restrictions. At one point Holmes noted the cacophony, saying that she was "not sure there was much we could do about it."

Rightly or wrongly, lawyers on the opposing sides of Courtroom 55 frequently created the impression that they were fighting the criminal charges against Meng and Huawei in British Columbia courts when, in fact, Canada's role in the whole affair is to decide whether or not to extradite Meng. Her guilt or innocence as charged will be for the US to determine in the event of her extradition. A Canadian extradition hearing is a unique legal process. It is a hearing, not a trial, and there are no criminal consequences in Canada for the subject of an extradition proceeding. The standard for a presiding judge in making a decision is lower than the level of evidence required to convict or acquit at an actual trial. The extradition process is divided into two decision-making phases: the first involves the presiding judge deciding if there's enough evidence to warrant sending a person to stand trial in a foreign country; the second phase involves the federal minister of justice deciding whether the extradition should take place according to Canadian law and Canada's treaty obligations. It sounds straightforward, but Meng's extradition was anything but. The hearings turned into a proxy fight over US criminal charges as teams of Canadian lawyers on opposite sides made arguments on the merits of those charges. More broadly, the hearings served as a new front in the epic struggle between China and the United States for economic and political supremacy, one with serious repercussions not only for Meng and the Two Michaels, but for the futures of the internet and everyone who uses it.

* * *

Meng's defence team began by pursuing a "double criminality" challenge to her extradition, arguing that because Canada didn't have its own sanctions against Iran, the allegations against her didn't constitute a crime in Canada and she should be set free. Those arguments failed.[10] Her lawyers then concentrated on a Trump-based defence. In their view, Donald Trump tainted proceedings before the British

Columbia courts with his unprecedented political interference in the Meng case, and particularly his linking of the criminal case to US commercial trade negotiations with China. That Meng was being used as a bargaining chip in US trade talks with China, they maintained, was an abuse of process.

In their abuse of process motion to the court, Meng's legal team argued that the US extradition request should be rejected, without any consideration of its merits, as a politically-motivated campaign against the accused, Huawei, and China. The abuse was such that the Canadian government had relinquished its right to proceed, and the interests of justice required that the proceeding not be heard. The lawyers further argued that Meng's arrest in Vancouver was unlawful, that the US provided misleading information to Canada when it summarized the case against the executive and sought her extradition, and that the case does not conform to international law because her alleged actions in Hong Kong had no substantial connection to the US.

Meng's defence dug even further into the past than the US indictment. It noted that America's anti-Huawei efforts date back at least to 2010 when the US National Security Agency tried to hack into Huawei's servers at company headquarters in Shenzhen, China. Project "Shotgiant" had two main objectives: "(1) to find evidence of Huawei's alleged connections with the Chinese government; and (2) to collect technical information of Huawei's products, enabling US intelligence agencies to implant backdoors into Huawei's products."[11]

Two years later, the bipartisan US House of Representatives permanent select committee on intelligence issued a scathing condemnation of Huawei, accusing the company of being evasive about its relationship with the Chinese government and Chinese Communist Party, and finding "credible evidence" that Huawei had failed to comply with US laws. The report also criticized the company for failing to explain its ties to the Chinese military, its relationship with Western consulting firms, and for exhibiting "a pattern of disregard for the intellectual property rights of other entities and companies in the United States."

In 2017, under Trump, the US began targeting Huawei's 5G efforts. Congress adopted a series of measures that restricted the company's ability to do business in the US. A year later, Trump's National Security Council issued its own report that said China and Huawei posed a threat to 5G networks: "The report also suggested that the US's allies collaborate to counter China's 'Belt and Road' initiative, expecting to diminish Huawei's position in the global market."[12]

Meng's legal team cited more examples of Trump's intensified anti-Huawei actions throughout 2018. His government attempted to rally its allies to shun Huawei in their new 5G networks. A report by the US trade representative labelled "China's technology transfer, licensing, outbound investment, cyber intrusion, and other acts, policies and practices as detrimental to US interests." That document was released March 22, the same day Trump imposed tariffs on Chinese imports. Five months later, the indictment against Meng and Huawei was sealed in the Eastern District of New York, and in November 2018, the US Department of Justice launched its "China Initiative" to prosecute threats, hacking, economic espionage, and a host of other cyber evils "prior to the transition to 5G networks."[13] All of this on the eve of Meng's arrest on December 1.

Ten days after she was picked up, Trump gave a controversial and much-dissected interview to *Reuters*. Asked if he would be willing to intervene in Meng's case if it helped him get a trade deal with China, Trump said: "If I think it's good for the country, if I think it's good for what will be certainly the largest trade deal ever made—which is a very important thing, what's good for national security—I would certainly intervene if I thought it was necessary."

Richard Peck, the leader of Meng's defence team and one of Canada's leading criminal lawyers who successfully defended accused child pornographer John Robin Sharpe and Air India bombing suspect Ajaib Singh Bargi, called Trump's words "abhorrent" and maintained that they "cast a pall" over his client's proceedings. "With that utterance, Ms. Meng became a bargaining chip in this economic contest between these two superpowers. Those words amount to the opening salvo in this trade war. They reduce Ms. Meng from a human being to chattel. The notion that a person's liberty can be used in any way to advance a commercial transaction is anathema to our justice system, to this process, to the rule of law. It's a notion that strikes at the heart of human dignity."

Trump would go on to link the China trade talks to the fate of the Huawei prosecution three more times in public remarks between January and June 2019.[14] "There is a cumulative effect to the president's words," said Peck. "They are uttered on multiple occasions over a period of roughly six or seven months. These cannot be said to be offhand comments. They're repeated, the intent is stated, and the words are repeated."

The arrest of Meng did nothing to slow the Trump administration's efforts to block Huawei's progress. As her case wound its way through Canadian courts, Trump signed a May 2019 executive order barring the use of Huawei and Chinese equipment in the US. Then-attorney general William Barr joined in with what Meng's lawyers consider a "bellicose" speech to a Washington, D.C. conference on China hosted by the Centre for Strategic and International Studies. He described China's influence on the global 5G market as "an unprecedented challenge to the United States," and compared the US struggle with Huawei to the Second World War and "Russia's Cold War technological challenge."[15]

In June 2019, Meng's lawyers fired back and filed a lawsuit in BC Supreme Court alleging her rights against unlawful search and seizure had been violated. Yep, the CBSA officers, and US justice department officials arranged to "detain, search and interrogate" Meng as soon as she arrived at the airport "without arresting her, under the guise of routine customs or immigration related examination and then to use that opportunity to unlawfully compel her to provide evidence and information," Meng's lawyers would argue in their claim.[16]

One of the border agents demanded Meng's passwords and she agreed "believing she had no choice as the CBSA Officers had failed to advise her of the true reasons for her detention, her right to counsel, and her right to silence."[17] Then, CBSA officers "opened and viewed the contents" of the seized electronics, which they allege amounted to a violation of her privacy. The whole episode violated Meng's legal rights under the Charter—the right to "life, liberty and security of the person," which includes being secure against unreasonable search and seizure, arbitrary detention, and being allowed a right to a lawyer.[18]

"From the moment of her apprehension on the jetway, the Plaintiff was under the total control of the CBSA officers and had no freedom of movement. As the detention was unlawful, it was arbitrary," said the statement of claim.[19]

Meng's lawyers argued that the border agents conducted an "unlawful interrogation" of Meng "in two sessions over a sustained period." They alleged that the questions the CBSA asked were based on a briefing of the US charges, as well as documentation, provided by the RCMP "and/or representatives of the U.S. D.O.J. familiar with the details of the U.S. Charges."

Canada's Attorney-General rejected the claim.

* * *

Peck's major opponent in court most days was Rob Frater, a veteran litigator of the Canadian justice department. It fell to Frater to rebut the sweeping historical and geopolitical arguments that Peck and his team were advancing. For six years prior to Meng's arrest, Frater served as the chief general counsel for the justice department. He was the top lawyer on Canada's public payroll, and likely its most skilled. For decades, he had been a fixture before the Supreme Court of Canada, advocating and defending the government's positions on a wide variety of cases. Frater had hopes of retiring in 2021, but the Meng case would not permit that.

Frater's assessment of the defence arguments, in a nutshell, ran as follows: "Their arguments are: the comments of the former president were shocking, egregious, corrosive, poisonous. My characterization of this argument is really that they are adjectives in search of facts to support them."

Frater disagreed "that the United States is essentially at war with Huawei," and that the Meng case is "a manifestation of the war." He dismissed the context of Huawei's supposed "threat" to US national security as irrelevant, "because there is no way that we can get underneath that, assuming it's based on intelligence. Mr. Peck can't prove that it's false. I can't prove that it's true. The only thing [the court] can do is presume good faith . . . if it's true, it's a serious matter. But how can you use that as a fact that is somehow relevant to the abuse of process argument?"

As far as Frater was concerned, Peck was asking the court "to engage in litigation" that was beyond its scope. The broader political questions at the heart of Meng's case would have to be considered by Canada's justice minister, long after the legal arguments had been settled, presuming the court decides that Meng should be extradited. Only then, Frater argued, could the minister decide whether the case was politically tainted, and whether that warranted overturning the court's decision and setting Meng free. Frater added that he wasn't certain, based on the broad theory put forth by Meng's legal team, that even the justice minister could make such a determination, "but if it's anyone, it's him," not the court.

Frater further argued that Meng's lawyers had failed to meet the high legal threshold required to satisfy the court that an abuse of process had occurred. He referred to a Supreme Court of Canada precedent that said an accused person's right to a fair trial, or the integrity of the justice system itself, must be prejudiced in order to justify a stay of proceedings. He also said Meng and her "battalion of lawyers" had the means to adequately defend her against what were serious fraud charges.[20]

Summarizing his case, Frater lambasted "the thinness of evidence" that his legal opponents had put forth. "That evidence only got worse over time," he says, because Trump was no longer the US president. Everyone involved in the proceedings knows "that the elephant in the room in this case has always been the geopolitical winds swirling around it." The defence was attempting to "bring the elephant" into courtroom. He urged the court to "focus on the facts and the law and leave the politics to the politicians." He expressed that on the basis of fact and the application of the law, the court would dismiss the abuse of process motion.

Meng Wanzhou absorbed it all as she sat next to an interpreter in Courtroom 55 through the lengthy proceedings, watching silently, adorned with her GPS anklet and a mask.

CHAPTER THIRTEEN

Who's Abusing What

WHILE THE MAJOR HEADLINES generated by the Meng arrest concentrated on Chinese-American diplomatic tensions and commercial rivalry, a whole other dimension of the courtroom arguments centred on the particular circumstances of her arrival in Vancouver on December 1, 2018. The facts of those few hours, and Meng's every move and interaction, were parsed and dissected down to their subatomic particles. Their significance was interpreted, rearranged, and disputed by the opposing teams of lawyers. It is inconceivable that the entry to Canada by airplane of any other passenger has been subjected to such close scrutiny.

For Meng's lawyers, the circumstances of her arrest provided another set of arguments in support of the abuse of process motion that sought to dismiss her extradition proceedings. Team Meng believed that a group of RCMP officers and agents of the Canada Border Services Agency (with the spies of the Canadian Security Intelligence Service lurking in the background) conspired with the US Department of Justice and the Federal Bureau of Investigation to illegally detain, search, and interrogate Meng, seizing her two cellphones, Mac laptop, iPad, and a Cruzer flash drive in an unlawful three-hour search to illicitly gather information on behalf of the US government to aid their prosecution of her. All of this was said to have been done by customs' officers before Meng was formally arrested by the RCMP and taken to jail in handcuffs. Moreover, the conduct of the Canadian officials amounted to a flagrant disregard of a BC judge's order to the police to "immediately" arrest her:

> At nearly every stage of Ms. Meng's detention, the authorities prioritized gathering evidence for the FBI over their obligations to the Court and Ms. Meng. This misconduct showed a flagrant disregard for Ms. Meng's Charter rights and a cavalier attitude towards the authority and role of the Court in these proceedings. Collectively, the misconduct has had and continues to have the effect of undermining the integrity of our justice system."

This wrong can only be righted, the lawyers contended, with the issuance of a stay of proceedings, throwing out the extradition request and restoring to Meng her freedom.

The lawyers for the Canadian Department of Justice respectfully disagreed. They held that Meng's lawyers had no compelling evidence of the vast conspiracy they allege. Rather, the various branches of law enforcement followed established procedures, and any cross-border collaboration between Canadian and US officials was above board and in line with established practices of operational co-operation within the scope of the extradition treaty both countries have signed:

> The Applicant's argument is supported only by speculation and innuendo. She has failed to establish the existence of the conspiracy she alleges. The evidence tendered in connection with the 'second branch' allegations of abuse of process fails to demonstrate misconduct by foreign authorities, the Canadian Border

Services Agency (CBSA) or the Royal Canadian Mounted Police (RCMP). The evidence shows the opposite.

Rob Frater, representing the Canadian justice department, maintained that the stay of proceedings sought by Meng's lawyers "should only be granted in 'exceptional', 'rare' and the 'clearest of cases,' and that this case "is not such a case."

In the course of the proceedings, new details came to light about Meng's arrest, some trivial, some significant. It was learned, for instance, that on November 29, 2018, John Sgroi, the FBI's legal attaché in Ottawa, telephoned Sergeant Ken Kopp of the RCMP'S federal policing services national security unit, also in Ottawa, to request the Mounties arrest Meng when she touched down in Vancouver on December 1. The next morning, constables Winston Yep and Gurvinder Dhaliwal were in the middle of serving an arrest warrant at a local jail when they were told to get themselves to the downtown Vancouver offices of the department of justice. They were too quick to respond. The justice department lawyers weren't ready for them, so the officers went for lunch, returning at 2:15 p.m. to begin their meeting with federal lawyers John Gibb-Carsley and Kerry Swift.

Yep took between thirty and forty-five minutes to review a summary of Meng's case, and quickly realized this was going to be a high-profile matter. The FBI's top priority was for Canadian officials to seize Meng's electronic devices and place them in Faraday bags, which block radio signals, to prevent their contents from being wiped or altered remotely. Yep was presented with an already complete affidavit courtesy of the US government. It said Meng had "no ties" to Canada and that the RCMP needed to apprehend her immediately. Yep signed the affidavit at 4:30 p.m. BC Supreme Court Justice Margot Fleming issued Yep a provisional warrant to "immediately" arrest Meng and bring her before a judge within twenty-four hours.[1]

Meng's lawyers cried foul over the "no ties" characterization given that her family owns two Vancouver houses valued well into the millions, and she has a valid ten-year re-entry visa for Canada. She'd been to Canada fifty-one times in the previous decade and was arrested on her seventh visit that year alone. Her previous stop to Canada occurred only a month earlier, on October 5, 2018, less than two months after the sealed US arrest warrant had been issued in New York. Her lawyers complained that Yep's affidavit "suggested that Ms. Meng was making only a brief stop in Vancouver, providing a unique opportunity to arrest her before she 'escaped' a jurisdiction to which she otherwise had 'no ties'. In essence, the image portrayed was that the authorities had one chance to apprehend a 'fugitive' who would remain beyond the reach of the United States. In reality, the authorities knew, or ought to have known, that Ms. Meng was a 'global traveler' who frequently visited countries, including Canada, that had extradition treaties with the United States."[2] They pointed out that following the preparation of the US indictment, Meng had visited Paris, London, Warsaw, Singapore, and Brussels before landing in Vancouver. All of the countries she visited in that span have extradition treaties with the US. Meng's lawyers considered it "shocking" that Yep, a veteran officer, didn't do his own research to verify some of the American claims.[3]

In the assessment of Meng's defence team, the RCMP and CBSA conspired with American authorities and Canada's own spy agency, the Canadian Security Intelligence Service (CSIS), to delay Meng's arrest by several hours so the CBSA could confiscate her digital devices, and question her before the police formally arrested her.

This line of argument was based on the fact that Canadian border agents have far broader legal powers than police to search and interrogate incoming air travellers presenting themselves for arrival in a country. Once arrested by police, a person has the right to call a lawyer and the right to remain silent. A traveller seeking the privilege of entering Canada temporarily surrenders those rights in order to avoid a thorough search and seizure, with the authorities poking through toiletries and underwear and combing the contents of cellphones and computer hard drives. But there are limits, Meng's lawyers argued, to how far border services personnel can go before committing a blatant violation of someone's rights to unlawful detention and search and seizure under the Canadian Charter of Rights and Freedoms. Meng's lawyers believed the line was overstepped at a meeting between the RCMP and the CBSA agents at Vancouver airport at 9:30 a.m., less than two hours before Meng's plane landed.[4]

It was at that meeting, Meng's team argued, that the RCMP decided to let the CBSA conduct its screening of Meng rather than board the aircraft and immediately arrest her. The night before, Yep's boss, Sergeant Janice Vander Graaf, had spoken to airport officials and determined that the best course of action was to "go on the plane" to arrest Meng. That was the "preliminary plan." Yep, Dhaliwal, and their CBSA counterparts reversed course at their 9:30 a.m. pre-arrest huddle. The border agents had entered the meeting seemingly content to have the RCMP take over and arrest Meng, but Yep said he was concerned about passenger safety, a claim Meng's lawyers lambasted. Richard Peck all but called Yep a liar for saying his delay was due to safety concerns:[5]

> She was in her late 40s, had no criminal record and her alleged crime was known to be financial in nature. She was arriving in Vancouver on a plane, after having proceeded through airport security in Hong Kong. The FBI were watching her and had provided an innocuous description of her and her companion before her arrival. The idea that she could be a risk to several armed RCMP officers as she exited the plane is preposterous. It is submitted that their conduct was a calculated attempt

to prolong the period in which Ms. Meng was detained and deprived of her Charter rights, so that she could be criminally investigated. After all, that is what in fact occurred, offering the strongest evidence of the RCMP/CBSA's motives that day.[6]

In response, Yep insisted there was a risk "because there are lots of people around there," and added that he didn't think three hours was too long to wait.

Meng's lawyers drew a negative inference from the fact that Sergeant Ross Lundie, a senior RCMP officer based at Vancouver airport, had at least two telephone calls with Sherri Onks, the FBI's assistant legal attaché, while the CBSA search was underway. They had a similar view of the conversation the previous evening between Kopp, the RCMP sergeant who fielded the original extradition request from the US embassy, and an unidentified CSIS agent who discussed how the CBSA would be helping the RCMP in the Meng arrest.[7]

Crown prosecutors maintained that it made no difference whether or not Meng could have been arrested in another country, or why the US chose Canada for its request. The US was free to choose when it wanted to seek someone's extradition and decide which country to ask. "There is also no right for a person sought to be extradited from the country of his or her choice," they argued. "Simply put, the Applicant's assertion that her previous travel to countries with extradition treaties with the United States, including Canada, is irrelevant. That information could have no bearing on the issuing judge's determination as to whether to issue the warrant. There is no merit to the Applicant's claim that the Affidavit is misleading because it fails to disclose steps the Requesting State *could have taken* to request the Applicant's extradition, either earlier from Canada or at another time from a different country."[8]

The same prosecutors conceded that it was a mistake for CBSA to give the passcodes to the RCMP. But it was an honest mistake, not a fatal one, they argued, and certainly nothing that warranted the unusual and extreme remedy of ordering a stay of proceedings. As for the RCMP and the FBI being in communication and perhaps consulting while Meng was being processed, the prosecutors viewed this as completely acceptable under the circumstances, and not evidence of collusion between the organizations:[9]

> The evidence demonstrates that at all times US authorities acted lawfully. Their contact with Canadian authorities was for legitimate and lawful purposes. There is no evidence that US authorities attempted to coerce, direct, or even influence Canadian authorities on how to carry out their duties. There is no evidence of improper requests for information. Without evidence of a US-led conspiracy, or any other US misconduct, [Meng's] theory that the RCMP and CBSA misused their statutory and common law powers and procedures to gather information for a US investigation concerning the [Meng] must fail.[10]

As the lawyers trooped in and out of court, it raised an obvious question: what was Associate Chief Justice Heather Holmes making of all this? There would be no way of knowing for certain until she delivered her final decision in the case, which was a work in progress. Holmes occasionally tested the lawyers with queries from the bench. Often, she was professorial in her tone, seeking specific direction on how she ought to interpret a particular section of the law or an aspect of a legal precedent. Sometimes her interventions were more pointed. During one set of in-person arguments, Holmes told Meng's lawyers that it was "not exactly a grilling examination" to which the CBSA had subjected their client. Tony Paisana, one of Meng's lawyers, tried to rebut the suggestion: "The fact that they didn't do a great job of violating your rights doesn't mean that they didn't violate your rights."

Holmes also raised questions about the conduct of a senior RCMP officer, Staff-Sergeant Ben Chang, who had dealings with an FBI counterpart, John Sgroi, in the days following Meng's arrest. The defence argued that Chang violated the extradition law by sharing the serial numbers of Meng's cellphones, iPad, and laptop with the FBI. They relied on a handwritten note from the RCMP's Janice Vander Graaf on December 12, 2018. At 1:20 p.m., she wrote in her notebook, "received info re: exhibits and moving forward. Gurv [Cst. Dhaliwal] advised Ben Chang had email and provided serial #'s to Legat [John Sgroi], Gurv believed it was Ben who had the discussions [with] US re: them putting forward request for acquisition [*sic*] of the exhibits from us/intake."[11]

Chang later swore in an affidavit that he did not send any information to the FBI. Soon after, he retired and moved to Macau, the high-rolling island off the southern Chinese coast, where he works in security at a casino. Meng's lawyers wanted to cross-examine Chang about the affidavit, but he sent word back through a lawyer that had no intention of testifying in the case. Meng's lawyers said that Chang's unprecedented snub of the courts meant that his refusal to help the FBI should be disregarded. The Crown meanwhile urged Holmes not to infer anything negative about Chang's conduct. Holmes suggested she saw that differently, telling Crown lawyer John Gibb-Carsley: "Generally, retired officers testify . . . and that's not happening here."[12]

* * *

The final piece of the abuse of process defence employed by Meng's lawyers was that the American extradition request was a violation of international law because her alleged crimes had no direct connection to the United States. Vancouver lawyer Gib van Ert, who served as the executive legal officer to the Supreme Court of Canada between 2015 and 2018, where he was top aide to two chief justices, Beverley McLachlin and Richard Wagner, led this argument before Justice Holmes. He maintained that the US had no jurisdiction to prosecute Meng because her alleged misconduct at her August 2013 meeting with HSBC executives took place in Hong Kong and involved a bank based there and in the United Kingdom. "If any laws were broken that day, that is the concern of China, in whose territory the events occurred," van Ert posited.[13] He also tried to debunk the assertion that because the transactions between Huawei and the bank involved US dollars, a practice known as "dollar clearing," a connection was somehow established to the United States. Van Ert pointed to a report that said the transactions in this case amounted to just US$2 million over thirteen months, a paltry sum in light of the US$4.5 trillion in transactions cleared through the American system every day. Moreover, Meng didn't initiate any US dollar clearing and HSBC decided to use American funds without any input from Huawei.[14]

Lawyers for the Canadian government flatly rejected that argument, claiming the case had an overwhelming connection to the US. Crown lawyer Rob Frater argued that the August 2013 meeting took place at Meng's request after the *Reuters* news stories said Skycom had sold US-made equipment in Iran in violation of US sanctions. "Why did that meeting take place?" he asked, before answering his own question: "At the request of Ms. Meng—a senior executive to senior executive meeting [between] client and nervous banker."

Frater found it significant that Meng used a PowerPoint presentation to show Huawei was complying with the sanctions, and played down any connection between Huawei and Skycom: "The overriding message is: 'If you continue to provide US banking services, you will not incur any legal risk.' It is a strong prima facie case, in our submission, that Ms. Meng knows what she is doing."

Frater also rejected the argument that the low amount of US "dollar clearing" rendered it irrelevant. The heart of the allegations against Meng boiled down to the fact she lied and committed fraud, he said, which created the possibility that the bank would run afoul of US sanctions. "The lies in Hong Kong are not about risks in Hong Kong; they are about risks primarily in the United States."[15]

By April 2021, the Meng Wanzhou extradition hearing appeared poised to enter its final phase. The lawyers were due back in court on April 26, 2021, to make their final three weeks of submissions to Holmes, this time on the merits of the actual case, and whether there was enough evidence to justify committing Meng for extradition. That would have left Holmes in position to rule on the case by late summer or early fall. This schedule was upended, however, by an unforeseen development in a Hong Kong courtroom.

On April 12, 2021, a Hong Kong court gave its seal of approval to a deal that would see HSBC share a trove of documents with Huawei related to Meng's all-important August 2013 meeting with its bank executives. It marked a dramatic reversal of fortune for Meng's defence: less than two months earlier, Huawei had made the same request to HSBC in the United Kingdom and been turned down. Why the sudden change of heart by HSBC's Hong Kong office? Nobody knows for certain. But the upshot was clear: for Meng's team, it was an opportunity to learn more about the obscure meeting on which American prosecutors were basing their charges, information that might help persuade Justice Holmes to deny Meng's extradition on the grounds that US authorities misled Canada about the case in December 2018.

Two days after the Hong Kong court ruling, Team Meng filed a petition with the BC Supreme Court, urging Holmes to delay the restart of the extradition hearing to August 3, 2021, instead of the scheduled April 26 date, so they could comb through the new disclosure in hopes of finding new evidence detrimental to the government's case. "There is a reasonable likelihood," her lawyers argued, "that the Hong Kong HSBC Disclosure will be material to issues before this Court, including whether the Requesting State has failed to comply with its duty to be diligent, candid and accurate in certifying the evidence available for trial." They also expected that the Hong Kong documents would show that the US relied upon "manifestly unreliable evidence" and did not establish "a prima facie case of fraud." [16] Meng's counsel further argued that it wasn't safe to ask lawyers to travel from across Canada to Vancouver for in-person court proceedings when a third wave of the COVID-19 pandemic was in full bloom across Canada, with infections reaching record numbers.

Canadian prosecutors vehemently disagreed and moved to block the adjournment request. "Two and a half years from the start of these proceedings, countless hours spent fashioning a schedule agreed to by both sides, and mere days from reaching the finish line, the Applicant asks this Court to take a several months pause. Her request should be denied," the attorney general of Canada said in a written reply.[17] "The alleged need to gather information in Hong Kong is not based on any objective evidence that the documents obtained would be relevant or admissible in this proceeding. It is the latest in a series of attempts to turn these proceedings into a trial that should properly take place in the Requesting State."[18]

This disagreement brought lawyers Peck and Frater once more before Holmes. Peck reiterated that the recent disclosures of evidence went to the core of the American prosecution. (Huawei's lawyers in the US also sent a letter to the US Department of Justice alleging that they had not been "candid" with the Canadian courts about the strength of their case against Meng.[19]) Frater countered that Meng's lawyers were making an "eleventh hour" request which relied too heavily on the letters of Huawei's American lawyers, and that US prosecutors have vigorously denied the allegations against them. He accused the Meng team of "jurisdiction shopping" to find a court that would approve the disclosure of the documents: "Having received the answer 'no' from the UK court, then my friends went to Hong Kong and inexplicably, HSBC, which was the same litigant that appeared in the court in the UK, completely reversed its position after having won on every single point in the UK court. HSBC for reasons known only to itself turned around and decided to agree to an order."[20]

Holmes took two days to decide the issue. The parties reconvened by telephone on April 21. She granted the defence request and adjourned the proceedings to August 3.

The next day, lawyers for the Canadian prosecution released a revised version of their submission calling for Meng to be formally extradited to the US. The timing of the release appeared intended to reinforce the notion that they had a strong argument for Meng to be committed to stand trial in the US. The document outlined what appeared to be strong evidence against Meng that they said more than met the threshold required to send her south to stand trial. Their overarching position was that an extradition hearing is not a trial. They quoted a previous Supreme Court of Canada precedent stating that extradition hearings are "intended to be expeditious procedures to determine whether a trial should be held. In fact, in some contexts, a requirement for more 'trial-like' procedures at the extradition committal stage may 'cripple the operation of the extradition proceedings.'"[21] It does not matter "whether the case is strong or weak, or even whether it is 'unlikely to succeed at trial.' If there is an inference available on the evidence to satisfy the elements of the offence, the inference must be drawn, and committal ordered."[22]

The Canadian prosecutors summarized what a few key witnesses for the American prosecution would likely say at Meng's trial. The names of the witnesses were withheld but one worked for HSBC in Hong Kong and two worked for Skycom in Tehran. "HSBC Witness

B is expected to testify that, at the meeting, Ms. Meng called Skycom a third-party business partner of Huawei. Using a PowerPoint presentation, Ms. Meng misleadingly characterized the relationship between the two companies in a manner that suggested partnership and cooperation between two separate companies." Witness B is also expected to say that Meng was once a Skycom board member to "better manage our partner" and to "strengthen and monitor Skycom's compliance," but she later quit the board and Huawei sold its shares in Skycom. HSBC Witness B is further expected to testify that Meng said Huawei subsidiaries in "sensitive countries" would not open accounts or have business transactions with HSBC.[23]

A former account manager who worked for Huawei/Skycom in Tehran between 2008 and 2014 was expected to testify that the two companies were "indistinguishable entities in Iran." While a Skycom logo was on the outside of the company building, all logos inside the building were Huawei logos. All employees were given Huawei access badges, and they used email addresses using the domain name @huawei.com, and logged into a computer system using a Huawei. com portal. The witness also plans to testify to overheard conversations that Skycom was facing trouble and that someone "found out about the daughter of the Chairman."[24]

Another former Iranian employee, who worked at the company between 2011 and 2013, was also expected to confirm that no email addresses ended in @skycom.com and that no Skycom logos were visible around the building. This employee allegedly asked a human resources manager to provide an employment letter on Skycom letterhead in June 2013 to verify his or her work for the company; the employee was told that "Huawei Iran is Skycom."[25]

Another anticipated witness, FBI Special Agent Melissa Beresford, was "expected to testify that HSBC documents and email records demonstrate that Huawei employees controlled Skycom's bank accounts" if the case went to trial[26]

The revised Canadian document reminded Holmes that an extradition judge does not have to consider the "ultimate reliability" of evidence. "Reliability in the context of an extradition hearing means threshold reliability. The extradition judge does not consider ultimate reliability, which is left for trial where guilt and innocence are at issue."[27]

By late June 2021, Meng's team had finished combing through the new trove of documents from HSBC and played its hand. Her lawyers argued in a court filing that the new documents showed the US misled Canada with its original request because senior HSBC executives were well aware of Huawei's connections with Iran: "The Requesting State's case for fraud is based on the improbable theory that a global bank relied on a single line in a PowerPoint or a single PowerPoint presentation to make a business decision about one of its biggest customers. The new evidence shows HSBC to be the sophisticated institution it is, acting with full knowledge of Huawei's affiliates and their corporate history."[28]

Canadian government lawyers did not let this new claim sit unanswered. They fired back, declaring that this was just one more attempt by Meng's legal team to stage a trial within an extradition hearing. The new evidence added "nothing of substance," the prosecution argued in its filing, while once again urging Holmes to stick to the narrow confines of an extradition hearing. "The Applicant persists in her quest to have this Court try the case," the prosecution wrote. "Given the limited role of the extradition judge in a committal hearing, the proposed evidence is irrelevant."[29]

Holmes decided that the new documents were inadmissible to the extradition hearing, underscoring that Meng's extradition hearing would not become a trial within a trial, as the prosecutors feared. Holmes heard more in-person arguments from both sides over several weeks in August 2021 before the case was adjourned.

Part of a judge's role during the oral argument, apart from paying close attention and noting the key points, is also to challenge the position of counsel, to ask probing questions, and to justify the positions. The judge would want to be certain that she had grasped in their entirely the submissions of counsel and the reasoning behind their submissions.

In this case, Holmes held her cards close, as any judge would. However, observers and especially counsel always pay close attention to a judge's interventions and try to divine from them where the judge may be going. This case was no different. In the course of the hearing, the judge asked probing questions. Because of its high-profile nature and the enormous stakes involved, observers were microscopically examining the questions she asked and what those questions might tell us about how she might eventually rule. Some observers suggested that some of her questions indicated skepticism about the attorney general's position.[30] Perhaps. But it was difficult to read the tea leaves in this judicial cup.

CHAPTER FOURTEEN

Donald's Double Dealing

SIX MONTHS BEFORE THE Two Michaels were arrested in China, relations between Justin Trudeau and Donald Trump were at an all-time low. Canada had just hosted a G7 summer in Charlevoix, Quebec. Behind closed doors, the prime minister told Trump to his face that his punitive tariffs on Canadian steel and aluminum (25 per cent and 10 per cent respectively) were an insult to Canada's Second World War legacy. Canadian metal manufacturing flourished during the war and the country became a major supplier of the metals used to build US military hardware. Trump had invoked a seldom-used chapter of US trade law to declare the Canadian imports a national security threat.[1]

Trudeau reiterated his concerns, which his Liberal government had often expressed publicly, at the summit's closing press conference. He told reporters he didn't want Canada to be "pushed around" by the US.

Trump watched the Canadian prime minister's final press conference aboard Air Force One while on his way to Singapore for his nuclear summit with North Korea's Kim Jong-un. He did not like what he saw. He unleashed a Twitter blast at Trudeau, calling him "very dishonest and weak," and sabotaged the G7 summit by revoking US support for its final communique. The president seemed especially perturbed to be undermined by the Canadian leader when he was on the verge, at least in his own narcissistic mind, of becoming a nuclear peacemaker and perhaps laying the groundwork for a Nobel Prize. Trump's top trade advisor, Peter Navarro, kept up the attack on Trudeau the next day when he told one of the American Sunday morning political news programs that "there was a special place in hell" for the prime minister for the "stunt" that he pulled at his press conference.[2]

Trudeau had his defenders. Canadian senator Peter Boehm was in the room during the G7 talks as lead summit organizer. He said Trump's attack was groundless: "To my recollection, there's nothing that the prime minister said in his press conference that he did not say in the meeting with President Trump." That did nothing to assuage the Americans, however.[3]

After that spectacle, it seemed somewhat surreal, just twelve months later, to see Trump and Trudeau amicably posing together at a chaotic Oval Office photo opportunity. The leaders were face to face, seated in a pair of armchairs a few metres away from the stanchion holding back a throng of American and Canadian media that had stormed into the office as if trying to secure Juno Beach. As the cameras rolled and reporters jostled for position, Trump sat spread-legged in his usual alpha-male pose. Trudeau projected a poker-faced, almost Zen-like calm, ankles crossed, hands clasped. It was clear Trudeau wanted to just get through the session with a few perfunctory remarks and shut the doors for a private talk.

The Oval Office meeting was ostensibly meant to show Canada-US solidarity for the recently concluded negotiations for the Canada-US-Mexico Free Trade Agreement. Trump needed Trudeau to achieve a key plank in his election platform, sealing a new continental trade deal to replace the quarter-century old North American Free Trade Agreement (NAFTA), which he repeatedly described as the worst trade deal ever, and routinely threatened to rip up. He forced Mexico and Canada to the bargaining table and a deal was eventually struck after much insult and drama.

Even with the signatures of his trading partners, Trump did not have everything he needed. Congressional Democrats stood in the way. They wanted to study the deal, even though they were no fans of NAFTA themselves. More importantly, they were in no hurry to do Trump any favours. Later on this same day, Trudeau would meet the most powerful Democrat in Congress at her Capitol Hill office. California Rep. Nancy Pelosi, or "Crazy Nancy" as Trump called her, was the leader of the House of Representatives. She controlled its agenda and was disinclined to support the new trade bill and make it law. Trump needed Trudeau to visit his political opponent and talk some sense into her.

Trudeau needed to move the new NAFTA along, as well, to end the long acrimonious nightmare of negotiating with an unpredictable American president whose hatred of the deal posed an existential threat to a relatively seamless cross-border trade integral to North American prosperity.

With the journalists in the room, Trump used the opportunity to trumpet the latest economic news: "The market hit an all-time high today. The S&P just broke its record, so we're very happy about that. The stock market continues to do well. Jobs have been literally through the roof."

Trump then praised the new United States-Mexico-Canada Agreement, as the Americans called it. "And, speaking of jobs, we have the USMCA . . . And we've come a long way. It's a great agreement."

With that, Trump pivoted to his guest. It was as if the G7 debacle had never happened. "But it's an honour to have the Prime Minister of Canada, Justin Trudeau," said the president. "He's been a friend of mine. We've worked hard together. We worked, in particular, on the USMCA. And we hope to have bipartisan support. I think, Justin, you're going to be making the rounds at Congress later on."

Trudeau thanked "Donald" for the meeting. "It's an opportunity for us, as you say, to keep talking about how we've worked hard to build a great trade deal that's good for Canadian workers, good for American workers, good for Mexican workers as well."

The questions started flying at the leaders, not all of them about free trade. Two hours earlier, fresh news broke that Iran had shot down an American surveillance drone over the Strait of Hormuz. Was the US planning to strike back? Trump was presidential in his reply, attempting to tamp down the tensions, suggesting the whole thing may have been a mistake committed by somebody "who was loose and stupid."

Inevitably, the leaders were asked about the situation in China, followed by a series of question about China and the Two Michaels. It was a reasonable line of inquiry, given that the Americans had brought Canada into that mess with their request for the extradition of Meng Wanzhou. The Canadian reporters, especially, were determined to wind Trump up on the subject.

"Mr. President, what are your concerns about China and the Canadians who are detained, sir?"

"No concerns. We'll be discussing that. It'll be one of the issues that I think we'll be discussing right now with Justin."

An American reporter asked about the Federal Reserve and interest rates before a Canadian fired off another question about the Two Michaels.

"Will you help Justin Trudeau get a meeting with Xi Jinping at the G20 next week to talk about the detained Canadians?"

"Well, I don't know that he's trying to meet. Are you trying to get a meeting?"

"We've got a lot of things to discuss."

"He wants one," said a reporter, "but Xi won't meet with him."

"Well, otherwise, I'll represent him well, I will tell you," said Trump. "We have a meeting set up with President Xi, and it's obviously on the big transaction that we're talking about and negotiating. Our people are actually speaking now, and we'll see what happens with that. But anything I can do to help Canada; I will be doing."

"Are you planning to bring it up with President Xi when you meet with him?" another reporter asked.

"Excuse me?" said Trump.

"Are you planning to bring it up with President Xi when you meet with him?"

"I would. At Justin's request, I will absolutely bring that up."

And so, it became a matter of public record that Trump agreed to raise the issue of the Two Michaels when he met next with China's leader President Xi Jinping during the G20 leaders' summit in Osaka, Japan on June 28–29. Divining whether Trump followed through on his promise would become a mug's game in the days to come. Rumours and scenarios were rampant. Perhaps other, more pressing matters distracted Trump in his one-on-one with Xi. Perhaps he changed his mind about helping Trudeau, a politician he oscillated between beating up and embracing as a friend.

A week after the G20, Trudeau declared publicly that Trump had raised the case of the Two Michaels during his meeting with Xi. Later that evening, as the American Independence Day celebration in Ottawa was gearing up, American diplomats showed *The Canadian Press* a written statement from Trump's ambassador to Canada, Kelly Craft. It was terse and noticeably short on details, but it stated that Trump had in fact raised the Two Michaels with Xi in Osaka.[4]

In some quarters, Trump's offer to speak to Xi was received as mere bluster, but a former member of Trump's National Security Council, retired brigadier general Robert Spalding, insists otherwise.

Spalding, who had left the White House a year earlier, was familiar with how such a concept would have reached Trump's office: a plan would have been carefully crafted in talking points prepared by the NSC. While Trump often ignored briefing materials, Spalding was adamant in an August 2021 interview that if Trump raised the possibility of talking to Xi about the two imprisoned Canadians, it was because he had listened to what his intelligence advisers recommended. "I have no doubt if the president said he was going to bring it up, he brought it up."[5]

* * *

In another time, under another president who didn't make up foreign policy on the fly and base his diplomacy on personal affection or hatred for his counterpart, it could have been argued that the United States owed Canada a lot more than token expressions of diplomatic opprobrium at China's arbitrary imprisonment of the Two Michaels. After all, Canada had provided extraordinary assistance to the United States four decades earlier during another hostage crisis.

In February 1979, Ayatollah Khomeini and his Islamic revolutionaries seized power in Iran by toppling the dynasty of Shah Mohammad Reza Pahlavi. In the ensuing chaos, a mob of student revolutionaries who called themselves the Muslim Student Followers of the Imam's Line, stormed the gates of the American embassy compound in Tehran and took hostage more than seventy American officials. They wanted to exchange their hostages for the Shah, who had fled Iran and taken refuge in the United States. Thus began the biggest crisis of the Democratic presidency of Jimmy Carter.

As the students were getting organized in the US compound, six American diplomats managed to escape and make their way to the homes of two Canadian embassy officials, ambassador Ken Taylor and immigration officer John Sheardown, where they took refuge for almost two months. A plan was eventually hatched to smuggle these Americans out of the country using Canadian passports issued by the Canadian government and forged Iranian entry documents prepared by the CIA. A story was crafted about a Hollywood production crew from a fictitious company visiting Iran to assess locations for a phoney science fiction movie, *ARGO*.[6] Canadian Prime Minister Joe Clark signed off on the gambit.

With their Canadian passports and falsified immigration documents, the six Americans, posing as members of an eight-person film crew, successfully boarded a Zurich-bound Swissair flight from Tehran's international airport on Sunday morning, January 27, 1980. In 2012, the movie *ARGO*, produced by and starring Ben Affleck, dramatized the rescue of the six Americans and won a best picture Oscar. The film underplayed the contributions of the Canadians, including the fact that Ambassador Taylor had been spying for the US throughout the crisis at the request of President Carter.[7] Regardless, Taylor received the Congressional Gold Medal for his efforts. A CBC documentary, *Our Man in Tehran*, was released a year later to set the historical record straight.[8] Prime Minister Clark said the high-risk hostage caper was illustrative of "the close and quite fundamental bond between Canada and the United States despite our many and serious differences on other issues."[9]

* * *

"For the last century," Joel Simon, executive director of the Committee to Protect Journalists, wrote in the *New Yorker*, "the US government's official policy for responding to the kidnapping of American overseas for political purposes has been to refuse to negotiate." He traced the policy to 1973, when eight members of the Palestinian terrorist group Black September overran the Saudi embassy in Khartoum, Sudan, and took hostage several foreign diplomats, including two Americans.

Asked by reporters for his response, President Richard Nixon declared that "we will not pay blackmail." Within hours, the two American diplomats, along with a Belgian colleague, "were stood up against a basement wall and shot."[10]

Nixon's refusal to make concessions to terrorists has been the standard line for American presidents ever since. The Patriot Act of 2001 explicitly banned material support to any terrorist organization, including ransom payments by families or third parties. But the principle is more honoured in the breach than the observance.

The Obama administration initially took a tough line on hostage-taking and refused to pay ransom. When many Western aid workers, including Americans, were kidnapped by ISIS in Syria, Obama refused any concessions (two of the captives, James Foley and Steven Sotloff, were brutally murdered), although he did create the office of a special presidential envoy for hostage affairs to lead the government's response and an interagency body, the hostage recovery fusion cell, to coordinate government efforts.[11]

Obama's policy seemed to bend on January 17, 2016, when Iran released five American prisoners and, in apparent exchange, the United States transferred $400 million in cash to Iran. Donald Trump was swift to criticize the deal as a "ransom payment." (It occurred the same day that the Iran nuclear agreement was implemented.) It was a claim Trump would repeat throughout the 2016 election campaign: "Our incompetent Secretary of State, Hillary Clinton, was the one who started talks to give 400 million dollars, in cash, to Iran. Scandal!" he tweeted.

Other Republicans levelled the same accusation.[12] Republican Senator Marco Rubio, failed candidate for the Republican nomination, said on NBC's *Meet the Press* that Obama had "put a price on the head of every American abroad [and that] our enemies now know that if you can capture an American, you can get something meaningful in exchange for it." Republican Senator Ted Cruz told viewers on *Fox News* that a hard-line was a proven way to end a hostage crisis: "It is worth remembering, this same nation, Iran, in 1981 released our hostages the day Ronald Reagan was sworn into office."[13]

In fact, Reagan had little to do with the negotiations which led to release of the Americans held in Iran. Those negotiations were conducted by Jimmy Carter, for whom the safe release of the Americans was an overwhelming preoccupation. As Carter later reflected, "Of course, their lives, safety, and freedom were the paramount considerations, but there was more to it. I wanted to have my decisions vindicated. It was very likely that I had been defeated and would soon leave office as President because I had kept these hostages and their fate at the forefront of the world's attention and had clung to a cautious and prudent policy in order to protect their lives during the preceding fourteen months. Before God and my fellow citizens, I wanted to exert every ounce of my strength and ability during these last few days to achieve their liberation."[14] The negotiations had been arranged through the intermediary services of the Algerian government because neither side would talk directly to the other. The Iranians agreed to release the hostages in exchange for the return of $7.9 billion in gold and bank assets,[15] which were frozen in American banks.[16]

Obama administration officials denied any linkage between the $400-million payment and the return of the American hostages, although the state department's John Kirby admitted that his side did "in those endgame hours, hold back on payment until we knew that our Americans were safe and sound and, on their way out of Iran, because in the very last few hours, Iran was playing a few games with us."[17]

As *The Guardian* pointed out, the release of the five Americans was actually part of "a prisoner swap for a number of Iranian nationals held in the US for crimes including violating sanctions regulations".[18] And as *The Wall Street Journal* reported, the cash, which was carried on wooden pallets aboard an unmarked cargo plane to Iran, "represented the first installment of a $1.7 billion settlement the Obama administration reached with Iran to resolve a decades-old dispute over a failed arms deal signed just before the fall of the Shah in 1979. That settlement, reached before an international tribunal in The Hague, coincided with the formal implementation of the landmark nuclear agreement between Iran, the US, and other global powers.[19]

In short, there were precedents for Trump to cast aside the principle of "no concessions" in hostage-taking situations.

Before becoming a presidential candidate, Trump had advocated the hard-line of not negotiating for hostages.[20] Once elected, he was handed more than his share of hostage problems, and found plenty of opportunities to make concessions to secure the release of detained Americans.[21] By the end of his presidency, his administration had negotiated the release of some forty Americans. The cases included the rescue of Caitlan Coleman and her family, held captive by the Taliban for more than five years in Pakistan; American pastor Andrew Brunson, who had been imprisoned by Turkish authorities on trumped up charges that he had participated in the unsuccessful coup against Prime Minister Recep Erdogan; three UCLA basketball players who were arrested in China for shoplifting; and American graduate student Xiyue Wang, who had been imprisoned by Iranian authorities on charges of espionage.

Most of the high-profile hostage cases negotiated by Trump involved some sort of recompense, although the president was loath to admit it. The Turkish government agreed to the release of American pastor Andrew Brunson as Turkish-US relations began to thaw in the aftermath of the disappearance of Saudi journalist Jamal Khashoggi and US help with the investigation. Trump insisted there had been no deal—"I don't make deals for hostages," he tweeted—but then went on to promise that the US would reconsider its "very tough" sanctions on the country.[22]

One of the more surprising hostage deals was the Trump administration's prisoner swap with Iran to secure the release of Xiyue Wang, who had served four years of a ten-year prison sentence in Iran for espionage. During Wang's time in prison, relations between the two countries seriously deteriorated due to Trump's decision in May 2018 to withdraw the United States from the 2015 nuclear framework agreement, whereby Iran agreed to eliminate its stockpile of enriched uranium and dial back on its nuclear enrichment programs in exchange for sanctions relief from the European Union and the United States. Tensions were further heightened by what appeared to be planned attacks on oil tankers leaving Iran, and the downing of a US drone by the Iranian military. The plight of American hostages faded into the background as some feared Iran and the US were on the brink of war.

In 2019, however, Wang was exchanged for an Iranian stem-cell researcher, Masoud Soleimani, who had been arrested in the United States for trying to smuggle proteins for medical research without a US licence. The swap was arranged with the help of Swiss authorities and former UN ambassador Bill Richardson but was controversial within the administration because key US officials, including Brian Hook, the US special representative for Iran, and national security adviser John Bolton (at least until his sudden resignation), opposed negotiated prisoner releases with Iran.[23]

In 2020, Iran released US Navy veteran Michael White, who had been detained for two years on undisclosed charges. He was part of a prisoner deal in which the US set free a US-Iranian dual citizen and physician, Matteo Taerri, it had imprisoned for violating US export sanctions against Iran. At roughly the same time, an Iranian scientist, Sirous Asgari, was also released from US custody, although the administration denied the cases were linked. The *New York Times* reported that even one of the most hawkish members of the Trump administration "said he was pleased that the Iranian authorities has been 'constructive in this matter.'"[24]

The "Art of the Deal" was central to Trump's approach to hostage diplomacy. It was also something he openly bragged about. But there was no similar Trump deal with the Chinese over Meng Wanzhou and the Two Michaels, despite his professed desire to make one. Why not?

CHAPTER FIFTEEN

America's Hostage

TEN DAYS AFTER BEING detained by Canadian authorities in Vancouver, and one day after Michael Kovrig was detained, Trump said publicly he "would certainly intervene" in the justice department's case against Meng if it helped him win a favourable trade deal with China. Trump's December 11, 2018, interview with *Reuters* made it clear that in his mind, at least, the Meng case was not an independent legal proceeding divorced from politics. He also indicated that the White House had spoken with the justice department about the case, as well as Chinese officials, although he had received no word from the Chinese government about the case.[1]

On December 7, 2018, at a White House Christmas dinner, as John Bolton recalls, "Trump raised Meng's arrest, riffing about how much pressure this puts on China." As he leaned across the table to Bolton, he said the United States had arrested "the Ivanka Trump of China."

Wrote Bolton after leaving office: "I came within an inch of saying, 'I never knew Ivanka was a spy and a fraudster,' but my automatic tongue-biting mechanism kicked in just in time."[2]

The Meng issue would come up frequently in the president's internal discussions. According to Bolton, he saw Meng and Huawei as a bargaining chip in trade negotiations with the Chinese, "ignoring both the significance of the criminal case and also the far larger threat Huawei posed to the security of fifth-generation (5G) telecom systems worldwide." Security and the law, says Bolton, were routinely subordinated to "Trumps' fascination with a big trade deal."[3]

That goes a long way toward explaining why Trump, who had dealt his way out of many other hostage situations, was not willing to negotiate and make concessions to secure the release of the Two Michaels. This wasn't the usual situation where the US was negotiating to bring hostages home. From Trump's point of view, he was also holding a hostage: Meng Wanzhou. She was a prize that the erratic president would not easily surrender, even to help America's closest friend and neighbour. So, notwithstanding the president's proclivities and historical precedent, no deal was struck.

That Trump would see the Meng-Huawei dispute through the prism of his trade dispute with China is not surprising. The president had long accused China of unfair trading practices and stealing US intellectual property. China was the centerpiece of his "Make America Great Again" global strategy. The trade war began in July 2018 when the Trump administration slapped tariffs on $35-billion worth of Chinese imports to the United States. The Chinese retaliated by targeting $34 billion in US exports to China. More tariffs affecting every higher volumes of trade followed. The final shot in May 2019 saw the US level 25 per cent tariffs on some $200-billion worth of Chinese goods, which the Chinese retaliated against with their own tariffs at the same level on $60-billion worth of US goods. As the *New York Times* reported, "[a] yearlong trade war between the United States and China is proving to be an initial skirmish in an economic conflict that may persist for decades, as both countries battle for global dominance, stature, and wealth. . . . And even if a trade deal is reached, it may do little to resolve tensions between the world's two largest economies."[4]

Yet a month later, Trump and Xi agreed to restart trade talks with the hope of averting further escalation of the tariff war that was roiling both their economies.[5] That the two leaders would be meeting at the G20 in Osaka at the end of the month made the gathering highly significant.

In many ways, it was significant that Trump was attending the summit at all. He was allergic to these carefully staged gatherings of world leaders. He didn't much like international travel, either, and had skipped the previous year's APEC summit. But Trump had taken a personal liking to the summit's host, Japan's Prime Minister Abe, who he had visited earlier in April, and he relished the opportunity to talk trade with Xi.

At their Saturday meeting at the end of the summit, Trump and Xi agreed to resume talks and take a "time out" on further tariffs. At his press conference, Trump said: "We discussed a lot of things, and we're right back on track . . . We had a very, very good meeting with China. I would say probably even better than expected, and the negotiations are continuing." The president also announced he would remove some of the restrictions the US government had placed on Huawei.[6]

When asked about Meng Wanzhou, Trump said "We did discuss Huawei but didn't discuss her situation."[7] What Trump chose to disclose publicly clearly fell short of Canada's request, and amounted to the loss of an ideal opportunity to broker some kind of deal to release the Two Michaels, as the president had promised to do at his mid-June meeting with Trudeau.

* * *

As Trump was fighting his own trade battles with Xi, China was weaponizing its trade relations with Canada to force the release of Meng Wanzhou. On March 1, 2019, China revoked the registration for the venerable Canadian firm Richardson International, a major exporter of canola seeds to China, ending its business there. China alleged that the quality of the company's exports was insufficient, which the company disputes. "We think this is part of a larger Canada-China issue," Richardson's vice-president, Jean-Marc Ruest, told the CBC. "The Canadian government respects and supports our position, and the quality of our product, at the same time."[8]

More cancellations followed. On March 26, China suspended the canola shipment licence of a second major Canadian company, Viterra Inc. "Clearly, they want to keep punishing us," said Guy Saint-Jacques, a former Canadian ambassador to China. Exports worth $5 billion, or 17 per cent of all Canadian shipments to China, were jeopardized, a clear expression of displeasure over the Meng affair.[9]

The diplomatic rift widened in early May when China suspended two Canadian pork exporters' permits because of alleged labelling problems. Although Canada's Agriculture Minister Marie-Claude Bibeau downplayed the suspension as merely "an administrative issue" that was easily resolved, that didn't prove to be the case. Four days before Trudeau headed to the G20 in Osaka, and on the eve of Canadian justice minister David Lametti's meeting with US attorney general William Barr, China suspended Canadian beef and pork exports after an "investigation revealed 188 counterfeit veterinary health documents and the existence of 'obvious safety loopholes' in Canadian meat shipments. Again, Bibeau downplayed the severity of the situation, saying it was a "technical" and not a political issue.[10] She was unconvincing.

When Trudeau landed in Osaka, he and his team did not expect to meet with their Chinese counterparts in the "bilats" that occur on the edges of such meetings. Foreign Affairs Minister Chrystia Freeland's efforts to secure a meeting with her Chinese counterpart were sternly rebuffed. The tension between Trudeau and Xi was palpable at the televised opening ceremony. Xi was already seated at the table when Trudeau entered the room to take his assigned seat, which by alphabetical order placed him next to the Chinese leader. Xi, speaking to an aide, did not bother looking up as Trudeau sat down. Trudeau stared ahead instead of making any kind of gesture to engage his seatmate. He then turned his back to Xi not once, but twice. The first time, he looked over his left shoulder as if to summon an aide. He then swivelled his chair to his left and made a show of trying to get the attention of President Jair Bolsonaro of Brazil, who was nearby. Trudeau then removed his binder and briefing notes from his satchel while he fiddled with his earpiece for simultaneous translation. As *CBC/Radio-Canada* captioned its video of the event, "Malaise palpable entre Trudeau et Xi au G20."

Trudeau's aides defended the prime minister's behaviour by explaining that Xi and Trudeau had greeted each other prior to their on-camera greeting. There was an exchange between the two men after the working lunch, described by the Prime Minister's Office as "brief, constructive interactions."[11]

Whether the "constructive interaction" broke any ice is unclear, but Freeland did finally land a face-to-face meeting with the Chinese foreign minister during the ASEAN Summit in Bangkok, Thailand, right after Osaka. The two ministers discussed the issue of the Two Michaels and Meng Wanzhou's extradition process. "The fact we were able to speak and discuss these issues face to face, directly with one another, absolutely is a positive step," Freeland said.[12]

The damage Canada suffered when China blocked canola and pork and beef imports was considerable. A major drought in Europe allowed Canadian producers to partially make up for the shortfall in Chinese sales and the restrictions were eventually relaxed, but Canada's problems did not end there. Trump's subsequent "trade truce" with China, signed on January 16, 2020, left Canada dangling in the wind. The pact included formal pledges to tighten rules on intellectual property protection, pirated goods, and the theft of commercial property, to avoid currency manipulation, and open China's financial services sector to US companies. But it also committed China to buy an additional US$200 billion in American goods over the next two years, including US$40 billion to US$50 billion in agricultural products such as soybeans, canola, fresh and frozen pork, beef, wheat, corn, barley, and a range of machinery, all on preferential terms unavailable to Canadian producers. China's other purchase commitments under the deal included $54 billion in additional energy purchases, $78 billion in additional manufacturing purchases, $32 billion more in farm products, and $38 billion in services.

As the *Globe and Mail*'s Barrie McKenna reported, the deal was bad news for Canada's farmers: "Whatever China commits to buying from the US will inevitably come at the expense of other exporting countries. In farm products, Canada is among the countries most at risk of losing market share, along with Australia, New Zealand, Brazil, and Argentina. For Canada, some of the exports that could suffer include frozen pork, beef, soybeans, canola oil, lentils, beans, wheat, coal and seafood."[13]

Back home, the Trudeau government was also coming under pressure from an increasingly strident opposition bench that demanded a complete "reset" on China. Conservative Leader Andrew Scheer told his supporters "If this government isn't willing to stand up to China when two Canadians are unlawfully imprisoned and billions of dollars in trade is under attack, it never will." With a fall election in the offing, he added: "I will not allow Chinese state-owned enterprises, solely focused on the political interests of Beijing, unfettered access to the Canadian market."[14]

It was a refrain Scheer would return to in the fall in the run-up to the October election. Only this time, Scheer drew comparisons between China and the government's handling of the SNC-Lavalin affair, where the federal ethics commissioner had found Trudeau guilty of violating Canada's Conflict of Interest Act by improperly pressuring former Attorney-General Jody Wilson-Raybould to stop the criminal prosecution of SNC-Lavalin on corruption charges. To Scheer, Trudeau's willingness to intervene in the SNC-Lavalin judicial process undermined his hands-off stance on Meng's extradition process. "On the one hand, his message to the government of China with the case of the Huawei executive was that he could not interfere in the court case, that we have an independent proceeding when it comes to criminal-court proceedings," said Scheer. "And then he turns around and attempts to interfere in a criminal court case for his own political purposes." A Chinese government spokesperson levelled the same allegation.[15]

It wasn't just members of Her Majesty's loyal opposition who were climbing onto their soapboxes. Former senior Liberal government officials were also weighing in on what the government should do (or should have done). Former deputy prime minister John Manley, who served as Canada's foreign minister and minister of finance in the Chrétien years, suggested shortly after the Two Michaels were detained that the government should have used a bit of "creative incompetence" to deal with the situation: they should have found a way to allow Meng Wanzhou to board her flight to Mexico, so Canada could evade the issue of her extradition. Manley told CBC radio that the situation was not your usual "garden variety" extradition case of a wanted criminal, like a murderer or drug trafficker, but a highly politicized case that involved a US president who was suggesting publicly that Meng was a bargaining chip in US trade talks with China. "Yes, they accused Huawei of doing things that they ought not to have done," said Manley. "But before you arrest someone . . . you make awfully sure that this is really what it's claimed to be. And I think the president has made it pretty clear that's not what it was at all."[16]

Asked whether Canada had been "played for a fool," Manley answered in the affirmative. "This is not an extradition matter. This is actually leverage in a trade dispute and it's got nothing to do with Canada," he said. "It's got nothing to do with trade with Iran. Let's call this what it is—it's an attempt to get China to buy more soybeans from the mid-western United States.

Manley said it was a mistake for Canadian officials to get the prime minister involved. From time to time, governments "don't always do exactly everything we need to do," and the world is none the wiser for it. But once a prime minister is informed, "we're really obliged by our treaties to act in accordance with the law. The trouble with the prime minister having been informed, and I don't think he should have been, is to the Chinese that means this was political."[17]

Former Canadian prime minister Jean Chrétien also got into the act. He offered to serve as a special envoy to China to negotiate the release of the Two Michaels. He argued that if the government cancelled the extradition request, which the justice minister had the authority to do, it would help to "normalize diplomatic relations with China." Chrétien also enlisted his former chief of staff, Eddie Goldenberg, to carry the torch on the prisoner swap idea. As Goldenberg underlined in an interview with CTV, the government was faced with unpalatable choices. Goldenberg said an exchange was preferable, otherwise the Two Michaels would "rot" in Chinese jails for a very long time.[18] Former Conservative Prime Minister Brian Mulroney also chimed in to express his support for the proposed Chrétien mission.

Although Trudeau politely signaled that he was always ready to listen to former prime ministers, his foreign minister Chrystia Freeland delivered the government's answer to the swap idea, saying that it would set an extremely "dangerous precedent." The idea went nowhere.

CHAPTER SIXTEEN

The Disappeared

THE DAYS THAT MADE UP Michael Kovrig's new life in Chinese prison usually began at 6:30 a.m. when he and his fellow inmates were awakened. Breakfast followed, usually a bowl of boiled rice with some boiled vegetables. After lunch, there was a mandatory nap time for prisoners, but Kovrig has not napped his whole adult life so he used the quiet time to meditate.

For the first six months of his imprisonment, he lived in solitary confinement without access to books or other communication beyond a thirty-minute visit, roughly once a month, from Canadian embassy officials in Beijing. Then, in mid-2019, he was allowed books and letters. "So, a big part of his days, from what we understand, is spent reading," his wife, Vina Nadjibulla, said during an International Crisis Group podcast that marked his second full year in prison. The books, she said, were Kovrig's "main way of passing time and kind of the solace of his 'half-life' as he calls it."

The details of Kovrig's highly regimented routine in Chinese prison trickled out through his monthly consular meetings and in letters to Nadjibulla. Michael and Vina met two decades ago as graduate students at Columbia University in New York City. On one of their first days at school, she was sitting in the front row of an international economics class and he was in the back of the class. They met, became friends, and eventually they got married. Michael proposed at the United Nations in New York when he was stationed there with the Canadian embassy.[1] As she told the CBC in June 2020, they eventually separated, but remained married. As far as Vina is concerned, their connection has never been stronger. "He's my person, we have each other's back. And he is in a fight for his life. And I am in his corner."[2]

As a free man, Kovrig was deeply engaged with the world, endlessly curious and eager to remain connected to all that was happening east and west. An ardent internationalist, he was devoted to understanding how the world worked, and how to make it better. He was also creative. He played in a punk rock band when he was young. He took drama classes. He studied English as an undergrad. He had a thirst for travel, new peoples, new culture, new food. It was his way of being "in conversation" with the world, said Nadjibulla in 2020:[3]

> One of the things that he mentioned in one of his last letters was how much he looks forward to the day where he can rejoin the conversation, the broader conversation with life and with the world. Michael has been speaking of that, from the prison cell with respect to his own situation. He hopes that he will be able to come out from this experience, not only having survived it, but with a commitment to rebuild his life better, to contribute even more to society. He has devoted his professional life to being a public servant, to making the world safer. He was working with the International Crisis Group, an organization devoted to preventing deadly conflict. So, he hopes that he can continue to do that. And he can rejoin the broader conversation in the world with life and not just continue to be isolated and cut off in the way that he is[4]

He's trying to make sense of how these two years fit in the larger trajectory of his life. The last few years have been about himself, like kind of going deep within himself, as his environment is extremely barren, monastic. He often describes this as a concrete jungle or completely barren, external environment. He's getting to spend a lot of time in exploration of his inner character at what it means to be a good person.[5]

Through his letters, Nadjibulla gained insights about how a man she had known for two decades processed the trauma of his situation, how he is summoned the strength to overcome his circumstances. "He hopes that he will experience what few experienced, which is post-traumatic growth rather than post-traumatic stress, so that he will come out of this as someone who not only has survived, but someone who's been made better," she said. "He also says that he, on a daily basis, sometimes on an hourly basis, tries to change his anger into determination, and his grievance into fortitude and a kind of resilience. There is a constant struggle to stay in the frame of mind that allows him to survive, and also to make the most of this experience—to not be broken by it."[6]

Kovrig was drawing on something that his wife noticed when they were living together in New York City: his stubbornness. In a letter, Kovrig described how difficult it was to exercise and move around in a small concrete cell. Kovrig had asthma as a child and was not naturally strong, but his wife says he turned to martial arts and strength training twenty-five years ago, and that has stood him in good stead during his incarceration. So, there is lots of walking—seven thousand steps a day—and yoga, and push-ups.[7] "He often says that he doesn't like that type of exercise in a cell, kind of only being able to do limited things, but he knows that it is important for his mental strength to stay physically fit. So, he keeps moving as much as possible," she said.[8]

Kovrig also subjected his mind to a rigorous discipline. Books are crucial to him. He tried to fill in some of the gaps in his understanding of literature by reading Tolstoy's *War and Peace*. Nelson Mandela's autobiography, *The Long Walk to Freedom*, as well as books on philosophy have been on his reading list. He was particularly drawn to the stoic philosopher, Marcus Aurelius. He drew strength from St. Paul's "Letter to the Romans" in the New Testament. Nadjibulla describes his takeaway from Paul: "Suffering produces endurance, endurance produces character, character produces hope."

Kovrig also "draws tremendous strength from knowing that we are working on his behalf," Nadjibulla said. "In his letters, he quotes, philosophers and passages from the Bible and other things that give them inspiration." His goal, she said, is to "cultivate each day" to find serenity, and to live through each day with as much dignity as possible.[9]

He reread a favourite book from his life before imprisonment, Nassim Nicholas Taleb's *Antifragile: Things That Gain from Disorder,* and found new meaning in it. In the opening of his 2012 book, Taleb posits the following:

> Some things benefit from shocks; they thrive and grow when exposed to volatility, randomness, disorder, and stressors, and love adventure, risk, and uncertainty. Yet, in spite of the ubiquity of the phenomenon, there is no word for the exact opposite of fragile. Let us call it antifragile. Antifragility is beyond resilience or robustness. The resilient resists shocks and stays the same; the antifragile gets better."[10]

Nadjibulla said Kovrig read *Antifragile* before the pandemic and recommended it to friends as a book with a profound message for everyone trying to cope with the strain of COVID-19. "It's very much on the minds of many of us as we recover from the pandemic," he said, "and that kind of building better our economy, building better our future."[11]

Kovrig's resolve was tested when his consular visits were cut off from January to October 2020. China said it was because of COVID-19, so neither he nor Spavor were allowed visits from anyone for ten months. On March 13, 2020, the Chinese offered one perk. They allowed Kovrig a telephone call with his father, who was ailing from an unspecified illness at the time. It lasted just shy of seventeen minutes. Nadjibulla and Kovrig's sister, Ariana Botha, were also on the call.

"V, is that you?" came Kovrig's voice through her cellphone, set to speaker mode.[12]

"It was an incredible, incredible experience. I mean, probably one of the most profound moments of my life, certainly, to be able to hear Michael's voice after so many days of no contact," says Nadjibulla. "And it meant a lot because as it turned out, it was one of the only moments of contact for us in the year 2020."[13]

* * *

Canada's new ambassador, Dominic Barton, described his first meetings with Kovrig and Spavor after the pandemic had started, in October 2020, during his testimony before the House of Commons special committee on Canada-China relations two months later. This was the visit in which Barton was not allowed in the same room as the Canadians and spoke to them via video link. Neither of the imprisoned Canadians had heard about the COVID-19 pandemic sweeping the globe while they were isolated in prison, according to the ambassador. When Kovrig heard the news, he said it sounded like the zombie apocalypse had struck, adding that it reminded him of the movie, *Contagion,* which, in fact, became a runaway favourite on video streaming services during the lockdown.

"I have to tell you," said Barton, "I'm deeply inspired by their resilience and their mindset. It's incredible, given what they're going through. The other thing, and what I just realized, too, in talking with the families, they're Canadians who have families who are worried about them, who haven't seen them and are worried about their health, their mental health, but they're very strong. It's remarkable."[14]

In time, Kovrig also learned another key fact: that there is another Michael out there suffering the same fate as him. "I believe that has been communicated in consular visits," Nadjibulla says. "I think Michael understands that both of them are caught in this bigger situation. But his information is limited to what can be shared during consular visits."[15]

Less was known about Spavor's difficult life behind prison walls in Dandong. For his first one thousand days behind bars, Spavor's family remained largely out of the public eye, beyond occasional written statements, including from his brother, Paul, affirming his innocence and calling for him to be brought home. In December 2020, the *Globe and Mail* obtained a hand-written letter from Spavor asking for a few things, books and clothes mainly, that showed strong signs of the same active and curious mind as Kovrig. There were traces of Spavor's much-loved, and deeply missed, sense of humour, as he punctuated a request for new terry cloth headbands and wristbands with a smiley face.[16]

Spavor asked for quick drying clothes, including shirts and shorts with pockets, no zippers, and dark colours, and unscented deodorant. He also asked for a sleep mask, which lent credence to the widespread speculation that the lights stay on around the clock for both prisoners.

Like Kovrig, Spavor suggested that he was becoming more physically fit, losing weight, and gaining muscle. According to diplomats who visited him, he joked about being on an "extended sabbatical" and dubbed his surroundings in his early incarceration, where he was interrogated, the "Shenyang Sheraton."[17]

Spavor also had his own voracious reading list. He asked for large-print Chinese study guides, books on geography, politics, medicine, venture capital fundraising, entrepreneurial start-ups, prison biographies, biographies on The Beatles and former US president Bill Clinton, a copy of Gary Shteyngart's novel, *The Russian Debutante's Handbook*. He also wanted books on "true and amazing stories," books on "understanding" China and the Chinese people, and books on diplomatic history and "dealing with difficult people."[18]

There were strong signs that Spavor was also engaged in some deeply spiritual pursuits. He asked for books by the late Indian writer and philosopher Jiddu Krishnamurti, who wrote about meditation and the quest for positive social change. One article described Krishnamurti's work this way: "He stressed the need for a revolution in the psyche of every human being and posited that such a revolution could not be brought about by any external entity, be it religious, political, or social. It had to be brought about by a holistic transformation from within, and an insight into the various layers of one's consciousness."[19]

Spavor wanted a copy of Viktor Frankl's *Man's Search for Meaning*, a book that emerged in 1946 after its author had survived imprisonment in a Nazi concentration camp during the Holocaust. It's not known what specifically drew Spavor to Frankl, but there are plenty of clues. As Frankl wrote: "The one thing you can't take away from me is the way I choose to respond to what you do to me. The last of one's freedoms is to choose one's attitude in any given circumstance."[20]

Spavor also wanted Korean comic books.[21] His reading list, combined with the diplomatic reports of his resilience, suggests a man hanging on to who he was before his arrest: a gregarious, fun-loving world traveller with a serious purpose to connect with other people and learn from them.

In December 2020, Spavor was granted a rare privilege by his Chinese jailers. He was allowed to phone home at Christmas. It was the first time his family had heard his voice in two years.[22]

Three months later, one of Michael Korvig's recent jailhouse letters reached his family, providing another window into how his and Spavor's incarcerations had evolved over two years. Kovrig had spent his first six months in solitary confinement in a small cell. He had yet to breath anything resembling fresh air on a regular basis.

Balazs Sarkadi, his old Hungarian punk rock bandmate, saw Kovrig's March 2021 letter from prison. In it, Kovrig indicated he had an unspecified number of new Chinese cellmates, and hoped to make a good impression on them. "He kind of feels that he's kind of an ambassador of Canada in the prison because he is the Canadian guy, the only Canadian guy those Chinese guys ever met," Sarkadi said.[23] The only Canadians the cellmates had heard of was the extremely popular Ottawa-born comedian Mark Henry Rowswell, who is known throughout China by the stage name Dashan. And, of course, they knew about Dr. Norman Bethune. "He mentioned that, at least, they know that there are some other Canadians besides Darshan and this doctor," said Sarkadi.

Sarkadi said he believed Kovrig was keeping up his reading and health regime to keep his mind and body sharp. Able to watch videos with his cellmates, he joked that there was too much *Kung Fu Panda* on offer. His Chinese jailers also allowed a special treat—pizza—but when it arrived it contained pineapples. Kovrig is no fan of Hawaiian pizza, so the gesture was a bust.

As far as Sarkadi could tell, Kovrig was maintaining his sense of humour, so "he's not desperate yet." Sarkadi went on say that "he wrote that he is often lonely, but he's never alone. He feels that there are a lot of people outside that are trying to help. And I think that he still has hope that eventually these efforts will get him out."[24]

CHAPTER SEVENTEEN

Rock Takes a Turn

ALLAN ROCK IS MANY THINGS: a former Canadian justice minister, a former Canadian health minister, a university president, a law professor, and a former Canadian ambassador to the United Nations mission in New York City. Rock's United Nations job meant that he was something else that in 2018 became extremely significant: he was Michael Kovrig's former boss.

When Rock took over the UN mission from career diplomat Paul Heinbecker, he immediately noticed a low-level communications officer, Michael Kovrig. Rock found Kovrig to be extremely well-informed, "an interesting guy with a master's degree from Columbia University in international affairs, possessed of a very active intellect, curious, and ambitious." He quickly came to the conclusion that Kovrig was underemployed and began to use him for a variety of more challenging tasks at the mission. At one point, at the request of Canada's ministry of foreign affairs, Rock went on a speaking tour of Canada to talk about Canada and the United Nations. He took Kovrig with him on this ten-day cross-country jaunt and developed a greater appreciation for his wry sense of humor and conversational skills.

When Rock left New York, the two men stayed in touch. Kovrig used Rock as a referee for a position with the International Crisis Group to which he had applied. Rock was happy to provide a very positive reference and was delighted when Kovrig landed the job.

With both a personal and professional interest in Kovrig's welfare, Rock was anxious to do what he could to either have him released from Chinese prison or to have his living arrangements improved and, fortunately, he soon had an opportunity. In early November 2019, Rock led a delegation of former Canadian government officials, politicians, and academics to Chengdu, China for a below-the-radar meeting with Chinese officials. Ostensibly, the gathering was to discuss the future of Sino-Canadian relations, part of a polite, well-oiled "track two" dialogue that had been set in place prior to those bilateral relations breaking down in 2018. Rock felt strongly that he also had a chance to improve the fortunes of the Two Michaels.

The meeting had been organized by Gordon Houlden, head of the China Institute at the University of Alberta (CIUA). A soft-spoken, bespectacled former diplomat who speaks Mandarin, Houlden had spent much of his professional career working on China, including his efforts two decades earlier in organizing the first human rights dialogue between Ottawa and Beijing under the Liberal government of Jean Chrétien. He had held postings in both Hong Kong and Beijing, and also served as executive director (an ambassadorial-equivalent position) of the Canadian Trade Office in Taipei. Prior to joining the University of Alberta in 2008, Houlden was Director General of the East Asian Bureau, which was responsible for Canada's relations with China and neighbouring countries, in what was then called the Department of Foreign Affairs and International Trade, since renamed Global Affairs Canada.

As head of the China Institute, Houlden has continued to promote Sino-Canadian relations. As he remarked on his retirement as director of the centre in 2021, "My goal, in line with the original mandate of the China Institute, has been to use the China Institute to increase Canadian understanding of China, and to build a think tank which would enhance better understanding of China, and what China will mean for Canada in this 21ˢᵗ century."[1]

The rest of the delegation was a who's who of the Canadian foreign policy and political establishments, and one that straddled party lines. Apart from Rock, who had recently stepped down as president of the University of Ottawa, his job after serving as ambassador to the UN, it included the affable John Baird, who had held a variety of senior ministerial posts in Stephen Harper's Conservative government, including foreign minister; Ted Menzies, a former Conservative MP from Alberta who was Harper's junior finance minister; Phil Calvert, a former diplomat who had also served in China and also for four years as Canada's ambassador concurrently to Thailand, Cambodia, and Laos; Rob Wright, a former Canadian ambassador to China; Len Edwards, who had held three deputy ministerial posts (foreign affairs, international trade and agriculture) in the Canadian government and had also been Canada's ambassador to South Korea and Japan; and Yves Tiberghien, a career academic and the former head of the Institute of Asian Research at the University of British Columbia.

The members of the group unanimously saw merit in having an "informal dialogue" with the Chinese to advance the Canadian position on Meng and to address the situation of the Two Michaels. As Wright testified a few weeks later at the House of Commons special committee on Canada-China relations: "To the extent that we can influence the government of China on their form of detention, we [should] do so. What's the best way to deal with this? My own view is that little is achieved by shouting publicly, loudly, at the Chinese on these issues." Based on his own experience in China, Wright said, "headlines on the front pages of newspapers about Chinese actions and about the fact that Canadians were detained in Chinese prisons didn't help resolve the issue. What helped was deliberate, ongoing, diplomatic contact with Chinese officials, working with them to ensure that Canadian citizens were treated fairly, that we had access to them, and that they were given a fair hearing under Chinese law to the extent possible."[2]

The Chinese government chose to host the meeting at the luxurious Six Senses resort near the city of Chengdu, coincidentally the birthplace of Meng Wanzhou, in Sichuan province. The resort advertises itself as a place where you can reconnect with your six senses because "in this world of disconnection, reconnection doesn't happen on its own. You have to define how you want to connect." It was an ironic piece of sloganeering, given the context of the meeting that was about to unfold. The hotel's vast complex of villas, courtyards, gardens, and main facilities sits at the base of Qing Cheng Mountain and the nearby Dujiangyan irrigation system, which was built in the third-century BC and still controls the waters of the Minjiang River. The region is also famous for being the home of the ancient Chinese philosopher Zhang Ling, founder of Taoism, and for its hot and spicy food. If the Chinese government was sending some sort of signal with their choice of venues, it was lost on the Canadians, who were unaware of Meng's association with Chengdu.

The members of the Canadian delegation took separate flights to Chengdu via Beijing. They met at a Chengdu hotel and had breakfast together in a private area off the hotel's main dining room before boarding a bus for the two-hour ride to the Six Senses resort. They discussed for the first time what they regarded as their central purpose and the principal message they would convey to the Chinese. There was anything but unanimity about the way forward. Some members of the group felt that Canada had to cut Meng loose, otherwise there was no way to get the Two Michaels back. Others said wait a minute, you can't give in to a bully, and you can't set a precedent that would endanger the lives of Canadians around the world and give would-be hostage-takers the wrong message. The discussion continued on the bus ride.

After arriving at the resort around noon and checking into their comfortable accommodations, some members of the group spent the next several hours meandering along the mountain trails near the resort. Small temples were visible to them on the surrounding slopes and hills, which were shrouded in a cloudy mist.

At dinner, the group agreed to meet again, early in the morning. Over breakfast, it was agreed that Rock would serve as group leader and deliver the opening statement, which had been drafted and reviewed over breakfast. But as they were walking from the breakfast room to the meeting room, Rock turned to the group and said, "you know guys, I don't think I can sit there and read this because it's too formulaic. I will use this as a basis for speaking but won't recite chapter and verse." The group agreed. It was cool and wet outside as the Canadians made their way through the labyrinthian hotel complex to the meeting room.

* * *

The Chinese delegation was led by Wang Chao, president of the Chinese People's Institute of Foreign Affairs (CPFIA), and included a number of former military and diplomatic officials, notably Zhang Junsai, who had been China's ambassador to Canada and had just retired from the prestigious job of director general of the administration of Diaoyutai State Guesthouse from 2014 to 2019, and Jiang Shan, who had been minister counsellor (economic) at the Chinese embassy in Ottawa from 2007 to 2013. The talkative Jiang was well-liked, and viewed as having done a superb job promoting economic ties between the two countries.

After their introductions, Wang got down to business. His main subject was Meng and the Two Michaels. He brought a chill to the room by blasting Canada for being a lackey of the United States. He said that Meng's business interests were legitimate and that she'd done nothing wrong. Canada, he said, was unlawfully detaining Meng, the court process was unmeritorious, and she should be sent home immediately. How could Canada do such a thing to such a nice woman? he asked.

Wang stressed that there was no connection between Meng and the Two Michaels. As far as the Chinese were concerned, the Two Michaels had been engaged in espionage activities, which was why they were arrested. It was a refrain that other members of the Chinese delegation would repeat.

Edwards said it wasn't easy listening to this half-hour lecture from the Chinese, given how the Canadian delegation felt. "We got the full force of the Chinese position," he said. "The whole environment before Allan came in had turned extremely cold."[3]

Now it was Rock's turn. Given how the meeting was unfolding, it was clear Rock was the right choice to take the lead. Anyone who had seen him in action knew that there would be nothing casual or off-the-cuff about his delivery. A skilled lawyer, Rock is a careful master of his brief and attentive to detail. He leaned in over the boardroom table and, though jetlagged, carefully set out for the stern-faced Chinese officials the Canadian government's position. He explained that Canada's actions were dictated by its obligations under international law. Canada was complying with a request from a treaty partner to extradite someone who had been charged under US law and that had triggered the judicial process, which was now underway. He pointed out that Meng was free on bail, living in comfortable accommodations, and enjoying access to highly sophisticated and experienced legal counsel. He said that she was appearing in an open courtroom, where she had the opportunity to make every representation available to her in Canadian law in full public view. Rock explained that an impartial independent judge would evaluate the merits of the case and that only if the statutory test was met would she be committed for extradition. After that, it was up to Canada's minister of justice to determine in the ministerial phase of the process whether to surrender her for extradition. All of this, Rock underscored, was being done in accordance with the law.

Rock then pivoted to the situation of the Two Michaels. He reproached the Chinese for the inhumane conditions in which the Canadian detainees were being held, which stood in stark contrast to those of Meng. They were prisoners, he said, with no opportunity for bail or freedom pending the disposition of whatever complaint the Chinese had against them. He then politely but firmly reprimanded the Chinese for denying the Two Michaels proper legal counsel and for not informing them about the particulars of the Chinese government's complaint and justification for holding them. Their detention was indeterminate, he underlined, and they had no idea if or when they would be allowed to leave or under what circumstances. Rock implored his Chinese hosts to bring to bear whatever influence they could, as distinguished current or former members of the Chinese government, to improve the living conditions of Canada's detainees which, he emphasized, were unacceptable and "unworthy of the great people of this nation." As for Canada, he concluded, it would pursue what the Canadian government believed were its legal obligations under the rule of law because Canada, he underlined, is a nation that abides the rule of law.

After Rock finished speaking, Baird passed him a handwritten note. While in politics, Baird presented as a partisan pit bull, but behind the scenes he worked hard to build consensus across party lines on sensitive international issues. This was hardly his first non-partisan international foray: he had taken NDP and Liberal critics with him to Iraq in 2014 and featured them prominently in talks with the Iraqis. He wanted to do the same when he visited Ukraine after the Russian invasion in 2014, but Prime Minister

Harper shot down the idea, not wanting the opposition to share the spotlight. Baird also travelled to Ethiopia in 2010 to lobby for an imprisoned constituent, so he was no stranger to fighting for political prisoners in tense international meetings. "Hell has frozen over. I agree with you entirely," said the note. The gesture drew a quiet chuckle from Rock, a perfect illustration of the aphorism that "politics stops at the water's edge."[4]

The Chinese were implacable in response to Rock's presentation. They claimed that the Two Michaels were being held in the same conditions as all other prisoners, which Rock said amounted to "the same old bullshit."[5] But they had also done their legal homework on Canada's extradition law. Rock had argued that when it came to the proceedings in the British Columbia Supreme Court, the government's hands were tied, that Canada had a process and was following it in good faith under the rule of law. The Chinese hit back with section 23(3) of Canada's Extradition Act, which gives the minister of justice the authority "at any time [to] withdraw the authority to proceed and, if the minister does so, the court shall discharge the person and set aside any order made respecting their judicial interim release or detention."[6] As Rock recalled, the Chinese in effect said, "the minister of justice can, at any time, pull the plug on this damn thing, so don't try to tell us that you're stuck pursuing this, unquestioningly, to the bitter end. We're reading from your own legislation."

The Canadians were ready for the Chinese to exploit that inherent loophole in the government's argument. Rock parroted the line from the Department of Justice, that the section of the legislation the Chinese had cited was not necessarily intended for this kind of case. It would be an extremely rare circumstance in which the minister would prematurely halt any such proceeding.

As Rock confessed privately sometime later, it was "a non-satisfactory response" and "somewhat ironic."[7] In later months, he and former Supreme Court Justice Louise Arbour would adopt that argument themselves in an effort to free the Two Michaels. They put it to the federal government in no uncertain terms that although it could cite the rule of law to justify its unquestioning and unswerving decision to allow the continuation of the Meng proceeding, the rule of law also includes Section 23. "I spent twenty years arguing cases in court. And I certainly know that sometimes you argue cases you don't believe in," Rock says. "Sometimes you argue a case and put the best face you can on it, knowing that it's got weaknesses, feeling your heart sink when the other side identifies those weaknesses, trying your best to respond. But knowing that they've got a very good point." That was how he felt about Section 23.[8]

The rest of the morning was spent alternating from one side to the other, allowing everyone an opportunity to offer views. Baird reinforced many of Rock's arguments. Ted Menzies, whose principal preoccupation was trade relations, spoke forcefully, drawing on his experience in Asia and in government, talking about the considerations facing the government of Canada and how to manage them.

The two sides broke for lunch, and when they returned expanded the conversation to the broader aspects of the Sino-Canadian relationship, including economic relations, people-to-people ties, health, and human rights. Both sides expressed a desire to return to a position where there was a constructive relationship between the countries because both had much to gain. Edwards said the tone became noticeably warmer. He started noticing some positive signals during informal conversations with the Chinese delegation away from the formal talks. While the formal Chinese position was that Meng's case was in no way connected with their prosecution of the Two Michaels, Edwards was beginning to get the impression that China saw a much closer connection between the cases. "We had not heard that before. And when we picked it up in the corridor and dinner discussions, despite what was being said, in a formal meeting, about no connection and so forth, the Chinese were ready to talk to us on the basis of a connection. They were ready to talk about the situation of the Michaels if we were prepared to drop our proceedings."[9]

Rock said the Chinese recognized the strength and potential political clout of the Canadian delegation. It had seasoned ex-diplomats who knew China, three former cabinet ministers from the country's two main political parties. "We had people very knowledgeable about China. And so, I think they regarded us as a potential source of hope that there might be some influence brought to bear on the government of Canada to bring this episode to an end."[10]

The next day, the Chinese delegation played tour guide for their Canadian visitors. They visited panda bears at a local zoo and took a tour of a water conservation project. Edwards interpreted the hospitality and the new "friendliness" of the Chinese delegation as "part of the signaling that things could be put right" between the two countries.[11]

Something very concrete was also "put right" that day: the Chinese lifted their ban on Canadian pork. Edwards couldn't say for sure whether it had anything to do with how the previous day's talks had gone. Was it a sign from the Chinese that progress was possible or was it simply a coincidence? Either way, it buoyed the spirits of the Canadian delegation as they departed Chengdu and made their way back to Beijing for the final leg of their journey. "We were anxious to take credit for the lifting of the pork embargo. But then we realized that, at that time, we were on the verge of the Chinese New Year," Edwards recalls. That meant family get-togethers and festive dining. "Pork is so central to the Chinese diet," Edwards said. "There was a shortage of domestic pork because of the disease that afflicted their herds."

When the group returned to Beijing, it met with Lu Kang, the North American chief for the Chinese ministry of foreign affairs.

The Canadians continued to communicate the message that that the tit-for-tat reaction to detention of Meng Wanzhou was a miscalculation. As Houlden later remarked, they "did not see movement in the Chinese formal position," but he hoped that his hosts came away from the meetings with "a better understanding of the Canadian position."[12]

When the group reassembled after meeting Lu at the Canadian embassy in Beijing, it came to the consensus that it was time to bring the Canadian legal proceedings to an end, not least because the Meng case had become so politicized with President Trump treating her as a bargaining chip in trade negotiations. Some members of the group felt that the Chinese were quietly signalling that they, too, would like to put the case behind them. The Canadians worked on a script that would be shared in a call with ambassador Dominic Barton, who was in Canada for consultations with his government and had no opportunity to meet directly in Beijing. Rock was tasked to make the call with Barton, which took place in the padded "secure" room in the bowels of the embassy, out of earshot of any hidden Chinese listening devices.

CHAPTER EIGHTEEN

Let's Make a Deal

THE OUTBREAK OF THE coronavirus pandemic in Wuhan, China became a matter of public knowledge in late 2019 as reports of the mysterious illness began to emerge. Cases began spreading to other countries, and some responded by introducing travel restrictions. Canada was praised by the Chinese government for not following the US example of a travel ban, which went into effect at the end of January. "Most countries appreciate and support China's efforts to fight against the novel coronavirus," declared a Chinese foreign ministry spokesperson, "and we understand and respect them when they adopt or enhance quarantine measures at border entry. In the meantime, some countries, the US, in particular, have inappropriately overreacted."[1]

Canada also went out of its way to help support China's response to the pandemic by sending sixteen tons of personal protective equipment (special clothing, face shields, masks, googles, and gloves) in early February. This was provided in collaboration with the Canadian Red Cross and the Red Cross Society of China. During discussions with his Chinese counterparts about the pandemic, Canada's then-foreign affairs minister, François-Philippe Champagne, said that he was using every opportunity available, including medical discussions, to raise the plight of the Two Michaels. But the government's critics, including former Canadian ambassador to China, David Mulroney, a well-known hawk on China, opined that playing nice wouldn't reap any dividends or concessions for Canada. "Anything that opens up the channels of communication is a good thing, and we should use the conversation to raise all of our priorities," Mulroney said. But he was skeptical about linking pandemic assistance to diplomatic hostages: "We don't play games when people are sick, and we shouldn't allow China to play games with us. Freeing the Michaels isn't a favour or quid pro quo; it is what we expect of law-abiding states."[2]

As the pandemic worsened and reports surfaced that COVID-19 had spread to other cities in China, including Beijing, where Michael Kovrig was being held, efforts intensified behind the scenes to see if there was a legal path for the government to secure the release of the Two Michaels. Rock joined with former Canadian Supreme Court Justice Louise Arbour to explore the options available to the government.

Louise Arbour is nationally and internationally renowned as one of Canada's best legal minds, smart, principled, fair-minded, tough, and a longstanding champion of human rights. Early in her legal career, Arbour served as vice-president of the Canadian Civil Liberties Association where she had launched a campaign for prisoners' voting rights. Later on, following a stint on the Ontario Court of Appeal, she was appointed chief prosecutor of war crimes before the International Criminal Tribunal in The Hague, where she successfully indicted Serbian leader Slobodan Miloševic and several other Serbian figures for crimes against humanity. In 1999, Arbour was appointed a justice of the Supreme Court of Canada, but she resigned her post in 2004 to become the UN High Commissioner for Human Rights following the death of Sérgio Vieira de Mello, who was killed in a terrorist attack on the UN's office in Baghdad.

In 2009, Arbour began a five-year stint as president and CEO of the International Crisis Group in Brussels. She never met future ICC employee Michael Kovrig but she was determined to help him.

Rock and Arbour approached the law firm of Greenspan Humphrey Weinstein LLP to secure a legal opinion on the extradition issues surrounding Meng's case. Brian Greenspan is one of Canada's most respected trial and appellate lawyers, whose opinion has often been sought on international and governmental investigations, including extradition, mutual legal assistance, and criminal cases. Greenspan's colleague at the firm, Seth Weinstein, is also a recognized authority on extradition and mutual legal assistance matters, and the co-author of a leading text on extradition, *Prosecuting and Defending Extradition Cases: A Practitioner's Handbook.*[3]

The results of the firm's investigation into the extradition issues were summarized in a lengthy and detailed letter to the minister of justice delivered under Brian Greenspan's signature on May 22, 2020. The letter offered five "compelling reasons" why it would be appropriate for the minister to intervene in the extradition appeal active in British Columbia's court.

"First, it is a mischaracterization to conceive of the judicial phase of an extradition proceeding as a prosecution," the letter stated. "Extradition is a matter of international relations and diplomacy, not domestic criminal law."[4]

Greenspan further argued that "extradition is fundamentally an executive determination" and while the justice department's international assistance group was usually tasked with arguing the case in court, that fact "neither detracts from nor diminishes the minister's unfettered exercise of his or her discretionary authority to subsequently withdraw the Authority to Proceed."

Neither the extradition act nor the treaty between Canada and the United States, Greenspan believes, "may affect the minister's exercise of discretion." Moreover, "the role of the minister of justice in extradition clearly includes a consideration of Canada's national interest and its international reputation or its commitment to fundamental principles of justice in a determination as to whether an Authority to Proceed should be withdrawn."

Finally, argued Greenspan, "there is a practical advantage to be gained by exercising ministerial discretion to withdraw the Authority to Proceed prior to committal being ordered, as the exercise of ministerial discretion at this stage is virtually unreviewable. If Canada's national interest dictated that Ms. Meng ought not to be extradited, the withdrawal of the Authority to Proceed would provide to the public and the international community a clear and transparent decision, without the necessity of expressing reasons to decline surrender in accordance with the specific considerations set out in the extradition act."[5]

In tandem with the delivery of Greenspan's letter to the government, Rock and Arbour sent their own confidential missive in the form of a memorandum to the prime minister, clerk of the privy council, and the ministers of foreign affairs and the justice.[6] It addressed two questions: "Does the Minister of Justice have the unfettered authority under the extradition act to bring to an end before committal the extradition proceeding involving Meng Wanzhou? In other words, can he? And, secondly, is this an appropriate case for the minister to exercise that authority? In other words, should he?"[7]

The answer to the first question, the memorandum argued, was expressed in Greenspan's letter of opinion. But Rock and Arbour's answer to the second question spoke to the broader foreign policy considerations relevant to the case:

Withdrawal had been called for as a means of appeasing China. Some have styled withdrawal as a way to set up a sort of 'prisoner exchange,' as though the current circumstances were akin to a

Cold War capture by each side of the other's spies. The government has expressed the reasonable concern that withdrawal for those reasons would not only create the impression that China had 'bullied' Canada, but also set a dangerous precedent that would put at risk the liberty and lives of other Canadians who might thereafter be seized by the Chinese, or others, for leverage and for political 'ransom.' In other words, Canada doesn't respond to blackmail.[8]

Rock and Arbour argued that the government had "left unexplored" the question of what was in Canada's best interests. "The government could reasonably conclude that ending the extradition proceeding is necessary or desirable in support of a geo-political priority. In that light, withdrawal by the minister can be seen as the exercise of authority that he plainly has, in a responsible move by a sovereign state to advance its own strategic interests that go well beyond the four corners of the Meng proceeding, the United States-Huawei controversy, and the Canada-China dispute."[9]

Canada's support of a prosecution that defends American sanctions against Iran, in the views of Arbour and Rock, was "undermining" its own foreign policy towards Iran. Canada had supported the nuclear deal struck between the West and Iran to prevent the latter from enriching enough uranium to build nuclear weapons. Canada's policy has been "to preserve to the extent possible the joint comprehensive plan of action (JCPOA)." Canada did not support President Trump's decision to pull the United States out of the JCPOA in 2017, which saw the Americans abandon the four other members of the UN Security Council (Britain, France, China, and Russia), as well as Germany, which signed the treaty with Iran. The memorandum stated that "those punitive American sanctions against Iran are at the very heart of the request by the United States to Canada to undertake the Meng extradition." Thus, support of

American foreign policy on Iran undermines Canada's interests with Iran in two ways: Canada supports international efforts to prevent Iran from becoming a nuclear state, and Canada hopes to some-day re-establish its own diplomatic relations with Iran, which were broken off in 2012.[10]

Canada's lack of diplomatic relations with Iran, say Arbour and Rock, hampered its ability to fully help the Canadian victims of Ukraine International Airlines Flight 752 disaster on January 8, 2020. The Iranian military shot down the airliner killing all 176 people on board, including fifty-five Canadian citizens and thirty permanent residents. "Consular support by the Canadian government for victims' families, pursuit of fair and reasonable reparations, and the completion of a thorough and independent investigation would all be facilitated by the presence of diplomatic representation."[11]

The memorandum then pointed to the material health risk that the Two Michaels faced as a result of the exploding COVID-19 pandemic during a prolonged judicial appeals process. "There is concern about the vulnerability of the Two Michaels to the COVID-19 virus, about whether measures have been taken to manage the risk of infection, and about the availability of medical care should that be required," it said. "In these circumstances, Canada's national interest surely dictates that the government should do everything possible to shorten the period during which our citizens are at risk. Again, the purpose here is not to please (or appease) the government of China, but rather to address Canadian interests first and foremost."

Rock and Arbour concluded on a personal note, saying the continued passage of time would only make things more difficult on the Two Michaels if the minister did not act. "If anything were to happen to either of them, how could the minister and the government ever explain their failure to act when it was within their power to do so?" They also fired a lawyerly broadside at their fellow lawyer, then-justice minister Lametti, suggesting that his interpretation of the extradition proceedings reflected poorly on his legal skills. It was also a full-frontal attack on the Trudeau government's slavish adherence to its non-interference "rule of law" mantra for allowing the extradition case to proceed without politically intervention:

> More importantly, the minister would be in full compliance with the rule of law in exercising his authority under the act in the best interests of the country. In fact, abdicating the exercise of that authority, without considering the merits of putting an end to the proceeding, rests on a profound misunderstanding of what the law requires. That is the affront to the rule of law, which seems to have been misconstrued by many here as requiring in all cases blind deference to judicial process."[12]

Arbour had another legal connection to the Meng case. During her tenure on the Supreme Court of Canada two decades earlier, she wrote a ruling that has become a precedent in extradition cases, including Meng's. It addressed whether a Canadian court had the right to deny a US extradition request on the basis of an abuse of process. In April 2001, Arbour held the pen in the high court's 7-0 ruling that blocked the extradition of several men wanted in Pennsylvania on fraud charges related to a telemarketing scheme. The judge appointed to hear the case said the fugitives would face an "absolute maximum jail sentence" if they were tried in his court. A prosecutor in the case urged the suspects to abandon their extradition fight and face trial in Pennsylvania, otherwise, he warned, "you're going to be the boyfriend of a very bad man." Arbour ruled that those comments amounted to an abuse of process, and wrote that "conduct by the requesting state, or by its representatives, agents or officials, which interferes or attempts to interfere with the conduct of judicial proceedings in Canada is a matter that directly concerns the extradition judge." She added that litigants are protected from "unfair, abusive proceedings through the doctrine of abuse of process." Arbour then granted the men's request for a stay of proceedings, which halted their extradition to the US. [13]

Rock and Arbour got no response to their 2020 letter to the federal government, not even a polite, pro-forma acknowledgment that it had been received. The Trudeau government chose not to offer a basic courtesy to two Canadians who had served their country with great distinction.

* * *

On Friday, June 19, 2020, a month after the combined work of Rock, Arbour, and Greenspan was delivered to the Canadian government, Chinese prosecutors formally charged the Two Michaels with espionage under Article 111 of the Criminal Law of the People's Republic of China—indictments that could lead to life imprisonment. By that time, they had been in jail eighteen months. Prime Minister Justin Trudeau said he was "very disappointed" and that he would keep pressing China to release the two men. [14]

Days later, Rock and Arbour displayed their frustration with the government's refusal to act or even respond to their memo in an interview with the *Globe and Mail.* They said they could not understand why the government was so intent on adhering to the position that it had no legal authority to set Meng free. Rock speculated that one of the reasons for the government's reluctance was the political fallout from the SNC-Lavalin scandal, which saw Trudeau and senior officials in his office try to interfere in the prosecution of the company by department of justice officials. Rock said "the Canadian government made missteps in the SNC-Lavalin affair, but that the lesson of that episode is playing out wrongly, and to the detriment of Mr. Kovrig and Mr. Spavor, both of whom China charged last week with espionage." Rock said SNC-Lavalin was a "traumatizing event" for the government. "My concern is, once bitten, twice shy. In SNC, they shouldn't have and they did. Here they can and they should, but they won't. Because they think they can't, and they're wrong."[15]

Arbour told the *Globe* that Team Trudeau was drawing the wrong lessons from the SNC-Lavalin debacle. The government was "confused again, but the other way around, about the role of the minister of justice and the attorney-general. The dominant role clearly is of the minister of justice, not the attorney-general, who has a small, very visible, very public part to play – that's the tail that shouldn't be wagging the dog."[16]

The same evening that the *Globe* interviews ran, Vina Nadjibulla broke her silence by appearing on CBC television to express her own frustration with the government. She had been in regular contact with Rock since Kovrig's arrest and had been reaching out to him for advice and support on a regular basis. In a poignant and emotional conversation with *The National's* co-anchor Adrienne Arsenault, Nadjibulla pleaded for the government to do more to get the Two Michaels out of prison. "Words are no longer enough," she said. "We as Canadians, as a Canadian government, have to take actions to bring him home."

Nadjibulla was a compelling and articulate witness to her husband's plight as she described the conditions of his imprisonment. She expressed "heartbreak" that he was confined to a single cell described in letters to his family as a "concrete desert," and that he had not been outdoors or "seen a tree or had fresh air to breathe for 560 days." Although she commended Canadian officials in China for working "tirelessly" on her husband's behalf, she also stressed that a lot more had to be done to secure their release: "This is about Canada and Canadian lives that are in harm's way. I am interested in Canada and Canadians standing up for Canadians and Canadian values." It wasn't about being tough or standing up to China, "I am interested in us being strong, but not antagonistic. We cannot win a race to the bottom with China, we cannot become aggressive and confrontational because confrontation is not a strategy," she said.[17]

The next day a group of former government officials, senior diplomats (including two former Canadian ambassadors to Washington), and academics sent a confidential letter to the prime minister suggesting that it was time to release Meng in exchange for the Two Michaels.[18] Allan Rock drafted the letter together with some of the signatories. The letter had been in the works for several days and went through multiple drafts to sharpen the message, which was that the health, if not the lives, of the Two Michaels were in jeopardy because of COVID-19 and the harsh conditions of their captivity. The government had a moral and political responsibility to secure their release. Crucially, it was within the power of the government to do so. The letter also pointed out that because the government was so worried about criticizing China on other matters such as Hong Kong or the Uyghurs because of potential negative repercussions for the Two Michaels, its entire China policy was on hold, if not completely paralyzed. It argued that fears about offending Washington were greatly exaggerated. Trump had already politicized the case against Meng with his comments about using her as a bargaining chip with Beijing, and the US was well into an election year and preoccupied with other matters. The letter did not argue, as some have claimed, that Canada had to follow a policy of naively conciliating China.[19] Rather, its central point was that the continuing situation of the Two Michaels meant that Canada had no policy towards China at all:

> There is no question that the US extradition request has put Canada in a difficult position. As Prime Minister, you face a difficult decision. Complying with the US request has greatly antagonized China. Putting an end to the extradition proceeding may irritate the US. In normal circumstances, the safer choice would be to stay close to our ally, our friend, and our

principal trading partner. But these are not normal times, and this is not a normal case," their letter said. "Although the US government may voice its strong objections to the Minister's decision to end the extradition, it would not be the first time that Canada has parted ways with the US, including on much more momentous issues, such as refusing to join in their invasion of Iraq. Our strong bilateral relationship survived all of those controversies, each of them expressions by Canada of its sovereignty and national interest. We believe that Canadians will strongly support a decision to end the extradition proceeding.[20]

Those calling for the government to intervene pointed to another arrow in the government's legal quiver: Section 23(3) of the extradition act can be used to withdraw at any time the "authority to proceed" with an extradition that has been granted by department of justice officials.[21] If the minister does so, the court is obliged to discharge the person and set aside any order respecting their bail or detention. The Department of Justice acknowledged in July 2020 that in the last five years Section 23(3) had been used on occasion, but added: "No justice minister has personally intervened to withdraw an (authority to proceed) in an extradition."[22]

Among the signatories were Louise Arbour; Allan Rock; Lloyd Axworthy and Lawrence Cannon, former foreign ministers from the Liberal and Conservative parties; Ed Broadbent, the former leader of the New Democratic Party; and many other high-profile figures including Derek Burney and Michael Kergin, who had represented Canada in Washington; and former G8 deputy defence minister and former UN ambassador Robert Fowler, who had been kidnapped by al-Qaeda while on a UN mission in Niger and held captive for 130 days.*

---

* One of the authors of this book, Fen Osler Hampson, was a signatory to the letter for the reasons outlined in it.

* * *

The letter was intended to be confidential and to advise the prime minister that he had options that his officials might not have brought to his attention. But the letter didn't stay confidential for long. Within twenty-four hours, it was leaked by an unknown source to a variety of Canadian news outlets.[23] Both the letter and photos of the Gang of 19, as they were now called, were plastered on television screens across the nation in what looked like a police lineup. Rock and his co-signatories knew immediately that their enterprise was doomed.

Barely twenty-four hours later, Prime Minister Justin Trudeau delivered his reply. He was unusually stern as he walked down the front steps of his Rideau Cottage residence for another of his frequent COVID-19 press conferences. On this day, he had little to say about the pandemic and instead delivered a firm message about the fate of the Two Michaels:

> I respect the distinguished Canadians who put forward that letter, but I deeply disagree with them. The bigger question is whether or not we want China or other countries to get the message that all they have to do to get leverage over the Canadian government is randomly arrest a couple of Canadians. That not only puts Canadians in difficulty now but puts them in difficulty and in danger in the coming years.[24]

Trudeau was clear that a hostage swap would set a terrible precedent. "We cannot allow political pressures or random arrests of Canadian citizens to influence the functioning of our justice system," he said. "It is not just the Two Michaels who are at question here. It is every Canadian who travels to China or anywhere else overseas."[25]

The prime minister was at least being consistent. He refused to negotiate when two Canadians, Robert Hall and John Ridsdel, were kidnapped and subsequently beheaded by militant groups in the Philippines. (Two other hostages, from Norway and the Philippines, were released after negotiations.)*

Robert Fowler, from his unique perspective having directly served prime ministers across the Canadian political divide, and having been an international hostage himself, believes the Hall-Ridsdel precedent dictated Trudeau's decision in dealing with China over the Two Michaels. "In those cases, the prime minister was faced with admittedly a very difficult decision," Fowler says." But he believes there comes a time when every leader has to take extraordinary action. "It is possible to say, yeah, well, that was then and, in those circumstances, and this is now, and in different circumstances, and I'm going to take a different position. But I think it takes enormous courage and self-confidence to do that."

In the case of the Two Michaels, that would mean a negotiated end to their captivity. Fowler is adamant that the Trudeau government's deference to the rule of law is wrong. "It is naive, simplistic, and in this case potentially murderous," said Fowler. "I don't know any country that always plays by the rules." [26]

Fowler also pointed out that US Secretary of State Mike Pompeo sent a tweet declaring the US government's commitment to winning the release of Americans held captive overseas: "Should the Canadian government be less mindful of the imperative of offering any less of a commitment to Canadians unjustly held captive abroad?"[27] Several months later, more than one hundred Canadian ex-diplomats also urged Trudeau to swap Meng for Kovrig and Spavor on similar grounds.[28]

But despite the inherent indifference to the plight of Two Michaels that it implied, many other Canadian voices spoke strongly against doing any sort of hostage swap with China, saying it would

---

* Historian John English recalled that Pierre Trudeau told his wife Margaret that if she were taken hostage, he would not bargain for her life.

only embolden and validate what had become known as hostage diplomacy.* The Macdonald-Laurier Institute, a Conservative Ottawa-based think tank, organized a letter to rebut to the Gang of 19. It was signed by thirty academics, diplomats, and China specialists which stated that the "arguments are not only wrong in principle but would involve Canada betraying important values and letting down a number of our key allies." It suggested a "prisoner exchange" involved a "false equivalence between Canada's legitimate arrest of Meng in accordance with our legal obligations and China's kidnapping of Kovrig and Spavor—an equivalence as spurious as it is heart-breaking." It also suggested that "such an exchange would be nothing less than the abandonment of the rule of law and acceding to the demands of hostage-takers."[29]

Public opinion at the time was clearly on the Trudeau government's side, providing it with a domestic political incentive to stay the course. Seventy-two per cent of those polled by the Angus Reid Institute support the government's position. That support ran across generational, gender, and party lines.[30]

Trudeau's implacability and adherence to this unwavering course of action caused widespread frustration among those that hoped to see him display some sort of flexibility to end the standoff with China. But the prime minister had also been receiving advice

---

* Some countries such as Britain have made a public display of refusing to negotiate when their nationals have been taken hostage abroad. But there is little evidence that they have fared any better in deterring future hostage-taking situations than countries, like Israel, which have negotiated hostage releases. A major study by the American RAND Corporation found no evidence that a "no-concessions" policy serves as an "effective deterrent" to future kidnappings or hostage-taking situations. See Brian Michael Jenkins, "Does the U.S. No-Concessions Policy Deter Kidnappings of Americans?" *Perspective* (Santa Monica, CA: The Rand Corporation, 2018). A much earlier internal study by the US State Department appeared to reach a similar conclusion. See Judith Miller, "Bargain with Terrorists?" *The New York Times*, July 18, 1976. Also see, Joel Simon, "A Smarter Way to Recover Hostages," *The Wall Street Journal*, January 4, 2019.

against political intervention. His national security adviser, Greta Bossenmaier, reminded him in a December 18, 2018, briefing note that there had never been an instance in the previous decade of a justice minister using the legal right to end an extradition case for political or diplomatic reasons. She said that only twelves cases, including nine from the US, had been denied by the minister at the political level. The grounds for refusing extradition varied and included severe health issues, and the "minor nature" of the particular offence. "Note there are no examples of the minister discharging a case for political or diplomatic reasons," Bossenmaier told the PM. She also made clear that when it came time for the justice minister to make a decision, the minister would have to decide based on the submissions of Meng's lawyers. Once more she cautioned: "The minister has broad discretion to decide, but her discretion cannot be exercised arbitrarily. Again, there are no examples of the Minister discharging a case for political or diplomatic reasons."[31]

One year after he sent the letter to the federal government suggesting political intervention, Brian Greenspan was still standing by his recommendation: "To dismiss an argument based upon . . . the fact 'well, we've never done it before,' begs the question, then why is it in the legislation? The legislation is pretty clear that the authority of the minister exists to intervene at any stage. And that's really the only opinion I expressed. I didn't express a view as to, or at least a strong view as to whether he ought to. But I expressed the view that the legislation was clear."

"Until I was asked to write the opinion," adds Greenspan, "they simply said, 'well, it's at the judicial stage, and we can't intervene.' At least we got them to change their position to 'we won't intervene,' rather than 'we can't intervene.' Because all I pointed out was it is incorrect as a matter of law and practice to suggest that you don't have the authority to intervene."[32]

In retrospect, the letter by the Gang of 19 may have had one small benefit. China, for the most part, publicly maintained that there was no connection between the Meng case and the arrests of the Two Michaels. But the day before Trudeau was forced to address the letter, China's foreign ministry acknowledged the possibility, ever so slightly, when he was asked at his department's daily media briefing in Beijing if releasing Meng would compromise Canada's justice system. Spokesman Zhao Lijian said Canada's legal system made it possible for the extradition process to be stopped. "Such options are within the rule of law and could open up space for resolution to the situation of the two Canadians," Zhao said, according to an English translation of his remarks posted on his department's website. "Once again, we urge the Canadian side to earnestly respect the spirit of the rule of law, treat China's solemn position and concerns seriously, stop political manipulation, immediately release Ms. Meng and ensure her safe return to China."[33]

CHAPTER NINETEEN

The West Steps Up

A STERN MESSAGE WAS DELIVERED to Beijing when diplomats from twenty-six nations assembled outside Beijing's Second Intermediate People's Court on Monday, March 22, 2021. It was both a show of solidarity for the Two Michaels and a protest that Canadian consular officials had been shut out of Michael Kovrig's trial, which was just getting underway. A somber-faced Jim Nickel took the microphone outside the courthouse. Nickel was a career foreign service officer and Canada's deputy head of mission in Canada's embassy in China. He had followed the case of the Two Michaels from the day they were arrested and was the key point man on consular engagement. Nickel spoke slowly and deliberately, and delivered a firm, unequivocal message. China wasn't living up to its international obligations as a signatory to the Vienna Conventions, which guarantees diplomats such as himself consular access to court proceedings for their citizens:

> We have asked for access to Michael Kovrig's hearings repeatedly, but that access has been denied. As you know, Michael Kovrig has been detained for more than two years now. He has been arbitrarily detained. And now we see that the court process itself

is not transparent. We are very troubled by this. But we thank those who have come out from the embassies here in Beijing and the international support that we've had for Michael, for Canada, and the call we are making here for their immediate release. Thank you very much.

Three days earlier, a similar show of diplomatic support had taken place outside the courthouse in the Chinese city of Dandong, on the North Korean border, where Michael Spavor was on trial and Canadian officials were again denied access to the proceedings. The only saving grace in both cases was that the Chinese police were not thumping journalists, diplomats, and demonstrators as they had in December 2015 at the trial of Chinese human rights lawyer Pu Zhiqiang–events Michael Kovrig documented at the time in his diplomatic report. International television cameras were permitted to record Nickel's speech.

"The host government is obliged to give us access under our international conventions and our bilateral consular agreement. But despite our repeated requests for access, we are being denied," Nickel continued. "The reason that has been given to us why we are being denied access to our citizens facing trial is that it is a so-called national security case and therefore it is a closed case and a closed courtroom."

William Klein, the US chargé d'affaires, followed Nickel and expressed America's strong support for the two detainees who he said would be treated "as if they were American citizens." And then, one by one, in a solemn understated show of international solidarity, a roll call was begun. A masked colleague of Nickel's addressed the twenty-eight assembled diplomats.

"We know Canada's here. The United States is here," the male diplomat said. "Other countries that are comfortable, if you can just shout out your name, just the country you're representing, everybody here can know."

And with that, the disparate collection of voices responded, firmly and resolutely, one by one:

"Netherlands."

"United Kingdom."

"Germany."

"Estonia."

"Lithuania."

"Spain."

More voices followed: Sweden, Denmark, Australia, Germany, France, Switzerland, the European Union, the Czech Republic, Italy, Ireland, Latvia, Spain, Austria, Norway, Lithuania and New Zealand and Belgium and Romania.

When the roll call ceased, Nickel turned to face the group. "I would like to thank everyone for coming out today. We appreciate deeply that you have demonstrated your solidarity and support for Michael Kovrig during these difficult times and you've come out to demonstrate your opposition to arbitrary detention which is a very important statement for all Canadians."

The roll call was an important moment in the efforts to win the release of Michael Kovrig and Michael Spavor. It showed that many Western countries stood solidly behind Canada, although Asian countries and the developing world pointedly refused to participate. It was a show of support that had not come easily, the product of a hard-won international campaign fought over several years under the direction of three successive Canadian foreign ministers. Some of the countries that showed up for the roll call, like Australia, Switzerland, and Spain, had previously been reticent about expressing a strong position on the matter or openly criticizing the Chinese. Spain had turned to Huawei to build its 5G network and was friendly towards China. Switzerland had long favored quiet diplomacy over public statements on human rights while it forged closer economic ties with Beijing. Australia, which had its own battles with the Chinese over

COVID-19 and Chinese claims in the South China Sea, had somewhat surprisingly only expressed mild "concern" about the plight of the Two Michaels, even though some Australians were pressing their government to take a firmer stand. It was therefore quite remarkable that so many countries had chosen to express their solidarity, visibly shaming the Chinese government, an unprecedented first in the annals of Canadian diplomacy.[1]

The effort to build the international coalition was launched soon after they were arrested. Just before Christmas in 2018, Canada's then-foreign minister, Chrystia Freeland, announced in a telephone call with reporters that Canada had begun to "work with a broad group of allies to raise this issue" and that Canada's envoys would be taking their plight to "governments around the world." She thanked the United States, the United Kingdom, and the European Union for issuing strong statements in support of the Canadian position while underscoring that "we absolutely believe this not only a Canadian issue," but "an issue that concerns our allies."[2]

Canada understood that it needed its friends and allies to stand up to Beijing. It also understood that its coalition-building would anger China, and it did. The Wolf Warrior warnings became more strident. The Chinese responses amounted to variations on two themes: 'don't do it or you will suffer consequences' and 'your allies don't scare us; we have many more in the world.'

Under Freeland's successor, François-Philippe Champagne, Canada continued to secure global support for release of the Two Michaels. The European Union, which was busy negotiating trade and investment deals with China, was a hard sell because nobody wanted to ruffle Chinese feathers with awkward conversations about human rights. After successive rounds of diplomatic appeals, however, the EU raised the situation of the Two Michaels directly at their 22nd bilateral Summit with China on June 22, 2020. Held via videoconference due to COVID-19, the meeting brought the European

Commission president Ursula von der Leyen, European Council president Charles Michel, and EU foreign policy chief Josep Borrell face to face with Chinese prime minister Li Keqiang, and China's supreme leader, President Xi.

Von der Leyen delivered a blunt message to her Chinese counterparts. She told them that although "the COVID-pandemic and a number of major bilateral and multilateral challenges clearly show the EU-China partnership is crucial, be it in terms of trade, climate, technology, and the defence of multilateralism," for "relations to develop further, they must become more rules-based and reciprocal . . . to achieve a real level playing-field." She expressed the EU's "grave concerns" at the steps taken by China to impose a democracy-crushing national security law on Hong Kong and "the deteriorating human rights situation, including the treatment of minorities in Xinjiang and Tibet." She and her colleagues also expressed their strong concerns about the arbitrary detention of a Swedish citizen, Gui Minhai, and two Canadians, Kovrig and Spavor.[3]

The same day, on the other side of the Atlantic Ocean, US Secretary of State Mike Pompeo also called on China to release the Two Michaels, saying that they had been arrested on charges that were "politically motivated and completely groundless." He also stressed that the United States stands with Canada in calling on Beijing for their "immediate release," and rejected "the use of these unjustified detentions to coerce Canada."[4]

With the inauguration of Joe Biden as Donald Trump's presidential successor, there were high hopes in Ottawa that Washington would offer more than sporadic words of protest to help secure the release of the Two Michaels. Trudeau had developed warm and close relations with Biden. As the Obama presidency was drawing to a close, Trudeau fêted Biden at a state dinner during an official visit to Ottawa in early December 2016. During dinner speeches, Biden called on Trudeau to join with the likes of Germany's Angela Merkel to defend the rules-based international order from the assault on it that eventually came from Donald Trump.[5]

Four years later, Trudeau was the first foreign leader to telephone Biden to congratulate him on winning the Oval Office. During the transition, Ottawa was rife with rumors that the US justice department might try to negotiate a deferred prosecution agreement with Huawei that would allow Meng Wanzhou to go home and lead to the handover of the Two Michaels. But it soon became clear that although Biden and his team were sympathetic to the Canadian cause, they weren't going to act precipitously.

Biden, however, did restore the US practice of making Canada the first official visit of a new president after being sworn in. The summit was held via video, with each leader and their top cabinet members addressing each other through massive flat screen televisions due to COVID-19. But the effort allowed the two leaders to reaffirm the special relationship between the two countries and herald a return to normalcy in Canada-US relations after the tumultuous Trump presidency. Discussions between the two leaders covered a wide range of issues, including the Two Michaels. In his closing remarks from the East Room of the White House, Biden named Kovrig and Spavor. "Human beings are not bartering chips," he said. "We're going to work together until we get their safe return."[6]

That same message was repeated by US Secretary of State, Antony Blinken, in his own virtual meeting days later with Trudeau and foreign affairs minister Marc Garneau. In discussions that included North American defence, security, and human rights in the West and around the world, the plight of the Two Michaels was again raised. In a post-meeting interview with CBC, Blinken said that "using people, human beings, as pawns for political purposes, is totally unacceptable conduct by any country," and that the United States "will continue to stand with Canada on that. I've made that clear in my own conversations with Chinese counterparts and we look forward to the day when they're able to return home."[7]

True to their word, Biden administration officials put the issue of the Two Michaels squarely on the agenda in their first meeting with their Chinese counterparts in Anchorage, Alaska in mid-March. White House national security adviser Jake Sullivan referred to the talks as "tough and direct," which was clearly an understatement. Dispensing with diplomatic niceties, both sides hammered each other mercilessly in their public opening remarks, although apparently the talks became more business-like after the TV cameras were turned off and the media left the room.[8] The *New York Times* reported that the "widening gulf of distrust and disagreements on a range of issues" will shape the global landscape for years to come, and mentioned President Xi's belief that "the East is rising, and the West is declining."[9]

The inflamed, angry tone of the meeting was clearly affected by the US announcement on the eve of the talks that it would sanction twenty-four Chinese officials for their role in suppressing human rights and political freedoms in Hong Kong. The US also issued subpoenas on a number of unnamed Chinese companies to get information on "possible national security risks." The Chinese retaliated by announcing that the trials of the Two Michaels would begin right away. It was another painful reminder that the Two Michaels were pawns in a bigger geostrategic struggle.[10]

Canada's ambassador to China, Dominic Barton, spent three weeks in Washington in April 2021 speaking to China's American envoy and top officials in the Biden administration. That included meetings with the White House national security council and various US departments, including state, justice, treasury, defence, and commerce. Asked later at the House of Commons special committee on Canada-China relations why his envoy to China had spent all that time in the United States, Foreign Affairs Minister Marc

Garneau explained that Barton was "very knowledgeable" about the situation of the Two Michaels, and that he was working with Kirsten Hillman, Canada's ambassador to the US:[11] "I can't go into details, but I can tell you that both are very actively working on the file with respect to the two Michaels."

Garneau also told the committee that Canada and the world were now viewing China much more critically. "China's increasing authoritarianism and coercive diplomacy are challenges for democracies around the world. All countries are reassessing and realigning their engagement with China, and Canada is no exception," the minister said. "Let me be clear. A path to any kind of long-term relationship with China implies the safe return of Michael Kovrig and Michael Spavor to Canada . . . Bringing them home is and must remain our top priority in our dealings with China, period."

In late 2021, Canada's foreign ministry offered additional details on the efforts they were making to win the release of the Two Michaels: "Our government continues to raise Michael Kovrig and Michael Spavor's cases with Chinese officials on a regular basis and Canada's partners have also raised the cases with Chinese officials since their detention began in 2018. To date, Canada's ongoing advocacy campaign for their release has included more than 1,280 interactions with Chinese officials and other governments and key stakeholders."

Despite that extended effort, the Chinese held firm.

CHAPTER TWENTY

New Provocations

ARNEAU'S PREDECESSOR AS foreign affairs minister, François-Philippe Champagne, broke free of COVID-19 travel restrictions in August 2020, flying to Europe on the first foreign trip of a Canadian politician in the pandemic era. Lebanon, the scene of a massive port explosion earlier in the month, was billed as his marquee destination, but there was another purpose behind the scenes of a four-day tour that would include Italy, Austria, Belgium, and the United Kingdom.

Champagne had barely got his feet on continental soil when an unexpected opportunity came his way in Rome. Noticing a news item that indicated his Chinese counterpart, Wang Yi, was also in Rome, the minister immediately started texting his officials and Italian contacts to see about arranging a meeting. Champagne decided to push for consular access to Korvig and Spavor, and for their release, in a face-to-face meeting with Wang Yi.

Wang agreed to meet at 9 p.m. local time in a hotel boardroom. The two foreign ministers sat opposite each other, unmasked, at a long, wide, rectangular table draped in a beige tablecloth and dotted with bottles of San Pellegrino and floral arrangements. Three masked officials flanked Wang, and two more joined Champagne.

In a photo posted on the Chinese embassy website in Ottawa, Wang is gesturing with both hands towards Champagne, who is listening, eyes down. According to the Chinese readout, 2020 marked fifty years since the two countries took the historic step of establishing diplomatic relations, and Canadian leaders "withstood pressure from various parties" to accomplish that "step in the right direction." Despite a relationship that has historically been free of disputes and conflict, "the Canadian side's detention of a Chinese citizen for no reason has caused serious difficulties in bilateral relations. As a Chinese saying goes, 'whoever started the trouble should end it.' The Canadian side should have a correct understanding of it. It is hoped that the Canadian side will act as an independent country and make a decision as soon as possible to remove the main obstacle in the development of China-Canada relations."

Champagne offered his version of the two-hour meeting in a December 2020 interview.[1] "In the end, it was robust, and robust in diplomatic terms . . . you can imagine that," Champagne said, seated in an armchair in his top-floor corner office at the Lester B. Pearson building, overlooking the Ottawa River and west Quebec. "They know our position. I repeated it in no uncertain terms. But the discussion also was around consular access." Champagne reminded Wang that China was a signatory to the Vienna Convention on diplomatic relations. "You have to restore access to Michael Kovrig and Michael Spavor and Mr. Schellenberg, despite COVID," he told Wang, so Canadians could "check on their well-being."

Asked about China's constant warnings to Canada not to try to build international support over the Two Michaels, Champagne emphatically defended his position. "I'll take no lessons from anyone, and certainly not from China, when it comes to defending and standing up for values and principles and defending Canadian interests and defending Michael Kovrig and Spavor," he said. He reminded the Chinese that the European Union, at its summit with

China earlier in the fall, had specifically mentioned the plight of Kovrig and Spavor and in their final communiqué called for their release. "It's one of the first times in recent history where you see the consular case of citizens being mentioned in a communiqué to say, 'We care.' So, my point is that we are going to stand united. That's what we have achieved."

The big win in the Rome meeting with Wang, said Champagne, was restoring consular access to Kovrig and Spavor, which he also credits to the hard work of Ambassador Barton. "It's a step," Champagne said. "Obviously, they should never be there in the first place. So, let's be clear with everyone."

* * *

Champagne's August 2020 trip, and a second one in early October, were also part of a clandestine diplomatic effort he had been mounting since he took on his new portfolio in November 2019: he was trying to build support for a new global initiative, a declaration against arbitrary detention in state-to-state relations. Officially, he had visited Austria for an update on the Organization for Security and Co-operation in Europe's efforts to broker peace in the full-scale war that had broken out between Azerbaijan and Armenia. He left Vienna with the first solid commitment by any country to the Canadian-inspired declaration. He also paid a successful visit to one of his top allies, British foreign secretary Dominic Raab in London.

Formally launched on February 15, 2021, the declaration called on all states "to prevent and put an end to: harsh conditions in detention; denial of access to legal counsel; torture; and other cruel, inhumane or degrading treatment or punishment." Announcing the initiative, Marc Garneau, an astronaut-turned-politician who succeeded Champagne in the foreign affairs portfolio, said the law applied to "all cases of arbitrary detention, whether they target

Canadian nationals, dual nationals, nationals or partners and other states." He also said that Canada would continue to "fight against arbitrary detention in state-to-state relations, now and for the future."[2] The announcement of the declaration was accompanied by strong statements of support by British human rights lawyer Amal Clooney, the executive director of Human Rights Watch, Kenneth Roth, and US secretary of state Blinken.

More than three dozen countries attended the launch, held over video conference. Austrian foreign minister Alexander Schallenberg offered a blistering statement of support for the new initiative: "If the question is: rule of law, or the law of the jungle, our answer must be clear. We have to prove again and again, that we stand by our values and that our joint commitment to human rights and to the rule of law does not know any lockdown. There is simply no room for discussion: arbitrary arrest and detention do not comply with international law. This practice must end." The United States, Britain, the European Union, Germany, Japan, Australia and others followed suit in voicing support.

As Garneau rolled out the announcement, he took pains not to point the finger directly at China or draw what was an obvious connection to the Two Michaels. The initiative was positioned as a broad declaration to stamp out an odious practice used by several countries. But there is no doubt it was born out of the China crisis and hatched in response to Champagne's relentless pressure on Canadian foreign affairs staffers to do more for the Canadian captives. In an exclusive briefing on the initiative with senior federal officials, a public servant, speaking anonymously, as is customary in such discussions, said it was Champagne as the minister who carried the ball forward in the effort to free Kovrig and Spavor.[3] "Everybody understands that he has spent the better part of the last year personally, shepherding this initiative. And he's made, I would say, hundreds of calls," the official said.

The Chinese embassy in Ottawa made the connection, too, and was not pleased. Envoys lambasted the appearance at the announcement of Roth, who drew a pinpoint connection between the new Canadian-led initiative and what was happening to the Two Michaels. "The Chinese government's detentions of the Canadians Michael Kovrig and Michael Spavor epitomizes this despicable practice," Roth said, adding that China had subjected Australian citizens to the same treatment. The Chinese embassy charged that Canada had "arranged" for Roth to be its mouthpiece to criticize China in what was a "fact-distorting and ill-intentioned" move. The Chinese statement affirmed that it had undertaken its own lawful prosecution of Kovrig and Spavor. "The Canadian side's attempt to pressure China by using 'megaphone diplomacy' or ganging up is totally futile and will only head towards a dead end." Once again, the embassy urged Canada to immediately release Meng so "she can return to China safe and sound."

Five days later, Cong Peiwu, China's latest ambassador to Canada, was on the telephone with *The Canadian Press*. The Chinese embassy had pitched an interview with him because Canada's official opposition was planning to introduce a motion in parliament that would declare China's treatment of its ethnic Muslim Uyghur population as genocide. The embassy wanted to get ahead of that, but it also wanted an opportunity to state the Chinese perspective on the arbitrary detention declaration. Cong turned it on its head:

> We must point out that Mme. Meng Wanzhou has been arbitrarily detained for over two years, despite the fact that she hasn't violated any Canadian law. This is the most accurate illustration of arbitrary arrest or detention of foreign nationals. So, the declaration looks rather like Canada's confession in the Meng Wanzhou case.[4]

In all, fifty-eight states and the European Union were founding endorsers of the declaration when it was launched (the number grew to sixty-six by the summer of 2021). Nevertheless, some critics felt it little more than empty words absent a commitment to direct, punitive actions. As former Canadian ambassador to Beijing Guy Saint-Jacques noted, if the signatories had decided to impose collective sanctions on China for its behaviour, they might have stood a better chance of getting Beijing's attention.[5]

Nevertheless, the declaration was a start, lifting out of existing international norms and law specific provisions to apply to the arbitrary arrest or detention of foreign nationals by other states. At the G7 meeting in London in May 2021, the declaration was not only reaffirmed but G7 members committed "to work together and with likeminded partners to deter those who conduct arbitrary detention to compel to action, or to exercise leverage over a foreign government, by amplifying the declaration against arbitrary detention in state-to-state relations." Those were diplomatic codewords indicating that the G7 recognized real action was a necessary accompaniment to reprobation. The G7 also invited "countries that have endorsed the declaration and other likeminded partners to actively consider taking part in the voluntary areas of cooperation and engagement outlined in the partnership action plan."[6]

The Chinese government swiftly denounced these and other comments critical of Beijing as representative of merely a "small" group of countries (the United States, Britain, Canada, France, Germany, Japan, and Italy): "The days when global decisions were dictated by a small group of countries are long gone."[7]

More tension developed between Canada and China over the latter's handling of the COVID-19 outbreak—specifically, its efforts to thwart the efforts of Taiwan, which it considers an illegitimate state, to gain information on the virus and share best practices for containing it through the World Health Organization. As a report of the

US-China economic security review commission, a US government body, noted, "as COVID-19 spread throughout the world in the early months of 2020, Beijing operationalized ties it had developed over decades within the world's premier public health organization to exclude Taiwan from the international response to the pandemic. Beijing's sway within the WHO, which has long refused to grant Taiwan membership, was apparent from the start of the crisis, when WHO officials ignored Taiwan's attempts to request information about the virus's potential for human-to-human transmission."[8] Canada and other Western countries pushed hard to have Taiwan included in important WHO meetings, further incurring Beijing's wrath. The Chinese told Canada to "butt out of its internal affairs."[9]

An unfortunate wrinkle for Canada on the COVID-19 front was that its government had earlier agreed to partner with a Chinese company to develop a vaccine. The collaboration was to have taken place between the Chinese vaccine-maker CanSino and Canada's National Research Council (NRC). Under the agreement, the NRC would issue a license to CanSino to use Canadian biological products for the new vaccine. CanSino also agreed to provide samples for the vaccine that would be carried out in clinical trials conducted by the Canadian Center for Vaccinology at Dalhousie University. As relations between Canada and China deteriorated, the Chinese government decided to block the shipments for the trial, and the deal went nowhere.

The Trudeau government's decision to partner with China on a vaccine came in for stiff criticism from the opposition benches. Conservative Leader Erin O'Toole denounced it for having "put all our eggs in the basket of China." He and others also criticized Trudeau for making Canadians wait in line for foreign-manufactured vaccines because there was no made-in-Canada vaccine. Trudeau defended the government's procurement program on the grounds that it "secured multiple options for the country."[10]

The Conservatives and Liberals pointed fingers at each other over the fact Canada had no domestic vaccine manufacturing capacity. The Conservatives said the previous Liberal governments under Jean Chrétien and Paul Martin failed to learn the lessons of the 2003 SARS pandemic. Trudeau blamed the Conservative government of Stephen Harper for allowing pharmaceutical companies such as AstraZeneca and Johnson & Johnson to lay off staff and shutter their operations in the previous decade.[11]

Still more tension developed over China's treatment of its Uyghur and Muslim communities in Western China. For years, stories had circulated in the Western press about Uyghurs being detained in "re-education camps" and used as forced labour, and of Uyghur women being sterilized. In addition, there were also a growing number of credible reports of torture, systemic rape, and mass arbitrary forced separation of children from their parents, all of which the Chinese government vigorously denied. A PBS documentary that was aired on its flagship show *Frontline* provided firsthand accounts of the horrors to which those who had been held in China's "re-education" camps were subjected. The documentary also investigated the Chinese government's growing use of state-of-the-art facial-recognition surveillance technologies and artificial intelligence to monitor and track the movements of Uyghurs and other Muslims living in the region which, as the show's producers argued, had global implications that go well beyond China's own brand of "digital authoritarianism."[12] The Chinese were quick to rebut the claims through a spokesperson who asserted "these [claims] are nothing but preconceptions without any proof. Xinjiang lawfully installs surveillance cameras at its urban and rural main roads, transportation junctions, and other public areas with the aim to improve its social governance and effectively prevent and strike against crimes."[13]

During a virtual press conference in November 2020 organized by Canada's Conservative opposition, Rukiye Turdush, a Canadian-

Uyghur activist, described in harrowing detail the lengths to which Chinese authorities will go, in China and on Canadian soil, to intimidate and silence discussion of the plight of the Uyghur people. Turdush spoke of being harassed by Chinese students after a speech at McMaster University in Hamilton in February 2019, for which he blamed the Chinese embassy. Chinese authorities also leverage their power over Uyghurs in Canada by intimidating their family members back in China, said Turdush. A familiar tactic was for Chinese police to visit their relatives back in Xinjiang province and share a video copy with their family in Canada. "They threaten them: 'If you tell the Canadian police, if you do something, your mother's going to die, your father's going to be arrested.'"[14]

The publication of the Xinjiang Papers, hundreds of pages of leaked Chinese government documents, exposed the vast scale of the detentions taking place under the direct instructions of Beijing. As the *New York Times* reported, the documents showed that "President Xi Jinping, the party chief, had laid the groundwork for the crackdown in a series of speeches delivered in private to officials during and after a visit to Xinjiang in April 2014." Xi called "an all-out 'struggle against terrorism, infiltration and separatism' using the 'organs of dictatorship' and showing 'absolutely no mercy.'" The documents also disclosed that the appointment of Chen Quanguo as the new party boss for the region produced an explosion in the number of internment camps and "growing surveillance and control of the Uyghur population."[15]

Irwin Cotler, a long-time human rights lawyer and advocate who also served as Canada's attorney-general and justice minister in the Paul Martin Liberal government, is also the founding director of the Raoul Wallenberg Centre for Human Rights. In an April 2020 interview, Cotler argued forcefully for Canada to level human rights sanctions with its allies against the Chinese individuals he says are perpetuating genocide against the Uyghurs. Such sanctions, named after the Russian whistleblower Sergei Magnitsky, who died in a Russian prison at the hands of Vladimir Putin, target the assets of individuals, freezing their overseas bank accounts and denying them travel rights. "We need to expose this ongoing culture of criminality and corruption and the impunity that attended, lest we become enablers. In my view, the international community has acted too long as bystanders to China's major human rights' violations."[16] A year later, the Wallenberg Centre issued a major joint-expert report documenting Chinese government abuses against the Uyghurs in the context of the 1948 genocide convention.[17]

Cotler pointed out that Canadian Uyghur human rights activist Huseyin Celil had been languishing in a Chinese prison for a decade and a half after he was arrested on a trip to Uzbekistan in 2006 and transferred to Chinese custody in 2007. Celil became a Canadian citizen in 2005, but China doesn't recognize his new nationality and hasn't allowed any diplomatic visits to check on his condition.

In late March 2021, the British government in tandem with the European Union, Canada, and the United States announced that it would be imposing sanctions against four senior Chinese government officials, including Chen Quanguo and the public security bureau of the Xinjiang Production and Construction Corps. The sanctions included asset freezes and travel bans and were part of a global movement to push China to account for its human rights violations, with thirty-nine countries also signing a joint statement at the UN.[18]

In announcing its own new sanctions, the Canadian government noted that "mounting evidence points to systemic, state-led human rights violations by Chinese authorities. This includes the mass arbitrary detention of more than 1 million Uyghurs and other Muslim ethnic minorities on the basis of their religion and ethnicity, as well as political re-education, forced labour, torture and forced sterilization." Garneau has pointed a finger directly at Beijing, stating that

Canada is "deeply concerned by the egregious human rights violations that are taking place in Xinjiang at the hands of the Chinese state."[19]

Although the Canadian government was prepared to levy sanctions against China for its treatment of Uyghurs and Muslim minorities, it was not prepared to formally accuse China of genocide. Conservative foreign affairs critic Michael Chong's non-binding resolution declaring that China was engaged in genocide against its Muslim people unanimously passed in the Canadian parliament by a 266-0 vote on February 22, 2021. The Trudeau cabinet abstained. Garneau was given the job of informing the House of Commons that Canada was "deeply disturbed by horrific reports of human rights violations in Xinjiang," but the cabinet would not support the resolution. Trudeau justified the decision in a press conference saying that genocide was an "extremely loaded" term and that the international community takes it "very, very seriously." He said it could only be used when it is "clearly and properly justified," so as not to diminish its value.[20] Trudeau's explanation fuelled speculation that the government didn't want to provoke the Chinese any further for fear of making the situation any worse for the Two Michaels. In any event, Trudeau was clearly bucking the trend when it came to public opinion. A poll indicated that an overwhelming majority of Canadians approved the parliamentary declaration and wanted to see sanctions against Beijing, including the transfer of the 2022 Winter Olympics to another country.[21]

The British government was also put on the defensive when a cross-party rebellion of Tory backbenchers joined with Labour opposition members to pass a non-binding resolution prohibiting trade deals with genocidal regimes (a similar motion received assent in the Netherlands). The British government took the position that genocide was a matter for international courts to decide.[22] It was clear that Prime Minister Boris Johnson was hoping to do trade deals with China in a post-Brexit world and didn't want to further antagonize Beijing. In stark contrast to both Canada and the UK, the Biden administration had few qualms about calling China's treatment of its Uyghurs genocide and did so openly in both the state department's annual human rights report and a forceful public rebuke by secretary of state Antony Blinken, who also urged US companies to ensure they weren't doing business in western China.[23]

Given these flash points in its relations with China, the Trudeau government began running interference on new provocations. *Politico* broke the story that Ottawa, the principal sponsor of the internationally recognized Halifax International Security Forum, was threatening to withdraw its funding if its organizers went ahead with awarding the John McCain Prize for Leadership in Public Service to Tsai Ing-wen, president of Taiwan, for being a "strong global advocate for democracy."[24] Three days after the story broke, the House of Commons unanimously passed a motion, again brought forward by Conservative MP Chong, to support her candidacy for the award. Trudeau responded by saying: "I have always supported Taiwan's meaningful participation in multilateral international forums in Canada and Canada continues to have strong and growing trade and people-to-people relations with Taiwan."[25]

CHAPTER TWENTY-ONE

A New Cold War

JOHN SUDWORTH, THE AWARD-WINNING BBC correspondent who had waded through that chaotic scene at the Pu trial on the December 14, 2015 to report on the police clampdown on journalists and diplomats—the same event Michael Kovrig documented as a diplomat—was forced to make a tough choice about his future in China. After nine award-winning years in China, he decided that the threats, surveillance, intimidation, and harassment he was being subjected to at the hands of Chinese authorities were no longer worth the risk of remaining. Sudworth and his team had seen their footage deleted by Chinese security officials after travelling to Xinjiang in 2020 to report on the Chinese re-education camps of ethnic Muslim Uyghurs. China had recently expelled correspondents from the *New York Times*, *Washington Post*, and *Wall Street Journal*. On March 31, 2021, Sudworth moved out of Beijing with his wife and children and relocated to Taiwan.[1]

The Foreign Correspondents Club of China said on Twitter that the "abuse of Sudworth and his colleagues at the BBC forms a part of a larger pattern of harassment and intimidation that obstructs the work of foreign correspondents in China and exposes their Chinese news assistants to growing pressure." Sudworth didn't give Chinese authorities any advance notice that he was leaving yet plainclothes Chinese police officers followed him and his family to the airport, including into its check-in area. Chinese foreign ministry spokeswoman Hua Chunying later told a press briefing "that Sudworth left without saying goodbye."[2]

Sudworth's departure was troubling for what it represented on a larger scale—the withdrawal of a leading international news agency from China in order to protect the safety of one of its journalists. In different roles, Sudworth and Michael Kovrig had reported in their own ways on the ramifications of Xi Jinping's China Dream. The veteran journalist had seen enough to perform the necessary risk assessment that led to what was undoubtedly a difficult decision. He could see trouble coming and he acted accordingly. In doing so, he avoided the real-life China nightmare that befell Michael Kovrig and Michael Spavor.

There has been much discussion since the arrests of Meng and the Two Michaels about how Western governments will deal with the reality of the new China. Western media will meanwhile continue to make their own choices.

* * *

As the legal saga played out in 2021, so, too, did efforts to persuade the Chinese to set the Two Michaels free, including a new initiative involving one of Canada's leading elder statesman. In mid-July 2021, former prime minister Brian Mulroney had a pointed and frank telephone conversation with the Chinese ambassador, Cong Peiwu. The envoy had been trying to connect with Mulroney to sound him out about the impasse in relations between their two countries. "Look, we know you well, and we respect you. You and Deng Xiaoping, in the beginning in 1986, built up quite a powerhouse of co-operation.

And my colleagues are obviously interested in what you might have to say," Mulroney recalled Cong telling him.[3]

Before the call, Mulroney had been fully briefed by Global Affairs Canada. When the time came to respond to Cong, Mulroney didn't hold back. He drew from his decades on the international political stage, and as a bare-knuckled labour negotiator before he became a politician.

"I don't know why you felt as though you had to do this. You're hurting yourself," Mulroney told him. "And as far as I'm concerned, you would gain much more by not asking for anything, and just freeing the Canadians. We know full well that they didn't do anything wrong. We know full well they were picked up on the sidewalks there to satisfy a political agenda in Beijing. You do yourselves a lot more good by instituting an initiative that would free the Canadians. It would gain you lots of plaudits around the world."

Mulroney realized he was talking to the new, more strident, more aggressive China, not the China of his political heyday in the 1980s and 1990s. The conversation with Cong was respectful and polite. Mulroney described Cong as a "smart guy," and he suggested the diplomat simply relay his message back to his political leaders in Beijing. Mulroney ended the call feeling optimistic, hopeful it could lead to a positive outcome.

Shortly after the arrest of the Two Michaels, Mulroney had suggested the federal government should enlist another ex-prime minister, his long-time political rival, Jean Chrétien, and his son-in-law, businessman André Desmarais, to travel to Beijing to break the ice on the impasse. Not only was Desmarais married to Chrétien's daughter, France, but he had taken over the mantle of his father, Paul, to become the deputy chairman, president, and co-chief executive officer of Montreal's Power Corporation, which has major business interests in China. Desmarais was also a board member of the influential Canada-China Business Council. "Andy Desmarais, in my judgment, has better connections and more influence in China than any other Canadian," said Mulroney. "The plan failed to launch. Prime Minister Justin Trudeau rejected it."

But on one matter Mulroney was crystal clear: he had never advocated for a prisoner swap of any kind. He backed the government's view that Canada's extradition treaty with the US is sacrosanct, not to be messed with to placate the Chinese, as painful as that implication would be for the Two Michaels. "Canada is a sovereign nation. We signed a treaty with another sovereign government. They've asked us to invoke it. We've invoked it," Mulroney said. "And that's what the Canadian government did. And so, to that extent we were like innocent bystanders in this. We were faithfully executing our assigned obligation to an international friend and partner."

But Mulroney also realized more needed to be done, and he drew a sharp parallel with how he and his fellow world leaders dealt with the former Soviet Union in the 1980s as they waged their final diplomatic battles of the Cold War, history-making overtures that would ultimately bring down the Berlin Wall. They needed to form a unified front behind the only country that had the power to take the lead and confront the Soviets directly: the United States.

"The only way to deal with the Soviet Union, which was aggressive, militaristic nuclear missiles pointed at us and our allies—was to really form a common front. Everybody would support the United States. NATO, NORAD, you name it," said Mulroney.

Mulroney was in the room when US President Ronald Reagan confronted Russian President Mikhail Gorbachev. "He said to him, 'Look, our position is very simple. We win, you lose.' And he kept that position. And they kept the pressure on. And the Cold War was won without a shot being fired."

Similarly, Mulroney believed the time has come for Trudeau to push US President Joe Biden "to give him that same kind of support, influence and power" to take the lead and directly confront China about reigning in its provocations, notably its military build-up in the South China Sea and its sabre-rattling against Taiwan.

This is how Mulroney envisioned the conversation between Biden and Xi:

"Look, I'm getting calls from everybody from the Philippines to you name it. The hegemony you seek to cast over your area, and the trouble in the seas, this has got to stop. This is uncivilized behavior, and we're not going to tolerate it."

After that tough conversation, Biden would add: "by the way, as an indication of your civility, I'd like to leave here with those two Canadians that were jailed. And I would urge you strongly to listen to me."

Days after the Mulroney interview, the Biden administration did indeed engage China on its own turf, in a meeting in the port city of Tianjin, but it was not the high-level showdown that the former Canadian prime minister envisioned. The US dispatched deputy secretary of state Wendy Sherman. China countered with its vice foreign minister, Xie Feng. Sherman raised ongoing US concerns about human rights violations in Hong Kong, Tibet, and Xinjiang. Xie blamed the US for seeing China as its "imaginary enemy" and blamed the Americans for the "stalemate" between them. Xie also made a very significant, and unexpected request: he called on the United States to abandon its extradition case against Meng in British Columbia.[4]

* * *

The way Robert Spalding sees it, the West is sleepwalking through the early days of a new Cold War with China over the future of information technology, control of the internet, and the very survival of democracy itself. The retired brigadier general and senior fellow at the Hudson Institute, a right-leaning Washington think-tank,

raised red flags about China's rise while serving the Obama admin-
istration in the Pentagon and on Trump's national security team.
Like Mulroney, Spalding draws parallels with the original Cold
War, particularly one of its most tense flashpoints: the 1960 shoot-
down by the Soviets the American U-2 spy plane flown by Francis
Gary Powers.

The American pilot had flown northwards across Central Asia
from a secret American airbase in Pakistan. Soviet radar detected a
plane that was supposed to be undetectable and shot it down. Powers
ejected from his burning aircraft and parachuted to safety, but he
was quickly arrested. He was imprisoned and stood trial, accused
of espionage. He pleaded guilty and was sentenced to three years in
prison and seven years of hard labour. But Powers would serve only
twenty-one months in Soviet prison. He gained freedom in one of
the time-honoured transactions of the Cold War: a prisoner swap.

Powers' dramatic walk to freedom in February 1962 is depicted
in the 2015 Steven Spielberg film, *Bridge of Spies*, that starred Tom
Hanks. Powers was swapped for imprisoned KGB spy Rudolf Abel
on the Glienicke Bridge that connected East Germany to West
Berlin. In Spalding's view, the Two Michaels would only come home
if Canada and the United States cross a metaphorical bridge of their
own: they must come to the realization that the rule of law, as they
know it, means nothing to China and the time has come to accept
the new geopolitical reality and negotiate a prisoner swap.

Spalding said Meng is nothing more than a Chinese spy, and
Beijing wants someone they view as a political prisoner returned to
them. "We tried to treat it as a purely legal thing. And that's not the
way the Chinese see it," Spalding said in an August 2021 interview.
"The whole thing is ridiculous on its face. We don't believe what
they're saying. They don't believe what we're saying. It's kind of this
holier-than-thou thing . . . We know that the Chinese don't have real
rule of law. Everybody knows that."

Spalding rejected any suggestion that the West would be compromising its democratic principle or its faith in its legal traditions. Instead, Canada, the US, and their allies should affirm their sovereignty and security in the face of China's weaponization of the internet and emerging 5G technology. In Spalding's view, these are much greater threats, along with Chinese attempts to subvert democracy, drive wedges between allies, and sow socio-economic unrest in the West.

Kovrig and Spavor are by no means spies, as Powers was, Spalding emphasized. "It's really about: how do we take care of our citizens?" He noted that when Francis Gary Powers returned home in 1962, he was welcomed as a hero. "These Two Michaels are heroes of the free world, and they have suffered," he said. "That's what we have to recognize: that they're basically the first Gary Powers of the second Cold War."

* * *

As the Two Michaels sat in prison, a number of prominent Canadians, impatient with the seemingly endless snakes-and-ladder game before the Canadian courts, argued that Canada should take the matter firmly in its own hands.

Derek Burney, a former Canadian ambassador to the US under Brian Mulroney, called on Canada to push the United States further on the issue. Burney said Canada needed to take a tougher stance with its southern neighbour to finally repatriate the Two Michaels. "The matter should not be left to dangle for years on end before the courts while the Two Michaels languish in jail. Canada should bring the matter to an end by telling the Americans they have thirty days to fix the problem in their own judicial system or we will intervene in the legal process and let Meng go free in exchange for the Two Michaels."[5]

Former hostage Robert Fowler was just as strident in his opposition to enlisting American help to solve what he sees as a Canadian problem. "Aside from the horrible damage being done to these two totally innocent guys, the thing I find most upsetting is this idea that the Americans or any number of foreign friends should somehow be responsible for fixing this for us. This is preposterous. This is our problem."[6] Fowler argued Ottawa should use its ministerial prerogative to intervene and end the Meng extradition proceeding, even if it offends the Biden administration.

A prisoner swap, of course, requires buy-in from both sides. Beyond vague innuendo, China had not publicly committed to trading the Two Michaels for Meng's release. Trudeau and his cabinet maintained from day one that they were not interested in doing deals; the rule-of-law is sacrosanct. Trudeau further maintained that a swap would endanger all Canadian travellers by making them possible targets.

It was also argued by some that even if Canada were to unilaterally set Meng free, it might not benefit the Two Michaels. Canadian senator Yuen Pau Woo understands China better than most Canadians. For many years, he headed the Vancouver-based Asia Pacific Foundation of Canada, Canada's premier think tank on Asia. Before that, he worked as an economist with the financial arm of the Singapore government where he had extensive dealings with China. He has an intuitive understanding of the Chinese viewpoint, and cautioned that a bilateral resolution of the Meng issue between the United States and China would not necessarily compel Beijing to free the Two Michaels. He told a student audience at Carleton University in the spring of 2021: "It will be extremely difficult for the Chinese to suddenly spring free Michael Spavor and Michael Kovrig, if we essentially say that this is bullshit, you know, your system is [corrupt], we just don't believe any of it and it's totally illegitimate. I think that it is going to be very difficult for the Chinese to spring them free because it would be basically recognizing that the Canadian side was right." [7]

Woo sparked controversy with a speech in the Senate in June 2021 in which he said Canada should stop criticizing China's human rights record because of its own poor treatment of Indigenous people. Woo's remarks came as Canadians were facing the shocking discoveries of mass graves of children who died at former residential schools decades ago. He was widely seen as parroting Beijing's line, which was to tell Canada to stop its accusations that China was abusing the human rights of its Uyghur Muslim population. Trudeau, who appointed Woo to the Senate five years earlier, denounced Woo's parallel. "In Canada, we had a truth and reconciliation commission," Trudeau said. "Where is China's truth and reconciliation commission? Where is their truth? Where is the openness that Canada has always shown and the responsibility that Canada has taken for the terrible mistakes of the past, and indeed, many of which continue into the present?"[8]

Whatever the difficulties, Canadian public opinion, by the summer of 2021, was warming to the notion of a prisoner swap to secure the freedom of the Two Michaels. A Nanos poll found that "that far more Canadians are in favour of the prisoner swap than they were when that idea was floated last June." Nanos reported 35 per cent of those surveyed were in favour of the trade, more than double the figure from nine months earlier, while 23 per cent say they are somewhat in support. Twelve per cent of respondents said they somewhat oppose the idea, while 23 per cent oppose it.[9]

As for US involvement, Meng's lawyer, Richard Peck, argued that nothing changed in US policy when the Republicans lost the White House to the Democrats in 2020. Joe Biden said that China had reduced Michael Kovrig and Michael Spavor to "bartering chips" in its struggle to free Meng, and that the US would try to free the Two Michaels.

Meanwhile in September 2021, the US, Huawei and Meng's lawyers resumed negotiations towards a possible deferred prosecution agreement. Were they to succeed, Meng would go free, but the fate of the Two Michaels would still hang in the balance.

CHAPTER TWENTY-TWO

Keeping the Faith

NEARING THE END OF HER third year under house arrest, Meng Wanzhou had all but left behind the mundane routine of Vancouver's Courtroom 55, and her ever-present GPS ankle bracelet and pink water bottle. With the outcome of her extradition hearing up in the air, the prospects of her returning to her former life of freedom and corporate globe-trotting were uncertain, at best. If sent to the US, the odds on her conviction would be high. If, on the other hand, she was allowed to return to China, she would have to face President Xi Jinping, who values loyalty to the state above profits and takes a dim view of business leaders who cause him trouble. "China has punished and shamed a series of tycoons who amassed enormous wealth and influence but were seen to overstep their bounds," the *New York Times* reported in April 2021. Those punishments include detentions and imprisonment and, in one case, execution.[1]

Her ordeal in Vancouver seemed at least to have helped Meng's bond with her father, Ren Zhengfei. He said he was proud of how she has held up under house arrest. "In the past, Meng Wanzhou might not give me a single call in a whole year. She wouldn't ask how I was, or even send me a text message," he said. "Now, our relationship has become much closer."

Still, Ren had not lost sight of the larger context that engulfed his family and his company. "She should be proud to have been caught in this situation. In the fight between the two nations, she became a bargaining chip," he says. "The experience of hardship and suffering is good for Meng and her growth. Under the grand backdrop of the . . . trade war, she is like a small ant being caught between the collision of two giant powers."[2]

All the same, Ren had not changed his opinion of Meng's business abilities. One year after her arrest, he was holding firm to the view expressed in his 2013 email: that he lacked a worthy heir within his family to succeed him at the helm of Huawei. He told *CNN Business* that his daughter was able to handle the role of chief financial officer but didn't have a strong enough background in technology and, perhaps more importantly, lacked the mettle of a true leader able to seize the reins of the entire Huawei operation. "Hardships like this one will have a major impact on a person's grit and character. However, when she returns to Huawei, it doesn't mean that she'll be given greater responsibilities." He expected that when Meng came back, "she'll continue to do what she has been doing all along."

* * *

Reflecting on his own experience after being freed as a hostage, Robert Fowler agreed that the that the reintegration challenges a freed hostage faces are huge. "It's so personal," he said twelve years after his own release as he reclined on a patio chair in his garden during the third wave of the COVID-19 pandemic. He recalled arriving at the US military hospital in Landstuhl, Germany, after he and Louis Guay had been freed by al-Qaeda. He was examined by a "thirty-something American shrink" in uniform. The young doctor declared him free of post-traumatic stress disorder. "You've been here thirty-eight seconds," Fowler shot back. "How do you know?"

The physician told him that 25 per cent of people are "essentially hardwired with a propensity, or an openness to PTSD," while the rest simply are not. The doctor broke it down with a stark example: a woman crossing the street has her purse snatched and gets PTSD; another woman is taken hostage by the Hells Angels for six months and doesn't."[3]

As Michael Kovrig and Michael Spavor approached their third anniversaries in captivity, preparations were underway to help them cope with whatever awaited them if and when they found their freedom. The friends and family of Spavor began to consider the challenges he would face as a free man. They realized it would be impossible for him to continue pursuing his passion for North Korea from Chinese soil, which used to be his livelihood. They created a GoFundMe campaign linked to the "Free Michael Spavor" website to raise $45,000 towards helping him restart his life. By late summer 2021, they had raised just over $35,000.

"We have created this GoFundMe to help Michael afford to pay legal costs he is likely to incur and for living costs when he is out. This episode could seriously affect his livelihood, possibly result in deportation and loss of possessions," the appeal said. "Knowing that he has support from outside is lifting Michael's spirits, despite very challenging circumstances. Michael is an earnest, genuine, and impossibly fun person, whom we believe has been detained in error. He deserves better, as does fellow Canadian detainee Michael Kovrig."[4]

In a closed-door proceeding on August 10, 2021, a Chinese court convicted Michael Spavor of spying and sentenced him to eleven years in prison. Counterintuitively perhaps, Spavor's supporters were encouraged by the verdict, seeing a glimmer of hope that he might be deported to serve his sentence in Canada.[5] "While we disagree with the charges," said a statement from Spavor's family, "we realize that this is the next step in the process to bring Michael home, and we will continue to support him through this challenging time."

Meanwhile, tributes, stories, and anecdotes were posted on the "Free Michael Spavor" website. They painted an endearing and entertaining portrait of a man who had an insatiable appetite for life. One friend, D.J. Ouellette, said Spavor was a combination of the young Hollywood actors Bradley Cooper and Chris Pratt, with the manic comedy of Bill Murray. Ouellette recalled a careening tour through Brussels with Spavor in search of the best Belgian chocolate. Spavor played "superlative roles as tour operator, travel guide, interlocutor, sign reader, survey taker, TV host, and comic relief," Ouellette wrote. "That's Michael. Wherever you go with him, there's a (makeshift) plan, but most always a connection, or one about to be made. New city? Know no one? No problem. With Michael, it's never a matter. Can't find your way? Want to know the price? Don't like the menu? Put away your iPhone and ask a stranger, chat up the clerk, and convince the chef to make you something special. Meet. Greet. Go for drinks or run for the door. People. Love them. Envy them. Entertain them. Befriend them. That's Michael. . . . He is loved by many in this world and deserves to be free to roam it again, experience its joy, and be the windy spark that he is."[6]

Spavor's brother Paul recalled the frenzied night that awaited him in South Korea when he first visited. Michael instructed Paul to be wearing a suit when his plane landed late that afternoon. They were going to a garden party at the Dutch embassy. "Why not?" thought Paul. "We are half Dutch, a blessing from our mom. The night led from consular conversations to more casual drinks with other comrade connections." In the early morning hours, drenched in a pouring rain, suitcase in tow, the Spavor brothers finally made it to Michael's apartment. They couldn't find the keys. Michael raced around the corner. "Moments later, a rooftop silhouette appeared, waved and disappeared again into the shadows," wrote Paul. He could hear roof tiles crashing to the ground, and then Michael appeared, victorious, at the front door. That's when they realized the keys were in the pocket of Paul's suitcase. "Never mind that," Paul wrote, "we were home!"[7]

John Glionna, a former *Los Angeles Times* foreign correspondent, wrote about meeting Spavor while stationed in Seoul in 2010. He found the young Canadian exactly the sort of "character" he wanted to get to know: "Michael knew things about the Korean peninsula. He'd been around, knew how things worked. He was like a young scholar who is also fun to have beers with. There's a swagger there, a sense of boundless adventure, but there's also this innocence and empathy. I remember questioning, to myself, his trips to North Korea but I believe in Michael and supported him. This was Michael Spavor; he knew what he was doing. Michael cared about people trapped in a country that has become a little more than a political jail. And now, I am sorry to see, my friend has himself ended up as a political pawn in the hands of the Chinese government."[8]

* * *

Brittany Brown, the International Crisis Group's chief of staff, discussed the efforts to rehabilitate a free Kovrig during a podcast interview with Kovrig's wife, Vina Nadjibulla. At first, Brown said, no one imagined Kovrig would be in detention for several years: "We were thinking, worst case scenario, three months, six months, or me as the optimist was thinking, Okay, we're going to get him out any day, now we're going to get a phone call that says he's on a plane on his way home."

"We started out thinking about the politics behind this," she continued, "and then we started thinking about the places where we could have impact. And we realized that one of the things that's going to be really important is how Michael is when he gets out. We've really spent a lot of energy thinking about preparing for his release. And that means things like everything that Michael has missed over the last two years, we have somebody who keeps a record of what's going on in the world. So that when Michael gets out, he has a record of what happened." That record includes everything from which football team won the World Cup to what has happened to Prince Harry. News, pop culture, "the big things that are happening."

Kovrig's co-workers also wrote him regular letters, quarterly, monthly, weekly, to share their thoughts. "I think we all think this could have been any one of us who happened to be in the wrong place at the wrong time and could have spent two years of our life you know, locked in a small cell," said Brown. "So, we did a lot of research on talking to folks who had been in situations that were similar to what Michael is going through right now. And we found that it was very important for his mental health, to feel connected to the outside world." Kovrig's friends knew that freedom could come as a shock to him. He used to be a private person; now he has become a public figure, and that might be unsettling. "His face is everywhere . . . we all know him now in a way that is pretty intimate . . . we know a lot about this individual who was kind of private. I think it's going to be really important in his healing, and as he tries to begin to reintegrate into the world."[9]

As the Two Michaels neared another dark milestone, one thousand days in captivity, Canada's *Globe and Mail* newspaper in late July 2021 launched a public advocacy campaign: it called on Canadians to mail letters of support for the two imprisoned men directly to its Toronto headquarters. The newspaper said it would forward those "hard copy or digital letters" directly to the Chinese embassy in Ottawa to mark the grim September 5, 2021, anniversary. "Throughout their detention, Mr. Kovrig and Mr. Spavor were interrogated in conditions similar to solitary confinement. Initially, guards even seized Mr. Kovrig's glasses," the newspaper wrote in its call for correspondence.[10]

The *Globe* campaign was one example of how the story of the Two Michaels seized Canadians.

Another came from Patricia Burnett, a songwriter on the Sunshine Coast of British Columbia, who wrote and recorded a plaintive piano ballad that begins *"Dear Michaels, Your journey has been too long, Dear Michaels, Captivity is so wrong, You need to know what's in our hearts, Across the sea so far apart . . ."*

Burnett was not alone in expressing her thoughts in music. Kovrig's former bandmates in Bankrupt continued to follow his case. After he was formally charged by the Chinese, the Hungarians posted on Facebook their view that "the only way out of this situation would be if the Canadian government agreed with the Chinese on a 'prisoner swap.' Let's hope this will happen very soon."[11] And in the summer of 2021, they released a song, "The Plane to Toronto", which they describe as the most important song they've written. It is intended to raise awareness of Kovrig's circumstances, and proceeds from it will go to Hostage International at the request of the prisoner's family. Its lyrics expressed hope that Kovrig would one day escape the nightmare of his "Kafka's Trial" and fly home to Toronto:

> Inside is hell, outside is heaven
> And the lights are on 24/7
> Hold on please, we're gonna get you home
> It's been a long time, but you've never been alone
> You've gotta know, bad times won't last forever[12]

Balazs Sarkadi of Bankrupt said he owed it to his friend to do whatever he could to help him. Because of Kovrig's influence, particularly through books and new musical references, Sarkadi was able to pursue a career as a music journalist in Budapest. "He did so much for me."

Sarkadi last saw his bandmate in April 2017. Kovrig's visit to Hungary happened to coincide with a Bankrupt performance. Their long-lost singer, Michael K., joined them on stage for a rendition of "Listen," without so much as a rehearsal, and nailed it in front of about fifty people crammed into a small club. Afterwards, the friends convened to the venue's upstairs bar for some quiet conversation.[13] Kovrig was on his way to his new job with the International Crisis Group, taking a leave of absence from the Canadian diplomatic corps. He was excited about the new job, and its possibilities. "He was really an idealist," Sarkadi recalled. "He really wants to make the world a better place."

* * *

They came slowly and tentatively at first, strolling over the grassy hill that led down to the main lawn of Windsor Park on the banks of the Rideau River in the Old Ottawa South neighbourhood of the Canadian capital. The rain that was threatening to drench them was holding off early on the Sunday morning of the Labour Day weekend that marked the unofficial end of this second summer of COVID-19. September 5, 2021 also marked one thousand days in captivity for Michael Kovrig and Michael Spavor. The Windsor Park arrivals continued to drift in, their numbers growing, answering the rallying cry on social media to gather and walk seven thousand steps, or roughly five kilometres, in honour of the Two Michaels. It drew upon the monastic ritual that Kovrig performed in his small Chinese prison cell to stay fit and sane.

Among them were the friends and family of the Two Michaels, current and former Canadian diplomats, Canadian senators, the foreign affairs minister and his shadow minister in the opposing political party, ambassadors and high commissioners and their diplomatic staff based in Ottawa from the United States, the European Union,

Germany, Britain, and Australia, and many more men, women and in some cases their children. Soon their numbers swelled to a few hundred, give or take. It was more than the organizers expected.

Pamela Isfeld, the president of the union that represented Canada's foreign-service officers, reminded the crowd that even though Kovrig was on a leave of absence from his government job to join the International Crisis Group, "he is still one of us. And he's not just a respected colleague, he's a beloved personal friend to many of us."

Isfeld said that while she had never met Spavor, "his friends and family are equally devastated by the hardships he is facing as result of his unjust and unfair imprisonment." Isfeld called for elected officials to try to find a way to do more to help them. She said the current impasse "presents our leaders with difficult choices, all of which could have profound consequences. And it's up to them to weigh these options. And we definitely do not envy them this responsibility. However, moments like these provide us with an important reminder that there is also a price to the status quo. And right now, that price is being paid by these two human beings: Michael Kovrig, and Michael Spavor."

Isfeld took note of the presence of Canadian diplomats, past and present, and their international colleagues who had shown up to march.

"As professional diplomats whose work requires us to live and work around the world, my members and I know that any of us could have been in the Two Michaels' shoes. I'm very happy to see as well, a number of diplomats accredited in Ottawa."

One embassy was not represented: China's. The day before the rally, the Chinese ambassador to Canada, Cong Peiwu, spoke on the phone to *The Canadian Press*.

"Recently, we have noted that a small number of people here in Canada have been hyping the so-called one thousand days of the detention of the Two Michaels, who are Canadian citizens, making unwarranted accusations against China's handling of the cases," Cong said. "This has severely interfered in China's traditional sovereignty, gravely violated the norms governing international relations and international law. The Chinese side firmly opposes that."

A few days earlier, the *Global Times*, the newspaper that is an organ of China's communist leadership, had released an "exclusive" story, based on anonymous sources, that reiterated what Dominic Barton, Canada's ambassador to China, had told reporters about a month earlier when Spavor received his eleven-year prison sentence: that Spavor's closed trial had heard evidence that he had photographed airplanes and other military equipment, and that he had shared the information with Kovrig.

Cong was pressed in the interview about whether he had more specific information about what Spavor and Kovrig may have done to violate his country's national security. He said the case had been thoroughly reviewed "by relevant Chinese competent authorities" and pointed to the *Global Times* report. "So, I haven't anything new to add."

Cong reiterated his government's official position that the cases of the Two Michaels and Meng Wanzhou were not linked. "However, I would like to suggest, as I always point out, that if the Canadian side takes resolute matters to correct its mistake and release Madame Meng at an early date, it will surely help the relationship between our two countries go back to normal."

In an interview before the march, Vina Nadjibulla, Kovrig's wife, reiterated what she had long been saying: that neither of the Two Michaels were spies, and that they had done nothing wrong. She renewed her push for the Canadian and American governments to do more to bring the Two Michaels home. She pointed to the upcoming G20 and United Nations Climate Change summits that were set for later in the fall of 2021. Both would bring the leaders of Canada, the United States, and China together face to face. Maybe, she hoped, they could talk it out. Perhaps, they would have a definitive court ruling from the Supreme Court of British Columbia on Meng's extradition to chew on as well.

She was dismissive of the anonymous allegations against Spavor and Kovrig that had surfaced again just days earlier in the Chinese government-controlled newspaper.

"There will be noise," she said. "But the focus since day one has been on bringing them home."

The time had come to mark the one-thousand-day milestone "to honour the strength and resilience that Michael and Michael Spavor have shown," Nadjibulla said.

"In one of his letters, Michael has said that we don't choose our circumstances. But we do have a choice in how we handle ourselves in those circumstances."

So it was that Nadjibulla waded into the growing throngs at Windsor Park with Paul Spavor, Michael Spavor's brother. Their families had forged a resilient bond of solidarity out of the public eye during the past one thousand days. It had been more than a year since Nadjibulla came out publicly to voice her concerns and begin her advocacy to free the Two Michaels. On this day, Paul Spavor ripped off that bandage, joined by several family members, as he offered his first public description of the pain that his family had been enduring. Minutes later, he was in front of the small scrum of journalists, holding court for the first time.

"He's very thankful for all the attention that everyone has had for him," Paul Spavor said. "It's difficult. One thousand days is a long time, and it wears on us, and particularly our father." He said it was important to mark the one-thousand-day milestone. "And Michael has come to understand the global profile of the whole situation. So, he's become a little more willing to have us speak."

Spavor said his brother was also coping with his predicament in similar ways to Kovrig. "He spends a lot of his time reading, meditating, yoga."

Spavor said he believed the government was doing everything it could to help his brother.

"They've been terrific. They've been very supportive. We've got great communication with a number of people. They've been working very hard for a very long time. We all know it's not a simple situation. But they've all been working very hard."

A few minutes later, Spavor was on a small stage, speaking to the assembled marchers through a loudspeaker. "It's important to mark this day. It's just another day, but it's another day that goes by without our Michaels being back with us. It's not an easy march for us," he said, reminding the crowd it was a difficult situation for his family "and especially for our father."

Spavor told the gathering that his family was drawing strength from their support "from all of you, from all the support we get from the government, from individuals from everyone around the world."

And he had a message from his brother about the outpouring of international support: "Michael is appreciative of that. He says he's in good spirits and very appreciative of all of this support that he gets."

Spavor ended his first public speech on behalf of his imprisoned brother with a quotation from Rudyard Kipling. He read this line to the crowd: "If you can fill the unforgiving minute with sixty seconds' worth of distance run, yours is the Earth . . ." The line comes near the end of Kipling's famous poem, "If", which at its essence is a meditation on overcoming adversity and staying true to oneself. Spavor ended his quotation just before reaching the end of the poem.

Spavor told the crowd he didn't want to say anything else after he chose to leave them with the truncated Kipling quote; he said he wanted "everyone to just reflect on that as we walk today, and we carry great hope for what we hope will come soon."

Spavor then gave the microphone to Nadjibulla. She told the Ottawa gathering that they were being joined in similar marches around the world—Brussels, Budapest, New York, Washington, Seoul and Singapore, as well as in Canada, in Calgary, Vancouver, and Toronto. Social media feeds would bolster her list with accounts of marches big and small in Canadian missions in far-flung locales such as Morocco and Laos, among others.

"I also would like to thank political leaders who are here today. It means a lot. And your presence here underscores what we have felt all along that Canadians and all political parties in this country are united in our call to bring them home," she said. "And our recognition that this is unjust, arbitrary and has to be brought to an end . . . I'd also like to note that this is not about partisanship or politics. This is about two Canadians, two innocent individuals and their families and everybody who loves them and cares for them and wants to bring them home."

Korvig, she said, "knows this event is happening" and was finding it a source of strength.

"He has faced the humiliations, the injustice, with dignity, remarkable strength," she said. "His humour is alive and that gives us a lot of reassurance.

"One of the things that he does in his cell, in his windowless small cell, every day is to pace seven thousand steps. He walks in circles, seven thousand steps, often holding a book reading, reciting songs, prayers, five kilometers of courage, prayer, and contemplation.

"And today, he will not be alone in that walk. We will accompany him."

And then they did.

The Ottawa marchers set out slowly in their orderly column through a gentrified downtown Ottawa neighbourhood, crossing traffic with the help of a police escort before reaching the closed Colonel By Drive on the east side of the Rideau Canal. They continued north as the familiar skyline of the Canadian capital came into view, the castle-like façade of the Chateau Laurier Hotel, the Peace

Tower on Parliament Hill partially obscured by a crane. The rain held off until they reached their endpoint at Major's Hill Park, the leafy treed expanse behind the hotel that overlooks the canal's intersection with the Ottawa River and the distant Gatineau Park foothills in the province of Quebec. The dark clouds above finally surrendered their rain. The downpour was short but heavy. And then it ended.

Nadjibulla offered one more thank-you to the crowd as she stood with the Spavors, and Kovrig's family members, including his sister Ariana Botha. They posed for a final round of photos with their banner and rejoined the crowd for more conversations and goodbyes.

A lone male voice started chanting: "Bring them home!" More voices immediately joined, and they grew into a fast-paced rhythmic chorus of voices and handclaps. "Bring them home, bring them home, bring them home . . ."

As if on cue, a flock of Canada geese flew across the sky in perfect formation and ascended westward somewhere towards Parliament Hill and the Ottawa River, a reminder of the soon-to-be changing season and the unstoppable flow of time.

Hours earlier, as he was about to end his first media scrum, Paul Spavor was asked what his hope was for his brother Michael, if he was released from prison one day soon.

"I expect it'll be a long path," he said.

"And that—that's all we know right now."

CHAPTER TWENTY-THREE

"Wonderfully Fantastic"

AFTER MORE THAN A thousand days of conflict and detention, the end came swiftly. Without public notice, Meng Wanzhou appeared by video link in a Brooklyn courtroom shortly after 1:00 p.m. on Friday, September 24. Her face filled the large flat screen television. A deferred prosecution agreement (DPA) between her and the US government was tabled in the United States District Court, Eastern District of New York,[1] the first in a series of carefully orchestrated moves.

The agreement allowed Meng to walk free if she admitted to wrongdoing as spelled out in a statement of facts filed to the court. It boiled down to this: Meng would admit she had misled a Hong Kong bank about the Huawei's relationship with Skycom in Iran, thus removing the bone of legal contention that had kept her under house arrest in Vancouver and the Two Michaels in Chinese prisons since December 2018.

The statement of facts targeted the pivotal August 22, 2013 meeting between Meng and an unnamed executive of a Hong Kong bank to address the allegations in *Reuters* reports earlier that year that Huawei was selling equipment in Iran through Skycom in violation of US law. The statement of facts noted that Meng described Skycom as a "business partner of Huawei" or a "third party" with which her company worked with in Iran.

"Those statements were untrue because, as Ms. Meng knew, Skycom was not a business partner of, or a third party working with, Huawei; instead, Huawei controlled Skycom, and Skycom employees were really Huawei employees."[2]

US Attorney David Kessler told the court that if Meng agreed to the terms of the deal all charges against her would be dropped on December 1, 2022, the fourth anniversary of her arrest in Vancouver.

The deferred prosecution agreement outlined one other key point: the US Department of Justice would "promptly notify the Minister of Justice of Canada that it is withdrawing its request for MENG's extradition."

The agreement was formalized and less than three hours later, Meng was back in person before Associate Chief Justice Holmes for a final court appearance in the British Columbia Supreme Court. Her lead lawyer, Richard Peck, introduced more than half a dozen of her lawyers and apologized for the ones who couldn't be there in person.

John Gibb-Carsley, the Canadian federal prosecutor, rose to address the judge.

"It appears that this extradition proceeding that commenced on December 1, 2018, has now reached its final chapter. The Attorney General of Canada comes before the court to respectfully request an order withdrawing the authority to proceed, discharging Ms. Meng, and vacating the bail order related to this proceeding."

Seven minutes later, after a series of exchanges with Holmes that sealed the matter, and after thanking various court officials and his legal opponents, Gibb-Carsley was done.

Holmes looked over at Meng's legal team.

"Mr. Peck, anything that you wish to respond to?" she asked. "Not suggesting you should."

Peck echoed the thanks of his colleagues and didn't push his luck.

Holmes turned to Meng and voiced her appreciation for the defendant's being "cooperative and courteous throughout the proceedings."

Meng replied in English: "Thank you, my lady."

With that, the judicial juggernaut known as the "United State of America versus Meng Wanzhou" was stopped in its tracks.

Moments later, Meng was standing free outside the Vancouver courthouse. She said she appreciated the court for its "professionalism and the Canadian government for upholding the rule of law." She lamented how her life had been turned "upside down" because of the case. "It was a disruptive time for me as a mother, a wife, and a company executive. But I believe every cloud has a silver lining. It was really an invaluable experience in my life. The greater the difficulty, the greater the growth."

She turned to leave, without taking questions.

* * *

Six months before these events, ambassador Dominic Barton had travelled from his post in Beijing to Washington to spend several weeks promoting discussions toward a deal among Meng's lawyers, the US Justice Department, and Huawei. It was no easy task. The issue was not a high priority in Washington at the time. Also, Huawei needed to be guided through the gamesmanship of criminal proceedings and plea bargaining, which was familiar territory to most US companies but not a Chinese multinational. Earlier efforts by Meng's lawyers in December 2020 to negotiate a deferred prosecution agreement while Trump was still in office had gone nowhere because Meng refused a guilty plea which was key to any deal.

Working with Kirsten Hillman, Canada's ambassador to the US, Barton pushed hard in the weeks after newly elected President Joe Biden and Prime Minister Justin Trudeau held their initial video summit. In their first phone call, Trudeau offered Biden his congratulations and was direct about doing something to help the Two Michaels. The Canadians were hopeful that the new administration would revisit the case with fresh eyes, although they were well aware of the political pressure Biden faced to keep the White House at arms-length from the Department of Justice. Biden came to power determined to rebuild public trust in American institutions, and undoing Trump's politicization of the justice department, which he attempted to run as his private law firm, was near the top of his list. Barton's efforts to find some sort of legal resolution to Meng's case faltered at that red line: the US Department of Justice was off limits to the White House.

Barton returned to Beijing empty-handed and disappointed at the reluctance of the Biden administration to move. One Canadian source with direct knowledge of the talks put it this way: "Things were made more difficult because Biden became more Catholic than the Pope about the Justice Department, trying to distinguish himself from Trump's interference with the administration of justice."[3]

As spring turned to summer, Canadian officials sensed a return to the old stalemate. The consensus was that there was no end in sight.

Behind the scenes, however, the US government had not given up on finding a way out of the Meng impasse. With a fall season of international summitry ahead—meetings that would include awkward photo-ops between Biden and Xi Jinping—both sides were motived to find a way out. The Americans knew the issue was important to the Chinese, not least because the Trump administration had delivered the Meng indictment three years earlier while President Xi was on the world stage at the G20 summit in Argentina. In a part of the world where maintaining "face"—面子 or miànzi—is culturally ingrained, the timing could not have been worse. When Xi learned of Meng's arrest he was livid. He took it personally, and he couldn't believe it happened. One Canadian government official described his view as: "We can't allow another country to take one of our senior executives."[4] As the years wore on, Xi's anger diminished and he became more amenable to finding a way out of the impasse which was undermining China's efforts to burnish its soft power credentials and pursue its broader international ambitions. Beijing also wanted to clean the slate before the 2022 Olympic Winter Games in Beijing

The turning point came over the summer when the British Columbia Supreme Court finished hearing evidence in Meng's marathon extradition hearing. Despite the Herculean efforts of her lawyers, it became apparent that her chances of avoiding extradition were slim. Associate Chief Justice Heather Holmes was due to return to court on October 21 to announce the date of her ruling. That deadline, some Canadian officials believed, increased Meng's interest in a deferred prosecution agreement and sped up negotiations.

While the Trump hangover was leading the White House to tread "extraordinarily carefully" on all matters relating to the Department of Justice, according to a senior US government official, there was a desire within the department to re-examine the merits of the Meng case as the new administration settled in.[5] Huawei's conduct was viewed as illegal but there was a growing realization that other banks and institutions that had run afoul of the Iran sanctions weren't being treated the same way. Troubled by elements of the Meng indictment, federal justice officials began to warm to the idea of a deferred prosecution agreement.

American and Chinese diplomats were soon discussing end-game scenarios. Wendy Sherman, the US deputy secretary of state, and David Meale, who had been assigned to the US embassy in Beijing in July 2021 as chargé d'affaires, were among the tight circle of American officials taking part in the talks, along with such senior

White House officials as national security adviser Jake Sullivan. Barton and Hillman were included in a series of meetings with White House and state department officials. Barton knew some of the key members of the administration from his days as head of McKinsey. The Two Michaels also had their personal champion in Robert Malley, Michael Kovrig's former boss at the International Crisis Group, who was Biden's special adviser on Iran. He remained keenly interested in their fate.

On September 9, 2021, Biden and Xi held a ninety-minute telephone call that the White House described in a public statement as a "broad strategic discussion in which they discussed areas where our interests converge, and areas where our interests, values and perspectives diverge."[6] China's accounts of the conversation characterized it as "candid and in-depth" and reported that Xi told Biden that American policies were causing China serious difficulties. Xi wanted to see relations between the two countries "get back on the right track," according to CCTV, the Chinese state broadcaster.[7] Biden pressed the Two Michaels case with Xi, although there was no mention of a deferred prosecution agreement.

Less than two weeks later, on September 21, China's desire to resolve the Meng situation was hinted at publicly for the first time. In his address to the UN general assembly, Xi said: "China has never and will never invade or bully others, or seek hegemony. China is always a builder of world peace, contributor to global development, defender of the international order and provider of public goods."[8]

As Chinese and American officials discussed the terms of a possible deal, they treated Meng's circumstances and those of the Two Michaels as entirely distinct. Rather than admit to a prisoner swap, they floated scenarios: *if this happened, what would happen next?* As the talks progressed, it was clear that the justice department was by now firmly behind a deferred prosecution agreement and that the

Chinese were ready for a resolution, but one large obstacle remained. The two sides simply didn't trust each other. Hence the carefully orchestrated chain of events that unfolded in that crucial twenty-four-hour period beginning on September 24.[9]

With the final details of the deferred prosecution agreement ironed out the previous evening, Meng was scheduled to make her back-to-back court appearances on September 24 and leave Vancouver on a chartered Air China jet late in the afternoon. Within a minute of her taking off, Kovrig and Spavor would board a charted jet out of Tianjin, accompanied by Barton, which flew them to Anchorage, Alaska, where they were met by two Canadian Forces Challenger jets—an extra one on hand in case one of them developed a mechanical failure.

As reported by Chinese state-owned media, the two men were discharged on bail for "medical reasons" but had to confess first to their crimes by writing confession and repentance letters. They also had to "strictly abide by the decision on bail" and if they violated the terms of their release China would "resume the trial of the alleged criminal acts."[10] Despite these announcements, intended for domestic political consumption, the Two Michaels signed nothing other than their medical discharge papers.

The exchange of the captives dominated the Chinese foreign ministry's daily press briefing two days later. A spokeswoman called Meng's arrest a "political frame-up and persecution against a Chinese citizen, an act designed to hobble Chinese high-tech companies as represented by Huawei." She also said that Meng was "arbitrarily detained" by Canada. President Xi was said to have given "personal guidance" on resolving the matter.

Canada also shaped the story for domestic political consumption. Kirsten Hillman denied in a television interview on CTV's *Question Period* that there was a quid-pro-quo with the Chinese to release the Two Michaels.[11]

"Two things happened simultaneously," Hillman explained. "The [deferred prosecution agreement] and the resolution to charges against Ms. Meng was a completely independent process. As the resolution for Ms. Meng was heading towards success and the parties to that discussion felt they were heading towards success, the Chinese government made its decision. And its decision was that it was no longer in its interest to continue holding the Michaels. They started the process in talking to our officials in Beijing about making arrangements about having the Michaels leave."

Hillman added that the Chinese government was feeling "incredible pressure" from Canada, the US, and their allies, both publicly and privately, to release the Two Michaels. "I think the Chinese government decided it was time to put this behind them and move on."

A US official sees the resolution somewhat differently. If American prosecutors were willing to shift their position on the Meng case, the Chinese would be required to respond "immediately" on the Two Michaels. That amounted to "wheels up, as opposed to, we'll look at this and review it over the course of the next month."[12]

The result was the simultaneous departure of two airplanes heading in opposition directions across the Pacific Ocean at 7:30 p.m., eastern time.

Prime Minister Justin Trudeau arrived in the West Block of Parliament Hill for a hastily called press conference a little more than an hour after the two planes took off.

"About twelve minutes ago, the aircraft carrying Michael Kovrig and Michael Spavor left Chinese airspace and they're on their way home," he announced to the world. "These two men have gone through an unbelievably difficult ordeal. For the past thousand days, they have shown strength, perseverance, resilience and grace and we are all inspired by that. I want to thank their families who have been there for them, supporting them in every way they could and supporting us in the work we've done to secure their release."

The prime minister thanked the "countless diplomats" and "our allies and partners around the world and the international community who've stood steadfast in solidarity with Canada and with these two Canadians."

"And finally, I want to thank Canadians who have kept them in our thoughts and remain determined in the core value that Canadians have of standing up for each other and looking out for each other. These two men have been through an unbelievably difficult situation, but it is inspiring, and it is good news for all of us that they are on their way home to their families."

The question of just where the resolution of Meng and the Two Michaels left relations between the West and China was allowed to dangle in the air. "I know that there is going to be time for reflections and analysis in the coming days and weeks," said Trudeau, "but the fact of the matter is I know Canadians will be incredibly happy to know right now, this Friday night, Michael Kovrig and Michael Spavor are on a plane and they're coming home."

* * *

Part of the answer to the future of US relations with China can be gleaned from Meng's deferred prosecution agreement, or at least what was left out of the document. Although it allowed Meng to go free, Huawei remains in America's legal crosshairs. There was no sign that the Biden administration was going to drop its charges or relax pressure on US allies to boycott Huawei from their 5G networks. If anything, Meng's admissions in her DPA will only strengthen the American legal case moving forward.

US Commerce Secretary Gina Raimondo told the *Wall Street Journal* before the prisoners were released that the US was going to continue its campaign to block Huawei from getting advanced computer chips for its 5G telecommunications gear, despite the fact that US authorities had decided a month earlier to allow Huawei to buy chips for its auto component business.[13]

President Biden's desire to stabilize relations with China and put them on a sustainable course after their steady deterioration during the Trump presidency will not change the fact that tensions remain between the nations on trade and technology, and on Taiwan and Hong Kong. These will not be easily resolved. Complicating matters further is Washington's new military alliance with Australia and the United Kingdom. Including a deal to sell nuclear-powered submarines to Australia, and clearly designed to counter China, it has not been well received in Beijing.[14]

The structural differences between the US and China remain profound. A US official said his government will focus on working more closely with its allies in the intelligence community on dealing with potential bad behaviour from Huawei and China. It is likely America will be "doubling down" on its investments in artificial intelligence, 5G, robotics and micro processing, "trying to run faster" than the Chinese in these crucial sectors.[15]

The fundamental trajectory of relations between the nations, then, still appears to many observers as headed for a new Cold War. And as former US Homeland Security Secretary Michael Chertoff notes, the outcome of the Meng affair may have created as much of a problem as it resolved: it will simply "embolden the Chinese government to view holding foreigners hostage as an effective negotiating tactic."[16][17]

As for Canada, its relationship with China has been broken since the Meng arrest. That albatross has been removed but diplomacy won't return to where it was before. As much as Trudeau, early in his government, wanted a stronger and more stable partnership with China, the battles over Meng and Canada's own trade disputes with China have left a residue of bitterness and suspicion that will not soon vanish.

The Trudeau government will have tough choices to make on how to deal with China on trade, investment, security, and technology, including Huawei's future in Canada. The Americans are also seeking clarity in Canada's position. That was underlined by remarks from Biden's nominee for ambassador to Canada, Comcast executive David L. Cohen, former chair of the board of the Jewish Federation of Greater Philadelphia, and a Democratic Party fundraiser. In his late September Senate nomination hearing, Cohen pointedly stated, "We are all waiting for Canada to release its framework for its overall China policy . . . As ambassador, if I'm confirmed, it's an appropriate role to be engaged in discussions and make sure that Canada's policies reflect its words in terms of the treatment of China."[18]

The Canadian government struck a theme of mutual co-existence post Meng. In remarks to Canadian media, Canadian foreign minister Marc Garneau said, "We will co-operate in areas where we need to co-operate such as climate change . . . And we will challenge China, whether it's on human rights or whether it's on arbitrary detention, when appropriate."[19] Canada's ambivalence was echoed in China where media announced that "Meng's release has brought a potential opportunity for reflection and adjustment of the relations among China, the US, and Canada," yet also warned darkly that "the entire Chinese society is psychologically prepared for worse ties with Washington."[20]

Whatever path the Trudeau government takes, it will have to tread carefully and look out for Canada's national interests while avoiding another turn as a pawn in the struggle for geopolitical supremacy between China and the United States. That is the crucial lesson of the saga of the Two Michaels.

* * *

If there was ever any doubt that Meng Wanzhou was considered royalty in China, the homecoming she received after her plane arrived in Shenzhen erased it. Having changed into a bright red dress, the official colour of her country, she appeared at the open door of the Air China 777 and paused to take in the welcome. Below her on the tarmac was a noisy, enthusiastic throng of about one hundred people. A red carpet had been rolled out. Music was blaring. A huge digital sign welcomed her home. Meng waved regally to her greeters and slowly descended the staircase. She was handed two separate bouquets of flowers by men in hazmat suits. China's ambassador to Canada, Cong Peiwu, who was on the flight with Meng, stood behind her.[21] The spectacle served as a reminder of the political dynamite that Canada had been handed in 2018 when the US government made its treaty request to arrest her in Vancouver.

On the plane ride over, Meng penned a note that read: "Under the leadership of the Chinese Communist Party, our motherland is becoming more glorious; without the might of the motherland, I would not have today's freedom."[22] She developed that theme after she arrived at a waiting microphone to address her supporters. Her remarks in Mandarin were broadcast to an estimated 100 million Chinese viewers. She paid tribute to Xi Jinping. "Chairman Xi cares about the safety of every Chinese citizen, and he also has my situation in his heart. I am deeply touched by this," she said.[23] "I have finally returned to the warm embrace of the motherland. As an ordinary Chinese citizen going through this difficult time, I always felt the warmth and concern of the party, the nation, and the people."

Meng departed and disappeared from public view to begin her mandatory COVID-19 quarantine.

China's foreign ministry issued a statement to mark her return. It was vintage Wolf Warrior, sounding as if the deferred prosecution agreement and the drama of the twin courtroom appearances a day earlier had never happened: "It has long been a fully proven fact that this in an incident of political persecution against a Chinese citizen, an act designed to hobble Chinese high-tech companies.

The so-called 'fraud' charges against Ms. Meng Wanzhou are purely fabricated. Even HSBC, the so-called 'victim' portrayed by the US side, has disclosed materials that are sufficient to prove Ms. Meng's innocence. What the United States and Canada have done is a typical case of arbitrary detention."

The statement made no mention of the Two Michaels.

* * *

At 6:00 a.m. on the morning of September 25, a Canadian Forces Challenger jet touched down in the darkness of Calgary's international airport, putting Michael Spavor and Michael Kovrig on Canadian soil for the first time in a very long time. They had been given only a few hours notice of their release before leaving China. Spavor sped down the staircase of the jet, followed by Kovrig. They walked together across the tarmac towards a waiting car and a man in a white shirt. Prime Minster Justin Trudeau exchanged hugs and elbow bumps with Kovrig and Spavor. With Barton and others standing by under the whir of idling jet engines, they spoke for several minutes. After the conversation, Kovrig dropped down into a push-up and kissed the ground.

Television cameras captured Spavor as he walked from the airport's private terminal building towards a waiting SUV to begin a new chapter of his life as a free man in his hometown of Calgary. He was wearing a gray blazer, black dress pants, and a white mask. He caught a glimpse of the cameras, gave an enthusiastic wave, and flashed a thumbs up before disappearing into the vehicle.

Kovrig climbed back into the jet for the plane ride to Toronto, just as his old bandmates had envisioned in their song. Later that day, he touched down at Toronto's Pearson airport and found his wife, Vina Nadjibulla, waiting for him on the tarmac. He saw her, set down his black backpack and a yellow plastic shopping bag bearing a LEGO logo, and took her in his arms. They held each other for thirty seconds. It seemed much longer.

A phalanx of journalists and their cameras waited patiently for Kovrig on the tarmac on the opposite side of a chain link fence. Dressed in a black t-shirt and jeans, he walked casually toward them, with Nadjibulla and his sister, Ariana Botha, at his side, and Dominic Barton trailing a few paces behind. Peeling away his white mask, Kovrig smiled broadly and spoke his first words to his fellow Canadians: "It's wonderfully fantastic to be back home in Canada."

"We'll have more for you later," he added in response to a series of shouted questions. Canadians would be hearing from him, but not on this day.

He smiled, turned, and, arm in arm with his wife and sister, began the long process of putting his 1,020-day ordeal behind him.

ACKNOWLEDGEMENTS

THE BOOK BENEFITED GREATLY from the insights, observations, and support of many people. We would like to acknowledge Vina Najibullah, who fought valiantly to secure the release of Michael Kovrig and Michael Spavor and to continuously remind Canadians and their government of their plight. Brian Mulroney, Allan Rock, Brian Greenspan, Robert Fowler, Robert Spalding, Len Edwards, Balazs Sarkadi, Karim Lebhour and Derek Burney, as well as many others who have chosen to remain anonymous also gave generously of their time to discuss key events and offer their own insights into the case of the Two Michaels. In course of writing this book and threading the needle on key events, we have also benefited enormously from the outstanding reporting of our colleagues in the media and have done our best to duly credit it. This includes Andy Blatchford, formerly of *The Canadian Press* and now of *Politico*, as well as Jim Bronskill, James McCarten, Amy Smart, and Laura Dhillon Kane of *The Canadian Press*, the *Globe and Mail's* Robert Fife, Steven Chase and Nathan VanderKlippe, the CBC's Jason Proctor, as well as international reportage from the BBC, *Reuters*, the *New York Times*, the *Washington Post* and elsewhere.

The Donner Foundation deserves special thanks for its financial support that allowed one of the authors, Mike Blanchfield, to take a leave of absence from *The Canadian Press* to work on the book. David Reevely, the former Ottawa bureau chief of *The Canadian*

Press, deserves special thanks for wholeheartedly approving that leave of absence. Blanchfield has covered the Meng-Two Michaels affair for *CP* since December 2018. Hampson has been a close student of Canadian foreign policy for many years, including Canada's relations with China, and the geopolitics of internet governance. Blanchfield remains forever grateful for the support and sacrifices of his wife, Kathy Cook, and their two young daughters during this memorable pandemic project. Hampson thanks his own family and colleagues for their support.

We offer a very special thanks to our publisher Sutherland House President Kenneth Whyte for believing in this project at the outset and encouraging us to pursue this story down its many different avenues. His wise counsel, incisive editorial guidance, and intuitive narrative storytelling talents have been critical in turning the manuscript into what we hope is a highly compelling account of two innocent Canadians who became the first victims in the new Cold War rivalry between the United States and China. We are also grateful to Sutherland House's Managing Editor Matthew Bucemi for his valuable editorial guidance and for keeping us on a tight writing and production schedule, and to Christopher Anthony for his research assistance.

This book is also our own "letter" to Michael Kovrig and Michael Spavor, with the hope they will have the opportunity to read it one day and gain some insight into the broad geopolitical reasons behind their imprisonment and learn what so many were doing to win their freedom.

NOTES

CHAPTER ONE

1 Jason Proctor, "RCMP officer who arrested Meng Wanzhou says he knew case was 'high profile,'" *CBC*, October 26, 2020.
2 Ibid.
3 Ibid.
4 Ibid.
5 The Canadian Press, "A timeline of events in the case of Meng Wanzhou," *National Post*, June 19, 2020.
6 "Affidavit of Constable Winston Yep," *Supreme Court of British Columbia*, November 30, 2018.
7 "MEMORANDUM OF FACT AND LAW: Application for Disclosure," *Supreme Court of British Columbia*, August 22, 2019.
8 Proctor, "RCMP officer who arrested Meng Wanzhou says he knew case was 'high profile.'"
9 Ibid.
10 Ibid.
11 Jason Proctor, "CBSA officer claims Meng Wanzhou was flagged for 'national security' concerns ahead of arrival," *CBC*, October 28, 2020.
12 Proctor, "CBSA officer claims Meng Wanzhou was flagged for 'national security' concerns ahead of arrival."
13 David Molko, "What we've learned from the Mounties and border officers who testified in Meng Wanzhou's extradition case," *CTV News*, November 27, 2020.
14 "MEMORANDUM OF FACT AND LAW: Application for Disclosure," *Supreme Court of British Columbia*, August 22, 2019.
15 Ibid.
16 Proctor, "RCMP officer who arrested Meng Wanzhou says he knew case was 'high profile.'"
17 Vipal Monga and Kim Mackrael, "Court Filings Shed New Light on Arrest of Huawei Executive," *The Wall Street Journal*, August 23, 2019.

CHAPTER TWO

1 Jason Proctor, "Status of Huawei CFO's husband question as he tries to post bail for wealthy wife," *CBC*, December 10, 2018.
2 "Affidavit of Wanzhou Meng," *Supreme Court of British Columbia*, December 4, 2018.
3 Ibid.
4 Ibid.
5 "Affidavit of Wanzhou Meng," *Supreme Court of British Columbia*, December 4, 2018.
6 Ibid.
7 BNN Bloomberg, "'Always very confident': Huawei's arrested CFO rose through ranks despite father's rebuke," *BNN Bloomberg*, December 6, 2018.
8 "Affidavit of Wanzhou Meng," *Supreme Court of British Columbia*, December 4, 2018.
9 Nathan VanderKlippe, "Meng Wanzhou: From high-school dropout to CFO and deputy chair at Huawei," *The Globe and Mail*, December 5, 2018.
10 Ibid.
11 Proctor, "Status of Huawei CFO's husband questioned as he tries to past bail for wealthy wife."
12 Richard P. Donoghue, "Re: In the Matter of the Attorney General of Canada on Behalf of the United States of America and Wanzhou Meng," *US Justice Department*, December 3, 2018.
13 *United States v. Meng*, Dec. 11, 2018, British Columbia Supreme Court 2255.
14 Ibid.
15 Ibid.
16 Ibid.
17 Government of Canada Privy Council Office, National Security and Intelligence Advisor to the Prime Minister, *Huawei Extradition Case*, Document No. WEBCIMS # 2018-FDP-00267, December 18, 2018. Document released under Access to Information Act.
18 Jason Proctor, "Meng Wanzhou is out on bail – but could be in legal limbo for years," *CBC*, December 11, 2018.

CHAPTER THREE

1 Amy Smart, "Huawei exec's lawyers call CSIS knowledge of multi-hour delay in arrest 'troubling'," *The Canadian Press*, June 12, 2020.
2 Author email interview.
3 The Canadian Press, "A timeline of events in the case of Meng Wanzhou," *National Post*, June 19, 2020.

4 Author interview.
5 https://gcrecords.bandcamp.com
6 Ibid.
7 "Michael Kovrig," *International Crisis Group*, n.d.
8 Author interview.
9 WION, "WION Gravitas: US & North Korea yet to come up with a roadmap; Was the Singapore Summit a success?" *YouTube*, June 12, 2018.
10 Ibid.
11 Author interview.
12 Author interview.
13 "Who is Michael Spavor?," *Free Michael Spavor*, n.d.
14 Ibid.
15 Jon Dunbar, "China, release our friend," *The Korea Times*, December 20, 2018.
16 "Michael Spavor: The detained Canadian close to Kim Jong-un," *BBC*, March 5, 2019.
17 Josh Smith and David Ljunggren, "Detained in China: Canadian businessman known for ties to North Korean leader," *Reuters*, December 13, 2018.
18 Smith and Ljunggren, "Detained in China."
19 Joshua Berlinger, "Second Canadian detained in China as diplomatic spat intensifies,'" *CNN*, December 13, 2018.
20 Jon Dunbar, "China, release our friend."
21 Ibid.

CHAPTER FOUR

1 Sarah Zheng, "Chinese court sentence Canadian Michael Spavor to 11 years after finding him guilty of spying," *South China Morning Post*, August 11, 2021.
2 Fan Lingzhi and Cao Siqi, "Exclusive: Canadian Spavor took photos, videos of Chinese military equipment, sent them to Kovrig and outside China, source said," *Global Times*, September 1, 2021.
3 "Who is Michael Spavor, the second Canadian to go missing in China?" *National Post*, December 13, 2018.
4 CBC News, "Ottawa could do more to free 2 Canadians jailed in China, Michael Kovrig's wife says," *CBC*, June 22, 2020.
5 Author interview.
6 Author email interview.
7 Peter Humphrey, "The Cruel Fate of Michael Kovrig and Michael Spavor in China," *The Diplomat,* December 10, 2019.
8 Ibid.
9 Ibid
10 Ibid.

11 Ibid.

12 Peter Dahlin, "Dahlin: Forced 'confessions' on TV violate Canadian law. Will Parliament or the CRTC act?," *Ottawa Citizen,* May 17, 2021.

13 Meng Wanzhou, "THERE IS ALWAYS GOOD IN PEOPLE!" *Huawei* press release, December 21, 2018.

14 Michael Bristow, "Meng Wanzhou: The Huawei exec trapped in a gilded cage," *BBC,* January 24, 2019.

15 Ibid.

16 Amanda Coletta, "Time to read and paint: Detained Huawei executive pens poetic letter from house arrest," *Washington Post,* December 2, 2019.

17 Ibid.

CHAPTER FIVE

1 BBC News, "China rights lawyer Pu Zhiqiang's trial ends amid scuffles - BBC News," *YouTube,* December 14, 2015.

2 Ibid.

3 "Michael Kovrig, email to David Hartman, Ram Kamineni, Zeynab Aliyeva," December 22, 2015. Document released under Access to Information Act.

4 Ibid.

5 Ibid.

6 John English, *Just Watch Me: The Life of Pierre Elliott Trudeau, Volume Two: 1968-2000* (Toronto: Alfred A., Knopf, 2009), 58.

7 Minister for International Trade, Secretary of State for External Affairs, Minister for External Relations, Memorandum to Cabinet, *A Canadian Strategy for China,* Document 5-0096-87MC(01), March 16, 1987. Document released under Access to Information Act.

8 Ibid.

9 Ibid.

10 James Rusk, "Mulroney, Chinese Premier Discuss Human Rights, Clergy," *The Globe and Mail,* May 12, 1986.

11 Minister for International Trade, Secretary of State for External Affairs, Minister for External Relations, Memorandum to Cabinet, *A Canadian Strategy for China,* Document 5-0096-87MC(01), March 16, 1987. Document released under Access to Information Act.

12 *The Cabinet Committee on Priorities and Planning, Minutes,* Document 12-89CMPP, June 6, 1989. Document released under the Access to Information Act.

13 *The Cabinet Committee on Foreign and Defence Policy, Minutes,* Document 8-89CMFDP, June 19, 1989. Document released under the Access to Information Act.

14　Ibid.

15　Fen Osler Hampson, *Master of Persuasion: Brian Mulroney's Global Legacy* (Toronto: Penguin Random House Canada, 2018), 87.

16　Ibid.

17　Jonathan Manthorpe, "CHINA TRADE MISSION: Chretien lauds students; PM says they will bring China into 21st century: [VALLEY edition]. *The Ottawa Citizen,* November 8, 1994.

18　Jack Aubry, "PM tackles China justice: A day after saying china's human-rights record is getting better, prime minister Jean Chretien urges China to improve its justice system as a step into the world economic system,"[final edition]. *The Gazette,* February 13, 2001.

19　Mike Blanchfield,"PM turns pitchman on mission to China," [final edition]. *Kingston Whig – Standard,* October 23, 2003.

20　"Jean Chretien's final 10 days," [final edition]. *The Ottawa Citizen,* December 13, 2003.

21　Global Affairs Canada, *Memoranda, telegrams, Cabinet submissions, correspondence and policy briefs regarding the Chretien government's decision to enter into a human rights dialogue with the People's Republic of China,* Number A-2015-01867, Jan. 1, 1997 to May 31, 1997. Documents released under Access to Information Act.

22　Ibid.

23　Ibid.

24　Ibid.

25　Ibid.

26　Global Affairs Canada, *Memoranda, telegrams, Cabinet submissions, correspondence and policy briefs regarding the Chretien government's decision to enter into a human rights dialogue with the People's Republic of China,* Number A-2015-01867, Jan. 1, 1997 to May 31, 1997. Documents released under Access to Information Act.

27　Ibid.

CHAPTER SIX

1　Mike Blanchfield, *Swingback: Getting Along in the World with Harper and Trudeau* (Montreal & Kingston: McGill-Queen's University Press, 2017).

2　Tonda MacCharles, "Harper in China: Free trade agreement with China in Canada's sights?" *Toronto Star,* February 11, 2012.

3　"What does Xi Jinping's China Dream mean?" *BBC,* June 6, 2013.

4　David Dollar, "Seven years into China's Belt and Road," Brookings Institution, October 1, 2020.

5　Theresa Fallon, "The New Silk Road: Xi Jinping's Grand Strategy for Eurasia,"

American Foreign Policy Interests: The Journal of the National Committee on American Foreign Policy 37, no. 3 (2015): 140–147.

6 Andrew Chatzky and James McBride, "China's Massive Belt and Road Initiative," Council on Foreign Relations, January 28, 2020.

7 Ibid.

8 Jane Perlez, "Tribunal Rejects Beijing's Claims in South China Sea," *New York Times*, July 12, 2016.

9 "Philippine foreign minister tells China to 'Get the F**k Out' over South China Sea dispute," *CNN*, May 3, 2021.

10 Willy Wo-Lap Lam, *Chinese Politics in the Era of Xi Jinping*, (New York and London: Routledge, 2015), 3.

11 Willy Wo-Lap Lam, *Chinese Politics in the Era of Xi Jinping*, (New York and London: Routledge, 2015), 295.

12 Michael Kovrig, email to David Hartman, Ram Kamineni, Zeynab Aliyeva, December 22, 2015. Document released under Access to Information Act.

13 Ibid.

14 Global Affairs Canada, Human Rights - *Updates (January 2017)*, January 2017. Released under Access to Information Act.

15 Mike Blanchfield and Andy Blatchford, "Influential, misinformed Canadian media hurts China-Canada relations: envoy," *Global News*, July 4, 2017.

16 Christopher Bodeen, "China widens personality cult around 'unrivaled helmsman' Xi," *Associated Press*, November 21, 2017.

17 Andy Blatchford and Mike Blanchfield, "China sees free trade with Canada as way to avoid future Norsat-like uncertainty," *City News*, July 5, 2017.

18 Mike Blanchfield and Andy Blatchford, "China wants no 'progressive' elements in any free trade deal with Canada: envoy," *National Post*, April 10, 2018.

CHAPTER SEVEN

1 John Feng, "'Good Riddance': China Chides Departing German Envoy Over U.N. Remarks," *Newsweek*, December 23, 2020.

2 Global Times, "FM spokesperson leaves post, likely to work for Chinese UN mission," *Global Times*, June 5, 2020.

3 Michelle Nichols, "'Good riddance,' China says as Germany leaves U.N. Security Council," *Reuters*, December 22, 2020.

4 Mike Blanchfield, "'White supremacy' a factor in detainees' cases, Chinese ambassador charges," *CBC*, January 9, 2019.

5 Ibid.

6 Susan Delacourt, "'Nobody is feeling good about' John McCallum's departure, says PMO source," *Toronto Star*, January 26, 2019.

7 Author interview; *Toronto Star*, December 5, 2017.

8 John Paul Tasker, "Canada's ambassador to China says Meng has strong defence to fight extradition," *CBC*, January 23, 2019.
9 Ibid.
10 *Maclean's*, January 24, 2019.
11 The Canadian Press, "McCallum firing leaves Canada's China strategy in disarray," *CTV News*, January 26, 2019.
12 Delacourt, "'Nobody is feeling good about' John McCallum's departure, says PMO source."
13 CBC News, "John McCallum puts Liberals on the defensive again with advice to China," *CBC*, July 11, 2019.

CHAPTER EIGHT

1 The Canadian Press, "On the agenda at the Trudeau cabinet retreat," *Maclean's*, April 24, 2016.
2 Special Committee on Canada-China Relations, House of Commons, "Evidence," Wednesday Feb. 5, 2020, No. 005, 1st Session, 43rd Parliament.
3 Walt Bogdanich and Michael Forsythe, "How McKinsey Has Helped Raise the Stature of Authoritarian Governments," *New York Times*, December 15, 2018.
4 Mike Blanchfield, "Chinese envoy lauds virus co-operation with Canada, amid chill in relationship," *BNN Bloomberg*, February 6, 2020.
5 Mike Blanchfield, "Chinese allow Michael Kovrig call to sick father amid COVID-19," *National Observer*, March 13, 2020.
6 Mike Blanchfield, "'Two Michaels' mark two jailed years in China, no development in their cases," *CTV News*, December 10, 2020.
7 "Bob Rae references George Orwell when it comes to his perspective on China," *Global News*, July 6, 2020.
8 Bob Rae (@BobRae48), "When China accused Canada of "bullying" China because of the extradition issue involving Mme Meng, this was my reply in the 3rd Committee of the UNGA . . .," Twitter, October 9, 2020, 6:23 p.m., https://twitter.com/bobrae48/status/1314692897875341313.

CHAPTER NINE

1 Chrystia Freeland, *Plutocrats: The Rise of the New Global Super-Rich and the Fall of Everyone Else* (New York: Penguin Press, 2012).
2 Yuval Noah Harari, "Yuval Noah Harari & Huawei CEO Ren Zhengfei in Conversation – Davos 2020," *YouTube*, January 22, 2020.
3 Ibid.

4 Ibid.

5 See: Ren Zhengfei, "The key to the future is open collaboration," *The Economist*, September 10, 2019.

6 Yuval Noah Harari, "Yuval Noah Harari & Huawei CEO Ren Zhengfei in Conversation – Davos 2020."

7 See: Li Hongwen, *Ren Zhengfei & Huawei: A Business and Life Biography* (London: LID Publishing.Com, 2017).

8 Rush Doshi, Emily de la Bruyère, Nathan Picarsic, and John Ferguson, "China as a 'cyber great power': Beijing's two voices in telecommunications," Brookings, Washington, DC, April 2021.

9 Klint Finley and Joanna Pearlstein, "The WIRED Guide to 5G," *Wired Business*, September 10, 2020.

10 Ibid.

11 McKinsey Global Institute, *Connected World: An evolution in connectivity beyond the 5G revolution*, Discussion paper, February 2020: iv.

12 Ibid, v.

13 See: Yun Wen, *The Huawei Model: The Rise of China's Technology Giant* (Urbana: University of Illinois Press, 2020).

14 Daniel Araya, "Huawei's 5G Dominance in The Post-American World," *Forbes*, April 5, 2019.

15 Francis Schortgen, "Weaponizing Globalization: Chinese High-Tech in the Crosshairs of Geopolitics," in W. Zhang et al., eds., *Huawei Goes Global* (London: Palgrave Macmillan, 2020), 44.

16 Jean-Marc F. Blanchard, "Helping Hands for Huawei: Dialing into China's Technology Policy to Understand Its Contemporary Support for Huawei," in W. Zhang et al., eds., *Huawei Goes Global* (London: Palgrave Macmillan, 2020), 57.

17 Keith Johnson and Elias Groll, "The Improbable Rise of Huawei," *Foreign Policy*, April 3, 2019.

18 Thomas D. Lairson, The International Political Economy of Huawei's Global and Domestic Environment," in W. Zhang et al., eds., *Huawei Goes Global* (London: Palgrave Macmillan, 2020), 26.

19 Martin Roll, "Huawei – Transforming a Chinese Technology Business to a Global Brand," *Martin Roll*, February 2018.

20 Denise Tsang and David Luigi Fuschi, "A Strategic Assessment of Huawei into the Fast Future," in W. Zhang et al., eds., *Huawei Goes Global* (London: Palgrave Macmillan, 2020), 88.

21 Stacie Hoffmann, Samantha Bradshaw and Emily Taylor, "Networks and Geopolitics: How great power rivalries infected 5G," in Chester A. Crocker, Fen Osler Hampson and Pamela Aall, eds., *Diplomacy and the Future of World Order* (Washington, DC: Georgetown University Press, 2021)

22 Johnson and Groll, "The Improbable Rise of Huawei."

23 Garrett M. Graff, "Inside the Feds' Battle Against Huawei," *Wired*, January 16, 2020.

CHAPTER TEN

1 Hoffman, Bradshaw and Taylor, "Network and Geopolitics."

2 Mark Chandler, "Cisco Suggests Huawei Release Court Report on Intellectual Property Misuse," *Cisco*, October 1, 2012.

3 Supercomm News Analysis, "Huawei in Spying Flap," *Light Reading*, June 25, 2004.

4 Evan S. Medeiros, Roger Cliff, Keith Crane and James C. Mulvenon, *A New Direction for China's Defense Industry* (Santa Monica, CA: RAND Project Airforce, 2005): 206, 218.

5 Steven R. Wiseman, "Sale of 3Com to Huawei is derailed by U.S. security concerns," *New York Times*, February 21, 2008.

6 Reuters Staff, "Huawei backs away from 3Leaf acquisition," *Reuters*, February 19, 2011.

7 Joann S. Lublin and Shayndi Raice, "Security Fears Kill Chinese Bid in U.S.," *The Wall Street Journal*, November 5, 2010.

8 David Barboza, "China Telecom Giant, Thwarted in U.S. Deals, Seeks Inquiry to Clear Name," *New York Times*, February 25, 2011.

9 United States. House of Representatives. Permanent Select Committee on Intelligence. Investigative Report on the U.S. National Security Issues Posted by Chinese Telecommunications Companies Huawei and ZTE. (112th Congress, October 8, 2012)

10 Michael S. Schmidt, Keith Bradsher and Christine Hauser, "U.S. Panel Cites Risks in Chinese Equipment," *New York Times*, October 8, 2012.

11 Doug Young, "Huawei, ZTE Banned From Selling to U.S. Government," *Techonomy.com*, April 2, 2013.

12 Garett M. Graff, "Inside the Feds' Battle Against Huawei."

13 National Security Council Power Point Deck, "Secure 5G: The Eisenhower National Highway System for the Information Age." In Jonathan Swan, David McCabe, Ina Fried, Kim Hart, "Scoop: Trump team considers nationalizing 5G network," *Axios*, January 28, 2018.

14 Finite State, "Huawei Supply Chain Assessment," June 27, 2019.

15 Roger Cheng, "Huawei CEO: Lack of US carrier support a big loss for you," *C/NET*, January 9, 2018.

16 Sara Salinas, "Six top US intelligence chiefs caution against buying Huawei phones," *CNBC*, February 15, 2018.

17 T.C. Sottek, "Google pulls Huawei's Android license, forcing it to use open source version," *The Verge*, May 19, 2019.

18 Carrie Mihalcik, "FCC bars Huawei, ZTE from billions in federal subsidies," *C/NET*, November 22, 2019.

19 Emily Birnbaum, "House passes legislation banning government from buying Huawei equipment," *The Hill*, December 16, 2019; and, Maggie Miller, "Senate unanimously approves bill to ban purchase of Huawei equipment with federal funds," *The Hill*, February 27, 2020.

20 David Shepardson and Karen Freifeld, "Trump extends U.S. telecom supply chain order aimed at Huawei, ZTE," *Reuters*, May 13, 2020.

21 Sareena Dayaram, "US companies allowed to work with Huawei on setting 5G standards," *C/NET*, June 16, 2020.

22 Joe McDonald, "China's Huawei says 2020 sales rose despite US Sanctions", *Associated Press*, March 31, 2021.

CHAPTER ELEVEN

1 Bojan Pancevski and Sara Germano, "Drop Huawei or See Intelligence Sharing Pared Back, U.S. Tells Germany," *The Wall Street Journal*, March 11, 2019.

2 Beryl Thomas, "What Germany's new cyber security law means for Huawei, Europe, and NATO," European Council on Foreign Relations, February 5, 2021.

3 HM Government, *Huawei Cyber Security Evaluation Centre: Review by the National Security Adviser*, December 2013.

4 Jack Stubbs and Michael Holden, "UK delay on Huawei 5G decision harming ties, lawmakers say," *Reuters*, July 18, 2019.

5 Max Colchester, "U.K. Allows Huawei to Build Parts of 5G Networks, Defying Trump," *The Wall Street Journal*, January 29, 2020.

6 Author interview, January 28, 2020.

7 Stu Woo, "Facing Pushback From Allies, U.S. Set for Broader Huawei Effort," *The Wall Street Journal*, January 23, 2020.

8 Author interview, January 28, 2020.

9 Paul Waldie, "Britain to purge Huawei from 5G network by 2027 in abrupt policy U-turn," *The Globe and Mail*, July 14, 2020.

10 "Digital, Culture, Media and Sport Secretary's statement on telecoms," *WIREDGOV*, July 14, 2020.

11 Toby Helm, "Pressure from Trump led to 5G ban, Britain tells Huawei," *The Observer*, July 18, 2020.

12 Reuters, "UK looks to remove China's CGN from nuclear power projects - FT," July 26, 2021.

13 Corinne Reichert, "Australian government bans Chinese vendors for 5G," *ZDNet*, August 23, 2018.

14 Saheli Roy Choudhury, "Former Australian PM Turnbull explains why his government banned Huawei, ZTE from selling 5G equipment," *CNBC*, March 28, 2019.

15 Eryk Bagshaw, "Huawei documents reveal China's grievance against Australia," *Sydney Morning Herald*, December 21, 2020.

16 Peter Hartcher, "China could have ordered Huawei to shut down Australia's 5G," *Sydney Morning Herald*, May 21, 2021.

17 Eleanor Ainge Roy, "Huawei tells New Zealand: banning us is like banning the All Blacks," *The Guardian*, February 13, 2019.

18 Keith Locke, "NZ shouldn't get caught up in the US game over Huawei," *The Spinoff*, February 3, 2020.

19 Rachel Thomas, "Andrew Little says New Zealand won't follow UK's Huawei 5G ban," *Radio New Zealand (RNZ)*, July 15, 2020.

20 Praveen Menon, "China, New Zealand sign upgraded free trade deal," *The Globe and Mail*, January 25, 2021.

21 "Huawei opens first R&D center in Canada," *Lightwave*, April 20, 2010.

22 "Huawei Canada Partners with Ontario Government to Hire Hundreds of Research Engineers," *Huawei* press release, March 8, 2016.

23 Iain Marlow, "Huawei appears set to open office in Kitchener-Waterloo," *The Globe and Mail*, January 23, 2015.

24 Ibid.

25 Greg Weston, "Chinese firm's Canadian contracts raise security fears," *CBC News*, May 15, 2012.

26 Jessica Vomiero, "Stephen Harper urges Canada to ban Huawei from 5G networks in Fox News appearance," *Global News*, December 7, 2018.

27 CBC Radio, "Huawei deal could give China 'enormous leverage,' warns former U.S. Homeland Security secretary," *CBC Radio*, May 6, 2019.

28 Susan Krashinsky Robertson and Joe Castaldo, "How Huawei built its brand in Canada," *The Globe and Mail*, December 11, 2018.

29 Sean Silcoff, Robert Fife, Steven Chase, and Christine Dobby, "How Canadian money and research are helping China become a global telecom superpower," *The Globe and Mail*, May 26, 2018.

30 Tom Blackwell, "Canadian governments give Huawei millions in funding while debate rages over its 5G role," *National Post*, February 3, 2020.

31 Robert Fife and Steve Chase, "Ottawa partners with Huawei to fund university research despite security concerns," *The Globe and Mail*, February 15, 2021.

32 "Huawei moving US research center to Canada," *Associated Press*, December 3, 2019.

33 Robert Fife and Steven Chase, "Ottawa launches probe of cyber security," *The Globe and Mail*, September 18, 2018.

34 Robert Fife and Steven Chase, "No need to ban Huawei in light of Canada's robust cybersecurity safeguards, top official says," *The Globe and Mail*, September 23, 2018.

35 Howard Solomon, "Canadian government IT security boss on Huawei: 5G review isn't over," *IT World Canada*, October 9, 2018.

36 David Sparling, "Beyond Huawei: The Urgency of Digital Security," *Johnson Shoyama Graduate School of Public Policy*, June 16, 2020.

37 David Ljunggren, "Canada looks set for a fight over C$1 billion compensation for Huawei gear," *Reuters*, September 13, 2020.

38 Mike Blanchfield, "No decision on Huawei and 5G before fall federal election: Goodale," *CBC*, July 30, 2019.

39 Pete Evans, "Bell, Telus to use Nokia and Ericsson, not Huawei, in building their next-generation 5G networks," *CBC News*, June 2, 2020; and Natalie Obiko Pearson, "Huawei snubbed by Canadian firms ahead of Trudeau's crucial 5G calls," *BNN Bloomberg*, June 3, 2020; and Tom Li, "Telus ditches Huawei for Nokia and Ericsson for its 5G network," *IT World Canada*, June 2, 2020.

40 The Canadian Press, "Parliament passes Conservative motion to demand government decision on Huawei and 5G," *CBC*, November 18, 2020.

41 Natalie Obiko Pearson, "Did a Chinese hack kill Canada's greatest tech company?" *Bloomberg Businessweek*, July 1, 2020.

42 Yuval Noah Harari, "Yuval Noah Harari & Huawei CEO Ren Zhengfei in Conversation – Davos 2020."

CHAPTER TWELVE

1 *United States of America v. Huawei Technologies, Huawei Device, Skycom Tech, Wanzhou Meng*, USDC (Superseding Indictment), filed January 24, 2019.

2 Ibid.

3 Ibid.

4 Ibid.

5 "U.S. Department of Justice, Huawei And Its CFO Meng Wanzhou Charged With Financial Fraud, Jan. 28, 2019," *USC US-China Institute, USC Annenberg*, February 11, 2020.

6 David E. Sanger, Katie Benner, and Matthew Goldstein, "Huawei and Top Executive Face Criminal Charges in the US," *New York Times*, January 28, 2019.

7 Ibid.

8 Prime Minister of Canada, "The Honourable Heather J. Holmes," *Prime Minister's Office*, June 22, 2018.

9 Malathi Nayak, "Frayed China- US Relations Put Canadian Judge in the Spotlight," *Bloomberg*, May 27, 2020.

10 Jolson Lim and Marco Vigliotti, "Huawei's Meng Wanzhou loses bid to end extradition process," *iPolitics*, May 27, 2020.

11 Ibid.

12 Ibid.

13 Ibid.

14 Ibid.

15 Ibid.

16 AMENDED NOTICE OF CIVIL CLAIM, No. S-192260 *Supreme Court of British Columbia*, June 3, 2019.

17 Ibid.

18 Ibid.

19 Ibid.

20 Amy Smart, "'Leave the politics to the politicians,' lawyer urges judge in Meng case," *The Globe and Mail*, March 4, 2021.

CHAPTER THIRTEEN

1 *Attorney General of Canada on behalf of the United States of America v. Wanzhou*, SCBC (Applicant's Reply: Second Branch of Abuse Process), filed March 10, 2021.

2 Ibid.

3 Ibid.

4 *Attorney General of Canada on behalf of the United States of America v. Wanzhou*, SCBC (Applicant's Reply: Second Branch of Abuse Process), filed March 10, 2021.

5 Ibid.

6 Ibid.

7 Ibid.

8 *Attorney General of Canada on behalf of the United States of America v. Wanzhou*, SCBC (Requesting State's Responding Submissions Re: Second Branch of Alleged Abuse of Process), filed March 3, 2021.

9 Jason Proctor, "Crown says lone breach of Meng Wanzhou's rights would not be enough to toss extradition," *CBC*, March 26, 2021.

10 *Attorney General of Canada on behalf of the United States of America v. Wanzhou*, SCBC (Requesting State's Responding Submissions Re: Second Branch Of Alleged Abuse Of Process), filed March 3, 2021.

11 *Attorney General of Canada on behalf of the United States of America v. Wanzhou*, SCBC (Applicant's Reply: Second Branch of Abuse Process), filed March 10, 2021.

12 Ian Young, "Canadian officer never sent Meng Wanzhou's phone information to FBI, extradition hearing is told," *South China Morning Post*, March 26, 2021.

13 Laura Dhillon Kane, "U.S. case against Huawei executive Meng Wanzhou breaks international law: defence," *Vancouver Sun*, March 29, 2021.

14 Laura Dhillon Kane, "'Dollar clearing' doesn't give U.S. jurisdiction to charge Meng Wanzhou: lawyer," *CTV News*, March 31, 2021.

15 Laura Dhillon Kane, "Meng Wanzhou extradition case has 'overwhelming' U.S. connection: attorney general," *Vancouver Sun*, April 1, 2021.

16 *Attorney General of Canada on behalf of the United States of America v. Wanzhou*, SCBC (Notice of Application For Adjournment), filed April 14, 2021.

17 *Attorney General of Canada on behalf of the United States of America v. Wanzhou*, SCBC (Attorney General of Canada's Written Submissions re: Adjournment), filed April 16, 2021.

18 Ibid.

19 Jason Proctor, "Meng Wanzhou claims delay in extradition case needed to review documents that could turn case 'on its head,'" *CBC*, April 19, 2021.

20 Amy Smart, "Huawei CFO's team asks judge for adjournment in final extradition hearings," *CTV News*, April 19, 2021.

21 *Attorney General of Canada on behalf of the United States of America v. Wanzhou*, SCBC (Attorney General of Canada's Revised Written Submissions re: Committal), filed April 6, 2021.

22 Ibid.

23 Ibid.

24 Ibid.

25 Ibid.

26 Ibid.

27 Ibid.

28 "APPLICANT'S AMENDED SUBMISSIONS – FOURTH APPLICATION TO ADDUCE EVIDENCE PURSUANT TO SECTION 32 (1)(c) OF THE *EXTRADITION ACT*," *Supreme Court of British Columbia*, June 24, 2021.

29 REQUESTING STATE'S WRITTEN SUBMISSIONS RE: FOURTH APPLICATION TO ADDUCE EVIDENCE PURSUANT TO SECTION 32 (1)(c) OF THE *EXTRADITION ACT*," *Supreme Court of British Columbia*, June 24, 2021.

30 Sean Fine, "B.C. judge takes aim at heart of case against Meng Wanzhou," *The Globe and Mail*, August 5, 2021; and Sean Fine, "Judge in Meng Wanzhou extradition hearing suggests American fraud charge is unusual," *The Globe and Mail*, August 12, 2021.

CHAPTER FOURTEEN

1 The Canadian Press, "Trudeau congratulates Joe Biden on victory in U.S. presidential election," *EnergyNow.ca*, November 7, 2020.

2 Eli Watkins, "Peter Navarro says 'there's a special place in hell' for Justin Trudeau," *CNN*, June 10, 2018.

3 The Canadian Press, "Trudeau congratulates Joe Biden on victory in U.S. presidential election."

4 Mike Blanchfield, "Trudeau shoots back at China's claim Canada is being 'naive' in courting allies," *CP24*, July 4, 2019.

5 Interview with the authors.

6 Joshuah Bearman, "How the CIA Used a Fake Sci-Fi Flick to Rescue Americans From Tehran," *Wired*, April 24, 2007.

7 David Haglund, "How Accurate is *Argo*?" *SLATE*, October 12, 2012.

8 Simon Houpt, "No Argo here: New doc sets the record straight on the Iranian hostage crisis," *The Globe and Mail*, September 17, 2013.

9 Canada Institute, "Revisiting Canada's Contribution to Resolving the Iranian Hostage Crisis," *Wilson Center,* April 8, 2005.

10 Joel Simon, "How Trump Has Reversed Decades of American Hostage Diplomacy," *The New Yorker,* February 7, 2020.

11 The White House, Washington, DC, *Report on U.S. Hostage Policy,* June 2015.

12 Saeed Kamali Dehghan and Mazin Sidahmed, "Trump attacks Clinton on 'scandal' of US paying $400m to Iran after nuclear deal," *The Guardian,* August 3, 2016.

13 Amanda Taub, "The Republican myth of Ronald Reagan and the Iran hostages, debunked," *Vox,* January 25, 2016.

14 Jimmy Carter, *Keeping Faith: Memoirs of a President* (Fayetteville: University of Arkansas Press, 1995), 6.

15 Bernard Gwertzman, "U.S. Promises Iran $5.5 Billion on Day Hostages Are Freed," *The New York Times,* January 11, 1981; and Mike Evans, "Obama's $400 million and Carter's $7.9 billion," *The Jerusalem Post,* August 8, 2016.

16 To the extent that Reagan as president-elect and his team were involved in the crisis, it may have been because, as principal former White House aide for Iran Gary G. Sick alleged after studying the evidence carefully, to delay the release of the hostages until just after Reagan's inauguration so that he and not Carter could take the credit. It turned out there may have also been a secret arms deal at part of the bargain. As Sick testified before the Senate Select Committee on Intelligence in 1991, "What this evidence shows is a consistent pattern of secret contacts between the Reagan-Bush campaign and Iran. The contacts began early in 1980, from about the moment that William Casey became the campaign manager for Mr. Reagan. They continued through the summer of that year in Madrid, where the first outline of a deal was reportedly proposed and accepted and where Israeli participation was first introduced. The terms of the bargain were reportedly made final in the second half of October in Paris. The hostages were released minutes after President Reagan had taken the oath of office, and arms began to flow to Iran from Israel, with U.S. government acquiescence, almost immediately thereafter" ("Statement of Gary G. Sick, November 22, 1991, S. 1003, "The October Surprise," Senate Select Committee on Intelligence, November 22, 1991. Available at: https://fas.org/irp/congress/1991_hr/index.html).

17 Lauren Carroll, "Donald Trump's Mostly False claim that $400 million payment to Iran was 'ransom,'" *PolitiFact,* August 24, 2016.

18 Ibid.

19 Jay Solomon and Carol E. Lee, "U.S. Sent Cash to Iran as Americans Were Freed," *The Wall Street Journal,* August 3, 2016.

20 David A. Graham, "The Iranian Humiliation Trump Is Trying to Avenge," *The Atlantic,* January 7, 2020.

21 Ibid.

22 Bethan McKernan, "Andrew Brunson: Turkey release US pastor after two years in prison," *The Guardian,* October 12, 2018.

23 Robin Wright, "The Real Deal Behind the U.S.-Iran Prisoner Swap," *The New Yorker*, December 8, 2019.

24 Farnaz Fassihi and Rick Gladstone, "Iran Frees Navy Veteran Held for Two Years," *New York Times*, June 4, 2020.

CHAPTER FIFTEEN

1   Steve Holland, Jeff Mason, and Roberta Rampton, "Trump says would intervene in arrest of Chinese executive," *Reuters*, December 11, 2018.

2   John Bolton, *The Room Where It Happened: A White House Memoir* (New York: Simon and Schuster, 2020), 305.

3   Ibid, 305–306.

4   Ana Swanson and Keith Bradsher, "U.S.-China Trade Standoff May Be Initial Skirmish in Broader Economic War," *New York Times*, May 11, 2019.

5   Peter Baker and Keith Bradsher, "Trump and Xi Agree to Restart Trade Talks, Avoiding Escalation in Tariff War," *New York Times*, June 29, 2019.

6   Ibid.

7   Jessie Yeung, Ben Westcott, Kevin Liptak, and Steve George, "G20 summit 2019: Trump meets leaders in Osaka, *CNN Politics*, June 29, 2019.

8   Pete Evans, "China halts canola shipments from major Canadian supplier," *CBC News*, March 5, 2019.

9   Rob Gillies, "China suspends license of Canadian canola company," *AP News*, March 26, 2019.

10 Kelsey Johnson and Rod Nickel, "China tells Canada to stop meat shipment over bogus documents," *Reuters*, June 25, 2019.

11 The Canadian Press, "Trudeau has 'brief, constructive interactions' with Chinese President Xi Jinping at G20," *CBC*, June 28, 2019.

12 The Canadian Press, "Freeland lands meeting with Chinese counterpart to talk about detainees," *CTV News*, August 2, 2019.

13 Barrie McKenna, "The U.S.-China trade deal is bad for Canada – and we can't do a thing about it," *The Globe and Mail*, January 12, 2020.

14 Steve Scherer, "Opposition leader says Canada needs 'reset' on China, attacks Trudeau," *Reuters*, May 7, 2019.

15 Andy Blatchford, "Scheer argues Trudeau hurt Canada-China relations with the SNC-Lavalin affair," *CTV News*, October 9, 2019.

16 CBC Radio, "Why former foreign minister John Manley thinks Canada botched Huawei affair," *CBC*, December 14, 2018.

17 Ibid.

18 CTV News, "Former Chretien official calls for a 'prisoner swap' with China," *YouTube*, January 20, 2020.

CHAPTER SIXTEEN

1 Ibid.
2 "Ottawa could do more to free 2 Canadians jailed in China, Michael Kovrig's wife says," *CBC*, June 22, 2020.
3 Atwood and Modirzadeh, "Episode 15."
4 Author interview.
5 Atwood and Modirzadeh, "Episode 15."
6 Ibid.
7 Ibid.
8 Author interview.
9 Mike Blanchfield, "Books, physical rigour stoke hope for Kovrig as 'two Michaels' mark two jailed years," *Toronto Star*, December 10, 2020.
10 Nassim Nicholas Taleb, *Antifragile: Things That Gain From Disorder* (New York: Random House, 2012).
11 Author interview.
12 Shannon Proudfoot, "A promise to Michael," *Maclean's*, January 13, 2021.
13 Author interview.
14 Canada. Parliament. House of Commons. Special Committee on Canada-China Relations, *Evidence*. (Meeting No.12, December 8, 2020). 43rd Parliament, 2nd session, 2020.
15 Author interview.
16 Nathan VanderKlippe, "Michael Spavor's wish list: Documents show how Canadians detained in China are seeking hope and comfort," *The Globe and Mail*, December 10, 2020.
17 Ibid.
18 Ibid.
19 Avinash De Sousa, "Mind and Consciousness as per J. Krishnamurti," *Mens Sana Monographs* 10, no. 1 (January–December 2012): 198–207.
20 "Viktor E. Frankl," *Goodreads*, n.d.
21 VanderKlippe, "Michael Spavor's wish list."
22 Ibid and Amanda Coletta, "Detained Huawei CFO enjoys private shopping and evenings at open-air theaters 'under the stars,' wants bail conditions eased," *Washington Post*, January 17, 2021.
23 Author interview.
24 Ibid.

CHAPTER SEVENTEEN

1 Director's Message, China Institute, University of Alberta. Available at: https://www.ualberta.ca/china-institute/about/directors-message.html.

2 Special Committee on Canada-China Relations, House of Commons, "Evidence," November 24, 2020, No. 008, 2nd Session, 43rd Parliament.

3 Interview with the authors.

4 Ibid.

5 Ibid.

6 Extradition Act, S.C. 1999, c. 18, Assented to 1999-06-17. Available at: https://laws-lois.justice.gc.ca/eng/acts/e-23.01/page-1.html.

7 Interview with authors.

8 Interview with authors.

9 Ibid.

10 Ibid.

11 Ibid.

12 Tom Blackwell, "Ex-ministers Baird, Rock part of delegation that warned Beijing Canadians are souring on China," *National Post*, November 14, 2019.

CHAPTER EIGHTEEN

1 Christy Somos, "China praises Canada, slams U.S. over coronavirus response," *CTV News*, February 3, 2020.

2 Mike Blanchfield, *The Canadian Press*, February 10, 2020.

3 Nancy L. Dennison and Seth Weinstein, *Prosecuting and Defending Extradition Cases: A Practitioner's Handbook* (Toronto: Edmond Publishing, 2017).

4 Letter to the Honourable David Lametti, Minister of Justice and Attorney General of Canada, "In the Matter of the United States of America and Meng Wanzhou," May 22, 2020.

5 Letter to the Honourable David Lametti, Minister of Justice and Attorney General of Canada, "In the Matter of the United States of America and Meng Wanzhou," May 22, 2020.

6 Memorandum prepared by Louise Arbour and Allan Rock, May 22, 2020.

7 Ibid.

8 Ibid.

9 Ibid.

10 Ibid.

11 Ibid.

12 Ibid.

13 United States of America v. Cobb, [2001] 1 S.C.R. 587.

14 Cate Cadell and Tony Munroe, "China charges two detained Canadians with suspected espionage, Trudeau 'very disappointed'," *Reuters*, June 19, 2020.

15 Sean Fine, "Ottawa has authority to free Meng Wanzhou now, former justice minister, Supreme Court justice say," *The Globe and Mail*, June 22, 2020.

16 Ibid.

17 CBC News, "Ottawa could do more to free 2 Canadians jailed in China, Michael Kovrig's wife says," June 22, 2020.

18 "A Letter to the Prime Minister of Canada," June 23, 2020.

19 John Ivison, "Trudeau should change tack on the two Michaels and negotiate for their release," *National Post*, June 2, 2021.

20 "A Letter to the Prime Minister of Canada," June 23, 2020.

21 Government of Canada, Extradition Act (S.C. 1999, c. 18). Available at: https://laws-lois.justice.gc.ca/eng/acts/E-23.01/

22 Ibid.

23 John Paul Tasker, Brennan MacDonald, "Former parliamentarians, diplomats pen letter calling on Canada to release Meng," *CBC News*, June 24, 2020.

24 John Paul Tasker, "Trudeau rejects calls to release Meng Wanzhou," *CBC News*, June 25, 2020.

25 Ibid.

26 Interview with authors.

27 Direct communication with the authors.

28 Steven Chase and Robert Fife, "More than 100 ex-diplomats urge Trudeau to swap Meng for Kovrig and Spavor," *The Globe and Mail*, September 18, 2020.

29 Levon Sevunts, "Do not appease China with 'prisoner exchange,' experts warn Trudeau," *Radio Canada International*, June 26, 2020.

30 "Meng and the Michaels: Most support PM's refusal to swap Huawei executive for imprisoned Canadians," Angus Reid Institute, June 29, 2020.

31 Government of Canada Privy Council Office, National Security and Intelligence Advisor to the Prime Minister, *Huawei Extradition Case,* Document No. WEBCIMS # 2018-FDP-00267, December 18, 2018. Document released under Access to Information Act.

32 Author interview.

33 Ryan Flanagan, "Releasing Meng to free Kovrig and Spavor would endanger Canadians abroad, Trudeau says," *CTV News*, June 25, 2020.

CHAPTER NINETEEN

1 Michael Fraiman, "At Michael Kovrig's trial, the world had Canada's back," *Maclean's*, April 14, 2021.

2 Peter Edwards, "Canada will work with allies to push China to release Kovrig and Spavor, Freeland says," *Toronto Star*, December 22, 2018.

3 European Commission, EU-China Summit: Defending EU interests and values in a complex and vital partnership, press release, June 22, 2020, Brussels. Available at: https://ec.europa.eu/commission/presscorner/detail/en/ip_20_1159.

4 Mike Blanchfield, "Pompeo calls on China to release two Michaels, says U.S. stands with Canada," *Associated Press*, June 22, 2020.

5 The Canadian Press, "US Vice-President Joe Biden in Ottawa for final official visit," *Global News*, December 8, 2016.

6 James McCarten, "Biden on China's detention of two Michaels: 'Human beings are not bartering chips,'" *The Canadian Press*, February 23, 2021.

7 National Post Staff, "'Totally unacceptable': U.S. secretary of state calls on China to free Two Michaels," *National Post*, February 28, 2021.

8 Humeyra Pamuk, David Brunnstrom, and Michael Martina, "'Tough' U.S.-China talks signal rocky start to relations under Biden," *Reuters*, March 19, 2021.

9 Lara Jakes and Steven Lee Myers, "Tense Talks With China Left US 'Cleareyed' About Beijing's Intentions, Officials Say," *New York Times*, March 19, 2021.

10 Jeanne Whalen, "On eve of China summit, Biden administration subpoenas Chinese companies on possible security risks," *Washington Post*, March 17, 2021.

11 Steven Chase, "Dominic Barton in 'regular contact' with Huawei to find a way to free two Michaels, Garneau says," *The Globe and Mail*, June 7, 2021.

CHAPTER TWENTY

1 Author interview.

2 Government of Canada, *Declaration Against Arbitrary Detention in State-to-State Relations,* December 2, 2021. Available at: https://www.international.gc.ca/news-nouvelles/arbitrary_detention-detention_arbitraire-declaration.aspx?lang=eng.

3 Author interview.

4 Mike Blanchfield, "Chinese ambassador says Canada is 'interfering in our domestic affairs' before MPs vote on Uighur genocide," *The Canadian Press*, February 21, 2021.

5 John Ivison, "Canada to lead global initiative against arbitrary detentions," *National Post*, February 15, 2021.

6 Foreign and Commonwealth Office (UK), G7 Foreign and Development Ministers' Meeting: Communique, 5 May 2021.

7 BBC, "G7 summit: China says small groups do not rule the world," *BBC News*, June 13, 2021.

8 Anastasya Lloyd-Damnjanovic, "Beijing's Deadly Game: Consequences of Excluding Taiwan from the World Health Organization during the COVID-19 Pandemic," US-China Economic and Security Review Commission, Issue Brief, May 12, 2020.

9 Mike Blanchfield, "China pushes back against efforts by Canada to get Taiwan access at WHO," *The Canadian Press*, May 11, 2020.

10 Mike Blanchfield, "Health experts tell Ottawa to hurry domestic vaccine funding amid China delays," *The Canadian Press*, July 24, 2020; and Mike

Blanchfield, "PM put all vaccine 'eggs' in one China basket, didn't consider other options: O'Toole," *The Canadian Press*, November 29, 2020.

11 Zi-Ann Lum, "Trudeau Blames Conservatives For Canada's Vaccine Manufacturing Decline," *Huffington Post*, November 25, 2020.

12 Priyanka Boghani, "The Story of Chinese Muslims Is A "Story That has Global Implications": Q&A With Filmmakers, *PBS Frontline*, April 7, 2020.

13 Liu Xin, "Xinjiang debunks lies in PBS documentary and biased Western media," *Global Times*, April 29, 2020.

14 Mike Blanchfield, "Canadians who say they've been targeted by foreign agents want co-ordinated response," *CTV News*, November 26, 2020.

15 Austin Ramzy and Chris Buckley, "'Absolutely No Mercy': Leaked Files Expose How China Organized Mass Detentions of Muslims," *New York Times*, November 16, 2019.

16 Author interview.

17 Newline Institute for Strategy and Policy and the Raoul Wallenberg Centre for Human Rights, *The Uyghur Genocide: An Examination of China's Breaches of the 1948 Genocide Convention*, March 2021. Available at: https://newlinesinstitute. org/wp-content/uploads/Chinas-Breaches-of-the-GC3.pdf.

18 The Rt Hon Dominic Raab, MP, Foreign, Commonwealth & Development Office, "UK sanctions perpetrators of gross human rights violations in Xinjiang, alongside EU, China and US," press release, March 22, 2021.

19 Global Affairs Canada, "Canada joins international partners in imposing new sanctions in response to human rights violations in Xinjiang," press release, Ottawa, Ontario, March 22, 2021.

20 Ryan Maloney, "Trudeau Explains Reluctance to Call China's Treatment of Uighurs A Genocide," *Huffington Post*, February 16, 2021.

21 Robert Fife and Steven Chase, "Canadian support harder line against China over treatment of Uyghurs," *The Globe and Mail*, March 7, 2021.

22 Zachary Basu, "U.K. Parliament declares China's treatment of Uyghurs to be genocide," *Axios*, April 22, 2021.

23 Colm Quinn, "Blinken Names and Shames Human Rights Abusers," *Foreign Policy*, Morning Brief, March 31, 2021; and Jonathan Ponciano, "Biden Secretary of State Condemns China's 'Acts of Genocide' Against Muslim Uyghurs," *Forbes*, April 11, 2021.

24 Betsy Woodruff Swan and Andy Blatchford, "Trudeau government threatens Halifax Security Forum over proposed Taiwan award," *Politico*, April 4, 2021.

25 Emerald Bensadoun, "House of Commons backs security forum award for Taiwan after report of funding threat," *Global News*, April 14, 2021.

CHAPTER TWENTY-ONE

1 BBC, "BBC China correspondent John Sudworth moves to Taiwan after threats," *BBC News*, March 31, 2021.

2 Ibid.

3 Interview with the authors.

4 Eva Dou, "Senior U.S. official visits China, in small thaw of relations with Beijing," *Washington Post*, July 26, 2021.

5 Author interview.

6 Interview with authors.

7 Steven Chase and Robert Fife, "Senator warns China might not free Spavor and Kovrig in Meng deal if Canada not part of effort," *The Globe and Mail*, April 12, 2021.

8 John Paul Tasker, "Invoking residential schools, B.C. senator says Canada should be careful about criticizing China," *CBC News*, June 29, 2021.

9 Ryan Flanagan, "Canadians warming to prisoner swap with China, split on balancing budget: Nanos survey," *CTV News*, April 4, 2021.

CHAPTER TWENTY-TWO

1 Raymond Zhong and Alexandra Stevenson, "Jack Ma Shows Why China's Tycoons Keep Quiet," *The New York Times*, April 22, 2021.

2 Kristie Lu Stout and Yuli Yang, "Huawei CEO says his daughter should be proud she became a 'bargaining chip' in the trade war," *CNN*, December 1, 2019.

3 Interview with the authors.

4 "Help for Michael," GoFundMe, https://www.gofundme.com/f/f4dxah-help-for-michael?utm_campaign=p_cp_url&utm_medium=os&utm_source=customer.

5 Joe McDonald and Ng Han Guan, "China sentences Canadian to 11 years in case tied to Huawei," *Washington Post*, August 11, 2021

6 D. J. Ouellette, "The Chocolate Run," *Free Michael Spavor*, January 22, 2020.

7 Paul Spavor, "Road Trip with my Brother," *Free Michael Spavor*, March 12, 2019.

8 John M. Glionna, "Swagger, and a sense of adventure," *Free Michael Spavor*, March 14, 2019.

9 Rob Malley and Brittany Brown, hosts, "Episode 15: Michael Kovrig: Two Years in Arbitrary Detention in China," Hold Your Fire! (podcast), October 12, 2020.

10 "Send a message to Michael Spavor and Michael Kovrig as they near 1,000 days in detention in China," *The Globe and Mail*, July 27, 2021.

11 https://www.facebook.com/bankruptrocks/photos/10163632527295408

12 https://bankrupt.bandcamp.com/track/the-plane-to-toronto

13 Author Interview.

CHAPTER TWENTY-THREE

1 United States District Court Eastern District of New York, United States of America against Wanzhou Meng, Defendant. Deferred Prosecution Agreement. Cr. No. 18-457 (s-3) (AMD) and Attachment A, "Statement of Facts," Brooklyn, New York, September 22, 2021.

2 Ibid.

3 Author interview.

4 Author interview.

5 Author interview.

6 Anne Gearan, "Biden and China's Xi speak for a second time amid rising tensions," *Washington Post*, September 9, 2021.

7 Ibid.

8 Statement by H.E. Xi Jinping President of the People's Republic of China at the General Debate of the 76th Session of The United Nations General Assembly, "Bolstering Confidence and Jointly Overcoming Difficulties To Build a Better World," September 21, 2021.

9 Author interview.

10 GT staff reporters, "Two Canadian confess guilt, granted bail for medical reasons before leaving China," *Global Times*, September 26, 2021.

11 CTV's *Question Period* for Sunday, September 26, 2021.

12 Author interview.

13 Bob Davis, "Commerce Secretary Gina Raimondo Aims to Strengthen Business Ties With China," *The Wall Street Journal*, September 24, 2021.

14 Julian Border and Dan Sabbagh, "US, UK and Australia forge military alliance to counter China," *The Guardian*, September 16, 2021.

15 Ibid.

16 Email communication with the authors.

17 Author interview.

18 Andy Blatchford, "Biden's pick for ambassador to Canada says U.S. waiting for Trudeau's updated China policy," *Politico*, September 23, 2021.

19 Quoted in Kristy Kirkup, "Homecoming of Michael Spavor, Michael Kovrig a welcome relief for Canada, but China rift runs deep after their detention," *The Globe and Mail*, September 26, 2021.

20 Global Times Editorial, "US elites should not misread Meng's release, incite hostility," *Global Times*, September 26, 2021.

21 Zhou Xin and Yujie Xie, 'Finally, I am home': Huawei's Meng Wanzhou lands in China to hero's welcome," *The South China Morning Post*, September 25, 2021.

22 Amanda Coletta, "Canada's 'two Michaels' back home after more than 1,000 days imprisoned in China as Huawei's Meng cuts deal with U.S.," *Washington Post*, September 25, 2021.

23 Zhou Xin and Yujie Xie, 'Finally, I am home': Huawei's Meng Wanzhou lands in China to hero's welcome," *The South China Morning Post*, September 25, 2021.